C
Europe

lonely planet

phrasebooks

Central Europe phrasebook
3rd edition – February 2007

Published by
Lonely Planet Publications Pty Ltd ABN 36 005 607 983
90 Maribyrnong St, Footscray, Victoria 3011, Australia

Lonely Planet Offices
Australia Locked Bag 1, Footscray, Victoria 3011
USA 150 Linden St, Oakland CA 94607
UK 72–82 Rosebery Ave, London, EC1R 4RW

Cover illustration
Europa by Yukiyoshi Kamimura

ISBN 978 1 74104 030 2

10 9 8 7 6 5 4 3 2

Printed by C&C Offset Printing Co Ltd, China

acknowledgment.

This book is based on existing editions of Lonely Planet's phrasebooks as well as new content. It was developed with the help of the following people:

- Richard Nebeský for the Czech chapter
- Gunter Muehl for the German chapter
- Christina Mayer for the Hungarian chapter
- Piotr Czajkowski for the Polish chapter
- Katarina Nodrovicziova for the Slovak chapter
- Urška Pajer for the Slovene chapter

Editor Branislava Vladisavljevic would also like to thank Elmar Duenschede (German) and Hunor Csutoros (Hungarian) for additional language expertise.

Lonely Planet Language Products

Publishing Manager: Chris Rennie
Commissioning Editor: Karin Vidstrup Monk
Editor: Branislava Vladisavljevic
Assisting Editors: Vanessa Battersby & Francesca Coles
Managing Editor: Annelies Mertens
Project Manager: Adam McCrow

Layout Designers: Clara Monitto & David Kemp
Managing Layout Designer: Sally Darmody
Cartographer: Wayne Murphy
Series Designer & Illustrations: Yukiyoshi Kamimura
Production Manager: Jennifer Bilos

contents

CONTENTS

4

Central Europe

Czech
German
Hungarian

Baltic Sea

Lithuania

Gdańsk

Kaliningrad
(Russia)

Belarus

POLAND

Poznań

⊛ **Warsaw**

Łódź

Wrocław

Ostrava

Kraków

Ukraine

PUBLIC

Brno

SLOVAKIA

Prešov
Košice

nna

Nitra

⊛ **Bratislava**

Miskolc

Győr

Debrecen

Moldova

⊛ **Budapest**

az

HUNGARY

Murlior

Szeged

e

Pécs

Romania

Croatia

Serbia

Bosnia and
Hercegovina

■ Polish
■ Slovak
■ Slovene

Note: Language areas are approximate only.
For more details see the relevant introduction.

EUROPE

central europe – at a glance

One of the rewarding things about travelling through Central Europe is the rich variety of cuisine, customs, architecture and history. The flipside of course is that you'l encounter a number of very different languages. Most languages spoken in Centra Europe belong to what's known as the Indo-European language family, believed to have originally developed from one language spoken thousands of years ago.

German belongs to the Germanic branch of the Indo European language family and is quite closely related to English. You should find that many basic words in German are similar to English words. The Slavic languages originated north of the Carpathians and are now divided into Eastern, Western and Southern subgroups Czech, Slovak and Polish all belong to the Western subgroup of the Slavic language family, while Slovene belongs to the Southern subgroup. Fortunately, (for travellers at least), all these Central European Slavic languages are written in the Latin alphabet. Hungarian is something of a linguistic oddity within Europe. Though classified as a member of the Finno-Ugric language group, making it a distant relative of Finnish, it has no other significant similarities to any other language in Europe – or the world for that matter.

did you know?

- The European Union (EU) was established by the Maastricht Treaty in 1992. It developed from the European Economic Community, founded by the Treaty of Rome in 1957. Since the 2004 enlargement, it has 25 member states and 20 official languages.
- The EU flag is a circle of 12 gold stars on a blue background – the number 12 representing wholeness.
- The EU anthem is the 'Ode to Joy' from Beethoven's Ninth Symphony.
- Europe Day, 9 May, commemorates the 1950 declaration by French Foreign Minister Robert Schuman which marked the creation of the European Union.
- The euro has been in circulation since E-Day, 1 January 2002. The euro's symbol (€) was inspired by the Greek letter epsilon (ε) – Greece being the cradle of European civilisation and ε being the first letter of the word 'Europe'.
- The Eurovision Song Contest, held each May, has been running since 1956. For the larger part of the competition's history, the performers were only allowed to sing in their country's national language, but that's no longer the case.

Czech

czech alphabet

A a uh	*Á á* a	*B b* bair	*C c* tsair	*Č č* chair
D d dair	*Ď ď* dyair	*E e* e	*É é* *dloh*-hair air	*Ě ě* e s *hach*-kem
F f ef	*G g* gair	*H h* ha	*Ch ch* cha	*I i* ee
Í í *dloh*-hair ee	*J j* yair	*K k* ka	*L l* el	*M m* em
N n en	*Ň ň* en´	*O o* o	*P p* pair	*Q q* kair
R r er	*Ř ř* erzh	*S s* es	*Š š* esh	*T t* tair
Ť ť tyair	*U u* u	*Ú ú* *dloh*-hair u	*Ů ů* u s *krohzh*-kem	*V v* vair
W w *dvo*-yi-tair vair	*X x* iks	*Y y* *ip*-si-lon	*Ý ý* *dloh*-hee *ip*-si-lon	*Z z* zet
Ž ž zhet				

czech

CZECH

čeština

introduction

Czech (*čeština* chesh-tyi-nuh), the language which gave us words such as *dollar*, *pistol* and *robot*, has a turbulent history. The Czech Republic may now be one of the most stable and well-off Eastern European countries, but over the centuries the land and the language have been regularly swallowed and regurgitated by their neighbours. In 1993 the Velvet Divorce ended the patched-together affair that was Czechoslovakia, and allowed Czech to go its own way after being tied to Slovak for over 70 years.

Both Czech and Slovak belong to the western branch of the Slavic language family, pushed westward with the Slavic people by the onslaught of the Huns, Avars, Bulgars and Magyars in the 5th and 6th centuries. Czech is also related to Polish, though not as closely as to Slovak – adults in Slovakia and the Czech Republic can generally understand one another, although younger people who have not been exposed to much of the other language may have more difficulty.

The earliest written literature dates from the 13th century upswing in Czech political power, which continued for several centuries. In the 17th century, however, the Thirty Years War nearly caused literature in Czech to become extinct. Fortunately, the national revival of the late 18th century brought it to the forefront again, at least until the 20th century, when first Nazi and then Communist rule pressed it into a subordinate position once more.

Many English speakers flinch when they see written Czech, especially words like *prst* prst (finger) and *krk* krk (neck) with no apparent vowels, and the seemingly unpronounceable clusters of consonants in phrases like *čtrnáct dní* chtr-natst dnyee (fortnight). Don't despair! With a little practice and the coloured pronunciation guides in this chapter you'll be enjoying the buttery mouthfeel of Czech words in no time. Czech also has one big advantage in the pronunciation stakes – each Czech letter is always pronounced exactly the same way, so once you've got the hang of the Czech alphabet you'll be able to read any word put before you with aplomb. Thank religious writer and martyr Jan Hus for this – he reformed the spelling system in the 15th and 16th centuries and introduced the *háček* ha-chek (ˇ) and the various other accents you'll see above Czech letters.

So, whether you're visiting the countryside or marvelling at Golden Prague, launch into this Czech chapter and your trip will be transformed into a truly memorable one.

pronunciation

vowel sounds

The Czech vowel system is relatively easy to master and most sounds have equivalents in English.

symbol	english equivalent	czech example	transliteration
a	father	*já*	ya
ai	aisle	*krajka*	*krai*-kuh
air	hair	*veliké*	*ve*-lee-kair
aw	law	*balcón*	*bal*-kawn
e	bet	*pes*	pes
ee	see	*prosím*	*pro*-seem
ey	hey	*dej*	dey
i	bit	*kolik*	*ko*-lik
o	pot	*noha*	*no*-huh
oh	oh	*koupit*	*koh*-pit
oo	zoo	*ústa*	*oo*-stuh
oy	toy	*výstroj*	*vee*-stroy
ow	how	*autobus*	*ow*-to-bus
u	put	*muž*	muzh
uh	run	*nad*	n d

word stress

Word stress in Czech is easy – it's always on the first syllable of the word. Stress is marked with italics in the pronunciation guides in this chapter as a reminder.

consonant sounds

The consonants in Czech are mostly the same as in English, with the exception of the kh sound, the r sound (which is rolled as it is in Spanish) and the rzh sound.

symbol	english equivalent	czech example	transliteration
b	**b**ed	*blá*to	*bla*·to
ch	**ch**eat	*odpočinek*	*ot*·po·**chi**·nek
d	**d**og	*nedávný*	*ne*·dav·nee
f	**f**at	*vyfotit*	*vi*·fo·tit
g	**g**o	*vegetarián*	*ve*·ge·tuh·ri·an
h	**h**at	*zahrady*	*zuh*·hruh·di
k	**k**it	*navěky*	*na*·vye·ki
kh	lo**ch**	*kuchyně*	*ku*·**khi**·nye
l	**l**ot	*loni*	*lo*·nyi
m	**m**an	*menší*	*men*·shee
n	**n**ot	*nízký*	*nyeez*·kee
p	**p**et	*dopis*	*do*·pis
r	**r**un (rolled)	*rok*	rok
rzh	rolled r followed by zh	*řeka*	*rzhe*·kuh
s	**s**un	*slovo*	*slo*·vo
sh	**sh**ot	*pošta*	*posh*·tuh
t	**t**op	*fronta*	*fron*·tuh
ts	ha**ts**	*co*	tso
v	**v**ery	*otvor*	*ot*·vor
y	**y**es	*již*	yizh
z	**z**ero	*zmiz*	zmiz
zh	plea**s**ure	*už*	uzh
'	a slight y sound	*promiňte*	*pro*·min'·te

tools

language difficulties

Do you speak English?
Mluvíte anglicky?   *mlu·vee·te uhn·glits·ki*

Do you understand?
Rozumíte?   *ro·zu·mee·te*

I understand.
Rozumím.   *ro·zu·meem*

I don't understand.
Nerozumím.   *ne·ro·zu·meem*

What does (knedlík) mean?
Co znamená (knedlík)?   *tso znuh·me·na (kned·leek)*

How do you ...?   Jak se ...?   yuhk se ...
  pronounce this   toto vyslovuje   *toh·to vis·lo·vu·ye*
  write (krtek)   píše (krtek)   *pee·she (kr·tek)*

Could you please ...? Prosím, můžete ...?   *pro·seem moo·zhe·te ...*
  repeat that   to opakovat   to *o·puh·ko·vuht*
  speak more slowly   mluvit pomaleji   *mlu·vit po·muh·le·yi*
  write it down   to napsat   to *nuhp·suht*

essentials

Yes.	Ano.	*uh·no*
No.	Ne.	ne
Please.	Prosím.	*pro·seem*
Thank you (very much).	(Mnohokrát) Děkuji.	(*mno·ho·krat*) *dye·ku·yi*
You're welcome.	Prosím.	*pro·seem*
Excuse me.	Promiňte.	*pro·min'·te*
Sorry.	Promiňte.	*pro·min'·te*

0	*nula*	nu·luh	16	*šestnáct*	shest·natst
1	*jeden* m	ye·den	17	*sedmnáct*	se·dm·natst
	jedna f	yed·na	18	*osmnáct*	o·sm·natst
	jedno n	yed·no	19	*devatenáct*	de·vuh·te·natst
2	*dva/dvě* m/f&n	dvuh/dvye	20	*dvacet*	dvuh·tset
3	*tři*	trzhi	21	*dvacet jedna*	dvuh·tset yed·nuh
4	*čtyři*	chti·rzhi		*jednadvacet*	yed·nuh·dvuh·tset
5	*pět*	pyet	22	*dvacet dva*	dvuh·tset dvuh
6	*šest*	shest		*dvaadvacet*	dvuh·uh·dvuh·tset
7	*sedm*	se·dm	30	*třicet*	trzhi·tset
8	*osm*	o·sm	40	*čtyřicet*	chti·rzhi·tset
9	*devět*	de·vyet	50	*padesát*	puh·de·sat
10	*deset*	de·set	60	*šedesát*	she·de·sat
11	*jedenáct*	ye·de·natst	70	*sedmdesát*	se·dm·de·sat
12	*dvanáct*	dvuh·natst	80	*osmdesát*	o·sm·de·sat
13	*třináct*	trzhi·natst	90	*devadesát*	de·vuh·de·sat
14	*čtrnáct*	chtr·natst	100	*sto*	sto
15	*patnáct*	puht·natst	1000	*tisíc*	tyi·seets

time & dates

What time is it?	*Kolik je hodin?*	ko·lik ye ho·dyin
It's one o'clock.	*Je jedna hodina.*	ye yed·nuh ho·dyi·nuh
It's (10) o'clock.	*Je (deset) hodin.*	ye (de·set) ho·dyin
Quarter past (10).	*Čvrt na (jedenáct).* (lit: quarter of eleven)	chtvrt nuh (ye·de·natst)
Half past (10).	*Půl (jedenácté).* (lit: half eleven)	pool (ye·de·nats·tair)
Quarter to (eleven).	*Třičtvrtě na (jedenáct).*	trzhi·chtvr·tye nuh (ye·de·natst)
At what time?	*V kolik hodin?*	f ko·lik ho·dyin
At ...	*V ...*	f ...
am (midnight–8am)	*ráno*	ra·no
am (8am–noon)	*dopoledne*	do·po·led·ne
pm (noon–7pm)	*odpoledne*	ot·po·led·ne
pm (7pm–midnight)	*večer*	ve·cher

Monday	pondělí	pon·dye·lee
Tuesday	úterý	oo·te·ree
Wednesday	středa	strzhe·duh
Thursday	čtvrtek	chtvr·tek
Friday	pátek	pa·tek
Saturday	sobota	so·bo·tuh
Sunday	neděle	ne·dye·le

January	leden	le·den
February	únor	oo·nor
March	březen	brzhe·zen
April	duben	du·ben
May	květen	kvye·ten
June	červen	cher·ven
July	červenec	cher·ve·nets
August	srpen	sr·pen
September	září	za·rzhee
October	říjen	rzhee·yen
November	listopad	li·sto·puht
December	prosinec	pro·si·nets

What date is it today?
   Kolikátého je dnes?   ko·li·ka·tair·ho ye dnes

It's (18 October).
   Je (osmnáctého října).   ye (o·sm·nats·tair·ho rzheey·nuh)

last night	včera v noci	fche·ruh v no·tsi
last week/month	minulý týden/měsíc	mi·nu·lee tee·den/mye·seets
last year	vloni	vlo·nyi

next ...	příští ...	przheesh·tyee ...
week	týden	tee·den
month	měsíc	mye·seets
year	rok	rok

tomorrow/yesterday ...	zítra/včera ...	zee·truh/fche·ruh ...
morning (early/late)	ráno/dopoledne	ra·no/do·po·led·ne
afternoon	odpoledne	ot·po·led·ne
evening	večer	ve·cher

weather

What's the weather like?	Jaké je počasí?	yuh·kair ye po·chuh·see
It's ...		
cloudy	Je zataženo.	ye zuh·tuh·zhe·no
cold	Je chladno.	ye khluhd·no
hot	Je horko.	ye hor·ko
raining	Prší.	pr·shee
snowing	Sněží.	snye·zhee
sunny	Je slunečno.	ye slu·nech·no
warm	Je teplo.	ye tep·lo
windy	Je větrno.	ye vye·tr·no
spring	jaro n	yuh·ro
summer	léto n	lair·to
autumn	podzim m	pod·zim
winter	zima f	zi·muh

border crossing

I'm here ...	Jsem zde ...	ysem zde ...
in transit	v tranzitu	f truhn·zi·tu
on business	na služební cestě	nuh slu·zheb·nyee tses·tye
on holiday	na dovolené	nuh do·vo·le·nair
I'm here for ...	Jsem zde na ...	ysem zde nuh ...
(10) days	(deset) dní	(de·set) dnyee
(three) weeks	(tři) týdny	(trzhi) teed·ni
(two) months	(dva) měsíce	(dvuh) mye·see·tse

I'm going to (Valtice).
Jedu do (Valtic).   ye·du do (vuhl·tyits)

I'm staying at the (Hotel Špalíček).
Jsem ubytovaný/á v   ysem u·bi·to·vuh·nee/a v
(Hotelu Špalíček). m/f   (ho·te·lu shpuh·lee·chek)

I have nothing to declare.
Nemám nic k proclení.   ne·mam nyits k prots·le·nyee

I have something to declare.
Mám něco k proclení.   mam nye·tso k prots·le·nyee

That's not mine.
To není moje.   to ne·nyee mo·ye

transcript

tickets & luggage

Where can I buy a ticket?
Kde koupím jízdenku?
gde koh·peem yeez·den·ku

Do I need to book a seat?
Potřebuji místenku?
pot·rzhe·bu·yi mees·ten·ku

One ... ticket to (Telč), please.	... do (Telče), prosím.	... do (tel·che) pro·seem
one-way	Jednosměrnou jízdenku	yed·no·smyer·noh yeez·den·ku
return	Zpáteční jízdenku	zpa·tech·nyee yeez·den·ku

I'd like to ... my ticket, please.	Chtěl/Chtěla bych ... mojí jízdenku, prosím. m/f	khtyel/khtye·luh bikh ... mo·yee yeez·den·ku pro·seem
cancel	zrušit	zru·shit
change	změnit	zmye·nyit
collect	vyzvednout	vi·zved·noht
confirm	potvrdit	pot·vr·dyit

I'd like a ... seat, please.	Chtěl/Chtěla bych ... m/f	khtyel/khtye·luh bikh ...
nonsmoking	nekuřácké místo	ne·ku·rzhats·kair mees·to
smoking	kuřácké místo	ku·rzhats·kair mees·to

How much is it?
Kolik to stojí?
ko·lik to sto·yee

Is there a toilet?
Je tam toaleta?
ye tuhm to·uh·le·tuh

Is there air conditioning?
Je tam klimatizace?
ye tuhm kli·muh·ti·zuh·tse

How long does the trip take?
Jak dlouho trvá cesta?
yuhk dloh·ho tr·va tses·tuh

Is it a direct route?
Je to přímá cesta?
ye to przhee·ma tses·tuh

Where can I find a luggage locker?
Kde mohu najít
zavazadlová schránka?
gde mo·hu nuh·yeet
zuh·vuh·zuhd·lo·va skhran·kuh

My luggage	Moje zavazadlo	mo·ye zuh·vuh·zuhd·lo
has been ...	bylo ...	bi·lo ...
damaged	poškozeno	posh·ko·ze·no
lost	ztraceno	ztruh·tse·no
stolen	ukradeno	u·kruh·de·no

getting around

Where does flight (OK25) arrive?

Kam přiletí let (OK25)? kuhm przhi·le·tyee let (aw·ka dvuh·tset pyet)

Where does flight (OK25) depart?

Kde odlítá let (OK25)? gde od·lee·ta let (aw·ka dvuh·tset pyet)

Where's (the) ...?	Kde je ...?	gde ye ...
arrivals hall	příletová hala	przhee·le·to·va huh·luh
departures hall	odletová hala	od·le·to·va huh·luh
duty-free shop	prodejna	pro·dey·nuh
	bezcelního zboží	bez·tsel·nyee·ho zbo·zhee
gate (12)	východ k letadlu	vee·khod k le·tuhd·lu
	(dvanáct)	(dvuh·natst)

Is this the ...	Jede tento/tato ...	ye·de ten·to/tuh·to ...
to (Mělník)?	do (Mělníka)? m/f	do (myel·nyee·kuh)
bus	autobus m	ow·to·bus
train	vlak m	vluhk
tram	tramvaj f	truhm·vai
trolleybus	trolejbus m	tro·ley·bus

When's the	V kolik jede	f ko·lik ye·de
... bus?	... autobus?	... ow·to·bus
first	první	prv·nyee
last	poslední	po·sled·nyee
next	příští	przhee·shtyee

At what time does the bus/train leave?

V kolik hodin odjíždí f ko·lik ho·dyin od·yeezh·dyee
autobus/vlak? ow·to·bus/vluhk

How long will it be delayed?

Jak dlouho bude mít zpoždění? yuhk dloh·ho bu·de meet zpozh·dye·nyee

What's the next station/stop?

Která je příští stanice/zastávka? kte·ra ye przheesh·tyee stuh·nyi·tse/zuhs·taf·kuh

Does it stop at (Cheb)?
Zastaví to v (Chebu)? · zuhs·tuh·vee to f (khe·bu)

Please tell me when we get to (Přerov).
Prosím vás řekněte mi · pro·seem vas rzhek·nye·te mi
kdy budeme v (Přerově). · kdi bu·de·me f (przhe·ro·vye)

How long do we stop here?
Jak dlouho zde budeme stát? · yuhk dloh·ho zde bu·de·me stat

Is this seat available?
Je toto místo volné? · ye to·to mees·to vol·nair

That's my seat.
To je mé místo. · to ye mair mees·to

I'd like a taxi ... · *Potřebuji taxíka ...* · po·trzhe·bu·yi tuhk·see·kuh ...
  at (9am) · *v (devět hodin* · f (de·vyet ho·dyin
    dopoledne) · do·po·led·ne)
  now · *teď* · teď
  tomorrow · *zítra* · zee·truh

Is this taxi available?
Je tento taxík volný? · ye ten·to tuhk·seek vol·nee

How much is it to ...?
Kolik stojí jízdenka do ...? · ko·lik sto·yee yeez·den·kuh do ...

Please put the meter on.
Prosím zapněte taxametr. · pro·seem zuhp·nye·te tuhk·suh·me·tr

Please take me to (this address).
Prosím odvezte mě na (tuto adresu). · pro·seem od·ves·te mye na (tu·to uh·dre·su)

Please ... · *Prosím ...* · pro·seem ...
  slow down · *zpomalte* · spo·muhl·te
  stop here · *zastavte zde* · zuhs·tuhf·te zde
  wait here · *počkejte zde* · poch·key·te zde

car, motorbike & bicycle hire

I'd like to hire · *Chtěl/Chtěla bych* · khtyel/khtye·luh bikh
a ... · *si půjčit ... m/f* · si pooy·chit ...
  bicycle · *kolo* · ko·lo
  car · *auto* · ow·to
  motorbike · *motorku* · mo·tor·ku

ČEŠTINA – transport

20

with ...	s ...	s ...
a driver	*řidičem*	*rzhi*·dyi·chem
air conditioning	*klimatizací*	*kli*·muh·ti·zuh·tsee
antifreeze	*nemrznoucí směsí*	*ne*·mrz·noh·tsee *smye*·see
snow chains	*sněhovými řetězy*	*snye*·ho·vee·mi *rzhe*·tye·zi

How much for	*Kolik stojí*	*ko*·lik *sto*·yee
... hire?	*půjčení na ...?*	*pooy*·che·nyee nuh ...
hourly	*hodinu*	*ho*·dyi·nu
daily	*den*	den
weekly	*týden*	*tee*·den

air	*vzduch* m	*vz*·dukh
oil	*olej* m	*o*·ley
petrol	*benzin* m	*ben*·zin
tyre	*pneumatika* f	pne·u·muh·ti·kuh

I need a mechanic.	*Potřebuji mechanika.*	*pot*·rzhe·bu·yi me·khuh·ni·kuh
I've run out of petrol.	*Došel mi benzin.*	*do*·shel mi *ben*·zin
I have a flat tyre.	*Mám defekt.*	mam *de*·fekt

directions

Where's the ...?	*Kde je ...?*	gde ye ...
bank	*banka*	*buhn*·kuh
city centre	*centrum*	*tsen*·trum
hotel	*hotel*	*ho*·tel
market	*trh*	trh
police station	*policejní stanice*	po·li·tsey·nyee *stuh*·nyi·tse
post office	*pošta*	*posh*·tuh
public toilet	*veřejný záchod*	ve·rzhey·nee *za*·khod
tourist office	*turistická informační kancelář*	tu·ris·tits·ka *in*·for·muhch·nyee *kuhn*·tse·larzh

Is this the road to (Cheb)?
Vede tato silnice do (Chebu)?   ve·de *tuh*·to *sil*·ni·tse do (*khe*·bu)

Can you show me (on the map)?
Můžete mi to ukázat (na mapě)?   moo·zhe·te mi to u·ka·zuht (nuh *muh*·pye)

What's the address?
Jaká je adresa?   yuh·ka ye *uh*·dre·suh

How far is it?
Jak je to daleko?   yuhk ye to *duh*·le·ko

How do I get there?
Jak se tam dostanu?   yuhk se tuhm *dos*·tuh·nu

Turn ...	*Odbočte ...*	od·boch·te ...
at the corner	*za roh*	zuh rawh
at the traffic lights	*u semaforu*	u se·muh·fo·ru
left/right	*do leva/prava*	do *le*·vuh/*pruh*·vuh

It's ...	*Je to ...*	ye to ...
behind ...	*za ...*	zuh ...
far away	*daleko*	*duh*·le·ko
here	*zde*	zde
in front of ...	*před ...*	przhed ...
left	*na levo*	nuh *le*·vo
near	*blízko*	*bleez*·ko
next to ...	*vedle ...*	*ved*·le ...
on the corner	*na rohu*	nuh *ro*·hu
opposite ...	*naproti ...*	*nuh*·pro·tyi ...
right	*na pravo*	nuh *pruh*·vo
straight ahead	*přímo*	*przhee*·mo
there	*tam*	tuhm

by bus	*autobusem*	ow·to·bu·sem
by taxi	*taxikem*	*tuh*·si·kem
by train	*vlakem*	*vluh*·kem
on foot	*pěšky*	*pyesh*·ki

north	*sever*	*se*·ver
south	*jih*	yih
east	*východ*	*vee*·khod
west	*západ*	za·puhd

signs

Vchod/Východ	vkhod/vee-khod	Entrance/Exit
Otevřeno/Zavřeno	o-te-vrzhe-no/zuh-vrzhe-no	Open/Closed
Volné pokoje	vol-nair po-ko-ye	Rooms Available
Obsazeno	op-suh-ze-no	No Vacancies
Informace	in-for-muh-tse	Information
Policejní stanice	po-li-tsey-nyee stuh-nyi-tse	Police Station
Zakázáno	zuh-ka-za-no	Prohibited
Záchody	za-kho-di	Toilets
Páni	pa-nyi	Men
Ženy	zhe-ni	Women
Horké/Studené	hor-kair/stu-de-nair	Hot/Cold

accommodation

finding accommodation

Where's a ...?	Kde je ...?	gde ye ...
camping ground	tábořiště	ta-bo-rzhish-tye
guesthouse	penzion	pen-zi-on
hotel	hotel	ho-tel
youth hostel	mládežnická	mla-dezh-nyits-ka
	ubytovna	u-bi-tov-nuh

Can you recommend somewhere ...?	Můžete mi doporučit něco ...?	moo-zhe-te mi do-po-ru-chit nye-tso ...
cheap	levného	lev-nair-ho
good	dobrého	dob-rair-ho
nearby	nejbližšíhu	ney-blizh-shee-ho

I'd like to book a room, please.
Chtěl/Chtěla bych
rezervovat pokoj, prosím. m/f
khtyel/khtye-luh bikh
re-zer-vo-vuht po-koy pro-seem

I have a reservation.
Mám rezervaci.
mam re-zer-vuh-tsi

My name is ...
Mé jméno je ...
mair ymair-no ye ...

Do you have a double room?
Máte pokoj s manželskou postelí?
ma-te po-koy s muhn-zhels-koh pos-te-lee

Do you have a ... room?	Máte ... pokoj?	ma·te ... po·koy
single	jednolůžkový	yed·no·loozh·ko·vee
twin	dvoulůžkový	dvoh·loozh·ko·vee

How much is it per ...?	Kolik to stojí ...?	ko·lik to sto·yee ...
night	na noc	nuh nots
person	za osobu	zuh o·so·bu

Can I pay ...?	Mohu zaplatit ...?	mo·hu zuh·pluh·tyit ...
by credit card	kreditní kartou	kre·dit·nyee kuhr·toh
with a travellers cheque	cestovním šekem	tses·tov·nyeem she·kem

For (three) nights/weeks.
Na (tři) noci/týdny. nuh (trzhi) no·tsi/teed·ni

From (2 July) to (6 July).
Od (druhého července) od (dru·hair·ho cher·ven·tse)
do (šestého července). do (shes·tair·ho cher·ven·tse)

Can I see it?
Mohu se na něj podívat? mo·hu se na nyey po·dyee·vuht

Am I allowed to camp here?
Mohu zde stanovat? mo·hu zde stuh·no·vuht

Where can I find a camping ground?
Kde mohu najít stanový tábor? gde mo·hu nuh·yeet stuh·no·vee ta·bor

requests & queries

When's breakfast served?
V kolik se podává snídaně? f ko·lik se po·da·va snyee·duh·nye

Where's breakfast served?
Kde se podává snídaně? gde se po·da·va snyee·duh·nye

Please wake me at (seven).
Prosím probuďte mě v (sedm). pro·seem pro·buď·te mye f (se·dm)

Could I have my key, please?
Můžete mi dát můj klíč, prosím? moo·zhe·te mi dat mooy kleech pro·seem

Can I get another (blanket)?
Mohu dostat další (deku)? mo·hu dos·tuht duhl·shee (de·ku)

Do you have a/an ...?	Máte ...?	ma·te ...
elevator	výtah	vee·tah
safe	trezor	tre·zor

The room is too ...	Je moc ...	ye mots ...
expensive	drahý	druh·hee
noisy	hlučný	hluch·nee
small	malý	muh·lee

The ... doesn't work.	... nefunguje.	... ne·fun·gu·ye
air conditioning	Klimatizace	kli·muh·ti·zuh·tse
fan	Větrák	vye·trak
toilet	Toaleta	to·uh·le·tuh

This ... isn't clean.	Tento ... neni čistý.	ten·to ... ne·nyi chis·tee
pillow	polštář	pol·shtarzh
towel	ručník	ruch·nyeek

checking out

What time is checkout?
V kolik hodin máme vyklidit pokoj?   f ko·lik ho·dyin ma·me vi·kli·dyit po·koy

Can I leave my luggage here?
Mohu si zde nechat zavazadla?   mo·hu si zde ne·khuht zuh·vuh·zuhd·luh

Could I have my ..., please?	Můžete mi vratit ..., prosím?	moo·zhe·te mi vra·tyit ... pro·seem
deposit	zálohu	za·lo·hu
passport	pas	puhs
valuables	cennosti	tse·nos·tyi

communications & banking

the internet

Where's the local Internet café?
Kde je místní internetová kavárna?   gde ye meest·nyee in·ter·ne·to·va kuh·var·nuh

How much is it per hour?
Kolik to stojí na hodinu?   ko·lik to sto·yee nuh ho·dyi·nu

I'd like to ...	Chtěl/Chtěla bych ... m/f	khtyel/khtye·luh bikh ...
check my email	zkontrolovat	skon·tro·lo·vuht
	můj email	mooy ee·meyl
get Internet access	přístup na	przhees·tup nuh
	internet	in·ter·net
use a printer	použít tiskárnu	po·u·zheet tyis·kar·nu
use a scanner	použít skener	po·u·zheet ske·ner

mobile/cell phone

I'd like a ...	Chtěl/Chtěla bych ... m/f	ktyel/khtye·luh bikh ...
mobile/cell phone for hire	si půjčit mobil	si pooy·chit mo·bil
SIM card for your network	SIM kartu pro	sim kuhr·tu pro
	vaší síť	vuh·shee seet'
What are the rates?	Jaké jsou tarify?	yuh·kair ysoh tuh·ri·fi

telephone

What's your phone number?
Jaké je vaše telefonní číslo?   yuh·kair ye vuh·she te·le·fo·nyee chees·lo

The number is ...
Číslo je ...   chees·lo ye ...

Where's the nearest public phone?
Kde je nejbližší veřejný telefon?   gde ye ney·blizh·shee ve·rzhey·nee te·le·fon

I'd like to buy a phonecard.
Chtěl/Chtěla bych koupit   ktyel/khtye·luh bikh koh·pit
telefonní kartu. m/f   te·le·fo·nyee kuhr·tu

I want to ...	Chtěl/Chtěla bych ... m/f	ktyel/khtye·luh bikh ...
call (Singapore)	telefonovat do	te·le·fo·no·vuht do
	(Singapůru)	sin·guh·poo·ru
make a local call	si zavolat místně	si zuh·vo·luht meest·nye
reverse the charges	telefonovat na	te·le·fo·no·vuht na
	účet volaného	oo·chet vo·luh·nair·ho

26

How much does … cost?	*Kolik stojí …?*	ko·lik *sto*·yee …
a (three)-minute	*(tří) minutový*	(trzhee) *mi*·nu·to·vee
call	*hovor*	*ho*·vor
each extra minute	*každá další*	*kuhzh*·da *duhl*·shee
	minuta	*mi*·nu·tuh

(Seven crowns) per minute.
(Sedm korun) za jednu minutu. (se·dm *ko*·run) zuh *yed*·nu *mi*·nu·tu

post office

I want to send a …	*Chci poslat …*	khtsi *po*·sluht …
fax	*fax*	fuhks
letter	*dopis*	*do*·pis
parcel	*balík*	*buh*·leek
postcard	*pohled*	*po*·hled

I want to buy a/an …	*Chci koupīt …*	khtsi *koh*·pit …
envelope	*obálku*	*o*·bal·ku
stamp	*známku*	*znam*·ku

Please send it by	*Prosím vás pošlete*	pro·seem vas *po*·shle·te
… to (Australia).	*to … do (Austrálie).*	to … do (*ow*·stra·li·ye)
airmail	*letecky poštou*	*le*·tets·ki *posh*·toh
express mail	*expresní poštou*	*eks*·pres·nyee *posh*·toh
registered mail	*doporučenou poštou*	*do*·po·ru·che·noh *posh*·toh
surface mail	*obyčejnou poštou*	*o*·bi·chey·noh *posh*·toh

Is there any mail for me?
Mám zde nějakou poštu? mam zde *nye*·yuh·koh *posh*·tu

bank

I'd like to …	*Chtěl/Chtěla bych … m/f*	kthyel/*khtye*·luh bikh …
Where can I …?	*Kde mohu …?*	gde *mo*·hu …
arrange a transfer	*převést peníze*	*przhe*·vairst pe·nyee·ze
cash a cheque	*proměnit šek*	*pro*·mye·nyit shek
change a travellers	*proměnit*	*pro*·mye·nyit
cheque	*cestovní šek*	*tses*·tov·nyee shek
change money	*vyměnit peníze*	*vi*·mye·nyit pe·nyee·ze
get a cash advance	*zálohu v hotovosti*	*za*·lo·hu v *ho*·to·vos·tyi
withdraw money	*vybrat peníze*	*vi*·bruht pe·nyee·ze

Where's a/an ...?	Kde je ...?	gde ye ...
ATM	bankomat	buhn·ko·muht
foreign exchange office	směnárna	smye·nar·nuh

What's the ...?	Jaký je ...?	yuh·kee ye ...
charge for that	poplatek za to	po·pluh·tek zuh to
exchange rate	devizový kurz	de·vi·zo·vee kurz

It's ...	Je to ...	ye to ...
(12) crowns	(dvanáct) korun	(dvuh·natst) ko·run
(five) euros	(pět) eur	(pyet) e·ur
free	bez poplatku	bez po·pluht·ku

What time does the bank open?
Jaké jsou úřední hodiny? — yuh·kair ysoh oo·rzhed·nyee ho·dyi·ni

Has my money arrived yet?
Přišly už moje peníze? — przhi·shli uzh mo·ye pe·nyee·ze

sightseeing

getting in

What time does it open/close?
V kolik hodin otevírají/zavírají? — f ko·lik ho·dyin o·te·vee·ruh·yee/zuh·vee·ruh·yee

What's the admission charge?
Kolik stojí vstupné? — ko·lik sto·yee vstup·nair

Is there a discount for students/children?
Máte slevu pro studenty/děti? — ma·te sle·vu pro stu·den·ti/dye·tyi

I'd like a ...	Chtěl/Chtěla bych ... m/f	khtyel/khtye·luh bikh ...
catalogue	katalog	kuh·tuh·log
guide	průvodce	proo·vod·tse
local map	mapu okolí	ma·pu o·ko·lee

I'd like to see ...
   Chtěl/Chtěla bych vidět ... m/f   khtyel/*khtye*-luh bikh *vi*-dyet ...

What's that?
   Co je to?   tso ye to

Can I take a photo of this?
   Mohu toto fotografovat?   *mo*-hu *to*-to fo-to-gruh-fo-vuht

Can I take a photo of you?
   Mohu si vás vyfotit?   *mo*-hu si vas *vi*-fo-tyit

tours

When's the next ...?	*Kdy je příští ...?*	gdi ye *przheesh*-tyee ...
day trip	*celodenní výlet*	tse-lo-de-nyee *vee*-let
tour	*okružní jízda*	o-kruzh-nyee *yeez*-duh
Is ... included?	*Je zahrnuto/a ...?* n/f	ye zuh-hr-nu-to/a ...
accommodation	*ubytování* n	u-bi-to-va-nyee
the admission charge	*vstupné* n	fstup-nair
food	*strava* f	struh-vuh
transport	*doprava* f	do-pruh-vuh

How long is the tour?
   Jak dlouho bude trvat   yuhk *dloh*-ho *bu*-de *tr*-vuht
   tento zájezd?   ten-to *za*-yezd

What time should we be back?
   V kolik hodin se máme vrátit?   f ko-lik ho-dyin se *ma*-me *vra*-tyit

sightseeing		
castle	*hrad* m	hruhd
cathedral	*katedrála* f	kuh-te-ura-luh
church	*kostel* m	kos-tel
main square	*hlavní náměstí* n	hluhv-nyee na-myes-tyee
monastery	*klášter* m	klash-ter
monument	*pamotnik* m	puh-mat-nyeek
museum	*muzeum* n	mu-ze-um
old city	*staré město* n	stuh-rair myes-to
palace	*palác* m	puh-lats
ruins	*zříceniny* f pl	zrzhee-tse-nyi-ni
stadium	*stadion* m	stuh-di-yon
statue	*socha* f	so-khuh

shopping

enquiries

Where's a ...?	Kde je ...?	gde ye ...
bank	banka	buhn-kuh
bookshop	knihkupectví	knyikh-ku-pets-tvee
camera shop	foto potřeby	fo-to pot-rzhe-bi
department store	obchodní dům	op-khod-nyee doom
grocery store	smíšené zboží	smee-she-nair zbo-zhee
market	tržnice	tr-zhnyi-tse
newsagency	tabák	tuh-bak
supermarket	samoobsluha	suh-mo-op-slu-huh

Where can I buy (a padlock)?
Kde si mohu koupit (zámek)?   gde si *mo*-hu *koh*-pit (*za*-mek)

I'm looking for ....
Hledám ...   *hle*-dam ...

Can I look at it?
Mohu se na to podívat?   *mo*-hu se nuh to *po*-dyee-vuht

Do you have any others?
Máte ještě jiné?   *ma*-te *yesh*-tye *yi*-nair

Does it have a guarantee?
Je na to záruka?   ye nuh to *za*-ru-kuh

Can I have it sent abroad?
Můžete mi to poslat   *moo*-zhe-te mi to *pos*-luht
do zahraničí?   do *zuh*-hruh-nyi-chee

Can I have my ... repaired?
Můžete zde opravit ...?   *moo*-zhe-te zde *o*-pruh-vit ...

It's faulty.
Je to vadné.   ye to *vahd*-nair

I'd like ...,	Chtěl/Chtěla bych	khtyel/khtye-la bikh
please.	..., prosím. m/f	... pro-seem
a bag	tašku	tuhsh-ku
a refund	vrátit peníze	vra-tyit pe-nyee-ze
to return this	toto vrátit	to-to vra-tyit

paying

How much is it?
Kolik to stojí?
ko·lik to sto·yee

Can you write down the price?
Můžete mi napsat cenu?
moo·zhe·te mi nuhp·suht tse·nu

That's too expensive.
To je moc drahé.
to ye mots druh·hair

What's your lowest price?
Jaká je vaše konečná cena?
yuh·ka ye vuh·she ko·nech·na tse·nuh

I'll give you (200 crowns).
Dám vám (dvěstě korun).
dam vam (dvye·stye ko·run)

There's a mistake in the bill.
Na účtu je chyba.
nuh ooch·tu ye khi·buh

Do you accept ...?	*Mohu platit ...?*	mo·hu pluh·tyit ...
credit cards	*kreditními kartami*	kre·dit·nyee·mi kuhr·tuh·mi
debit cards	*platebními kartami*	pluh·teb·nyee·mi kuhr·tuh·mi
travellers cheques	*cestovními šeky*	tses·tov·nyee·mi she·ki
I'd like ..., please.	*Můžete mi dát ..., prosím?*	moo·zhe·te mi dat ... pro·seem
a receipt	*účet*	oo·chet
my change	*mé drobné*	mair drob·nair

clothes & shoes

Can I try it on?	*Mohu si to zkusit?*	mo·hu si to sku·sit
My size is (40).	*Mám číslo (čtyřicet).*	mam chee·slo (chti·rzhi·tset)
It doesn't fit.	*Nepadne mi to.*	ne·puhd·ne mi to
small	*malý*	muh·le
medium	*střední*	strzhed·nye
large	*velký*	vel·keeh

books & music

I'd like a ...	*Chtěl/Chtěla bych ...* m/f	khtyel/khtye·luh bikh ...
newspaper	*noviny*	no·vi·ni
(in English)	*(v angličtině)*	(f uhn·glich·tyi·nye)
pen	*propisovací pero*	pro·pi·so·vuh·tsee pe·ro

Is there an English-language bookshop?
Je tam knihkupectví   ye tuhm knyih·ku·pets·tvee
s anglickýma knihama?   s uhn·glits·kee·muh knyi·huh·muh

I'm looking for something by (Kabát).
Hledám něco od (Kabátu).   hle·dam nye·tso od (kuh·ba·tu)

Can I listen to this?
Mohu si to poslechnout?   mo·hu si to po·slekh·noht

photography

Can you ...?	*Můžete ...?*	moo·zhe·te ...
develop this film	*vyvolat tento film*	vi·vo·luht ten·to film
load my film	*vložit můj film*	vlo·zhit mooy film
transfer photos	*uložit fotografie*	u·lo·zhit fo·to·gruh·fi·ye
from my camera	*z mého*	z mair·ho
to CD	*fotoaparátu*	fo·to·uh·puh·ra·tu
	na CD	nuh tsair·dairch·ko

I need a/an ... film	*Potřebuji ... film*	pot·rzhe·bu·yi ... film
for this camera.	*pro tento fotoaparát.*	pro ten·to fo·to·uh·puh·rat
APS	*APS*	a·pair·es
B&W	*černobílý*	cher·no·bee·lee
colour	*barevný*	buh·rev·nee
slide	*diapozitivní*	di·uh·po·zi·tiv·nye
(200) speed	*film s citlivostí*	film s tsit·li·vos·tyee
	(dvěstě)	(dvye·stye)

When will it be ready?   *Kdy to bude hotové?*   gdi to bu·de ho·to·vair

meeting people

greetings, goodbyes & introductions

Hello/Hi.	*Ahoj/Čau.*	uh·hoy/chow
Good night.	*Dobrou noc.*	do·broh nots
Goodbye.	*Na shledanou.*	nuh·skhle·duh·noh
Bye.	*Ahoj/Čau.*	uh·hoy/chow
See you later.	*Na viděnou.*	nuh *vi*·dye·noh

Mr/Mrs	*pan/paní*	puhn/*puh*·nyee
Miss	*slečna*	*slech*·nuh

How are you?	*Jak se máte/jnáš?* pol/inf	yuhk se *ma*·te/mash
Fine. And you?	*Dobře. A vy/ty?* pol/inf	*dob*·rzhe a vi/ti
What's your name?	*Jak se jmenujete/ jmenuješ?* pol/inf	yuhk se *yme*·nu·ye·te/ *yme*·nu·yesh
My name is ...	*Jmenuji se ...*	*yme*·nu·yi se ...
I'm pleased to meet you.	*Těší mě.*	*tye*·shee mye

This is my ...	*To je můj/moje ...* m/f	to ye mooy/*mo*·ye ...
boyfriend	*přítel*	*przhe*·tel
brother	*bratr*	*bruh*·tr
daughter	*dcera*	*dtse*·ruh
father	*otec*	*o*·tets
friend	*přítel* m	*przhe*·tel
	přítelkyně f	*przhe*·tel·ki·nye
girlfriend	*přítelkyně*	*przhe*·tel·ki·nye
husband	*manžel*	*muhn*·zhel
mother	*matka*	*muht*·kuh
partner (intimate)	*partner/partnerka* m/f	*puhrt*·ner/*puhrt*·ner·kuh
sister	*sestra*	*ses*·truh
son	*syn*	sin
wife	*manželka*	*muhn*·zhel·kuh

Here's my ...	*Zde je moje ...*	zde ye *mo*·ye ...
What's your ...?	*Jaké/Jaká je vaše ...?* n/f	*yah*·kair/*yuh*·ka ye *vuh*·she ...
(email) address	*(email) adresa* f	(ee·meyl) *uh*·dre·suh
fax number	*faxové číslo* n	*fuhk*·so·vair *chees*·lo
phone number	*telefonní číslo* n	te·le·fo·nyee *chees*·lo

occupations

What's your occupation?
Jaké je vaše povolání? — yuh·kair ye *vuh·*she *po*·vo·la·nyee

I'm a/an ... — *Jsem ...* — ysem ...

artist	*umělec/umělkyně* m/f	u·mye·lets/u·myel·ki·nye
businessperson	*obchodník* m&f	ob·khod·nyeek
farmer	*zemědělec* m	ze·mye·dye·lets
	zemědělkyně f	ze·mye·dyel·ki·nye
manual worker	*dělník* m&f	dyel·nyeek
office worker	*úředník* m	oo·rzhed·nyeek
	úřednice f	oo·rzhed·nyi·tse
scientist	*vědec/vědkyně* m/f	vye·dets/vyed·ki·nye

background

Where are you from?	*Odkud jste?*	ot·kud yste
I'm from ...	*Jsem z ...*	ysem s ...
Australia	*Austrálie*	ow·stra·li·ye
Canada	*Kanady*	kuh·nuh·di
England	*Anglie*	uhn·gli·ye
New Zealand	*Nového Zélandu*	no·vair·ho zair·luhn·du
the USA	*Ameriky*	uh·meh·ri·ki
Are you married?	*Jste ženatý/vdaná?* m/f	yste zhe·nuh·tee/fduh·na
I'm married.	*Jsem ženatý/vdaná.* m/f	ysem zhe·nuh·tee/fduh·na
I'm single.	*Jsem svobodný/á.* m/f	ysem svo·bod·nee/a

age

How old ...?	*Kolik ...?*	ko·lik ...
are you	*je vám let* pol	ye vam let
	ti je let inf	ti ye let
is your daughter	*let je vaší dceři*	let ye vuh·shee dtse·rzhi
is your son	*let je vašemu synovi*	let ye vuh·she·mu si·no·vi
I'm ... years old.	*Je mi ... let.*	ye mi ... let
He's ... years old.	*Je mu ... let.*	ye mu ... let
She's ... years old.	*Jí je ... let.*	yee ye ... let

34

feelings

Are you ...?	Jste ...?	yste ...
I'm/I'm not ...	Jsem/Nejsem ...	ysem/ney·sem ...
happy	šťastný/šťastná m/f	shtyuhst·nee/shtyuhst·na
hungry	hladový/hladová m/f	hluh·do·vee/hluh·do·va
sad	smutný/smutná m/f	smut·nee/smut·na
thirsty	žíznivý/žíznivá m/f	zheez·nyi·vee/zheez·nyi·va

Are you ...?	Je vám ...?	ye vam ...
I'm/I'm not ...	Je/Neni mi ...	ye/ne·nyi mi ...
cold	zima	zi·muh
hot	horko	hor·ko

entertainment

going out

Where can I find ...?	Kde mohu najít ...?	gde mo·hu nuh·yeet ...
clubs	kluby	klu·bi
gay venues	homosexuální	ho·mo·sek·su·al·nyee
	zábavné podniky	za·buhv·nair pod·ni·ki
pubs	hospody	hos·po·di

I feel like going	Rád bych šel ... m	rad bikh shel ...
to a/the ...	Ráda bych šla ... f	ra·duh bikh shluh ...
concert	na koncert	nuh kon·tsert
movies	do kina	do ki·nuh
party	na mejdan/	nuh mey·duhn/
	večírek	ve·chee·rek
theatre	na hru	nuh hru
restaurant	do restaurace	do res tow·ruh·tse

interests

Do you like to ...?		
go to concerts	Chodíte na koncerty?	kho·dyee·te nuh kon·tser·ti
dance	Tancujete?	tuhn·tsu·ye·te
listen to music	Posloucháte hudbu?	po·sloh·kha·te hud·bu

Do you like ...?	Máte rád/ráda ...? m/f	ma·te rad/ra·duh ...
I like ...	Mám rád/ráda ... m/f	mam rad/ra·duh ...
I don't like ...	Nemám rád/ráda ... m/f	ne·mam rad/ra·duh ...
art	umění	u·mye·nyee
cooking	vaření	vuh·rzhe·nyee
movies	filmy	fil·mi
reading	čtení	chte·nyee
sport	sport	sport
travelling	cestování	tses·to·va·nyee

food & drink

finding a place to eat

Can you recommend a ...?	Můžete doporučit ...?	moo·zhe·te do·po·ru·chit ...
café	kavárnu	kuh·var·nu
pub	hospodu	hos·po·du
restaurant	restauraci	res·tow·ruh·tsi
I'd like ..., please.	Chtěl/Chtěla bych ..., prosím. m/f	khtyel/khtye·luh bikh ... pro·seem
a table for (five)	stůl pro (pět)	stool pro (pyet)
the nonsmoking section	nekuřáckou místnost	ne·ku·rzhats·koh meest·nost
the smoking section	kuřáckou místnost	ku·rzhats·koh meest·nost

ordering food

breakfast	snídaně f	snee·duh·nye
lunch	oběd m	o·byed
dinner	večeře f	ve·che·rzhe
snack	občerstvení n	ob·cherst·ve·nyee
What would you recommend?	Co byste doporučil/ doporučila? m/f	tso bis·te do·po·ru·chil/ do·po·ru·chi·luh

I'd like (the) ..., please.	Chtěl/Chtěla bych ..., prosím. m/f	khtyel/khtye·luh bikh ... pro·seem
bill	účet	oo·chet
drink list	nápojový lístek	na·po·yo·vee lees·tek
menu	jídelníček	yee·del·nyee·chek
that dish	ten pokrm	ten po·krm

drinks

(cup of) coffee ...	(šálek) kávy ...	(sha·lek) ka·vi ...
(cup of) tea ...	(šálek) čaje ...	(sha·lek) chuh·ye ...
with milk	s mlékem	s mlair·kem
without sugar	bez cukru	bez tsu·kru
(orange) juice	(pomerančový) džus m	(po·me·ruhn·cho·vee) dzhus
soft drink	nealkoholický nápoj m	ne·uhl·ko·ho·lits·kee na·poy
(hot) water	(horká) voda f	(hor·ka) vo·duh
... mineral water	... minerální voda	... mi·ne·ral·nyee vo·duh
sparkling	perlivá	per·li·va
still	neperlivá	ne·per·li·va

in the bar

I'll have a ...	Dám si ...	dam si ...
I'll buy you a drink.	Zvu vás/tě na sklenku. pol/inf	zvu vas/tye nuh sklen·ku
What would you like?	Co byste si přál/přála? m/f	tso bis·te si przhal/przha·la
Cheers!	Na zdraví!	nuh zdruh·vee
brandy	brandy f	bruhn·di
champagne	šampaňské n	shuhm·puhn'·skair
cocktail	koktejl m	kok·teyl
a shot of (whisky)	panák (whisky)	puh·nak (vis·ki)
a bottle/jug of beer	láhev/džbán piva	la·hef/dzhban pi·vuh
a bottle/glass of ... wine	láhev/skleničku ... vína	la·hef/skle·nyich·ku ... vee·nuh
red	červeného	cher·ve·nair·ho
sparkling	šumivého	shu·mi·vair·ho
white	bílého	bee·lair·ho

What's the local speciality?
| Co je místní specialita? | tso ye *meest*·nyee spe·tsi·uh·li·tuh |

What's that?
| Co to je? | tso to ye |

How much is (500 grams of cheese)?
| Kolik stojí (padesát | ko·lik *sto*·yee (*puh*·de·sat |
| deka sýra)? | de·kuh see·ruh) |

I'd like ...	Chtěl/Chtěla bych ... m/f	khtyel/*khtye*·luh bikh ...
200 grams	dvacet deka	*dvuh*·tset de·kuh
(two) kilos	(dvě) kila	(dvye) *ki*·luh
(three) pieces	(tři) kusy	(trzhi) *ku*·si
(six) slices	(šest) krajíců	(shest) *kruh*·yee·tsoo

Less.	Méně.	*mair*·nye
Enough.	Stačí.	*stuh*·chee
More.	Trochu více.	*tro*·khu *vee*·tse

special diets & allergies

Is there a vegetarian restaurant near here?
| Je zde blízko vegetariánská | ye zde *blees*·ko ve·ge·tuh·ri·ans·ka |
| restaurace? | *res*·tow·ruh·tse |

Do you have vegetarian food?
| Máte vegetariánská jídla? | *ma*·te ve·ge·tuh·ri·ans·ka *yeed*·luh |

Could you prepare a meal without ...?
| Mohl/Mohla by jste | *mo*·hl/*mo*·hluh bi yste |
| připravit jídlo bez ...? m/f | *przhi*·pruh·vit *yeed*·lo bez ... |

butter	máslo n	*mas*·lo
eggs	vejce n pl	*vey*·tse
meat stock	bujón m	*bu*·yawn

I'm allergic to ...	Mám alergii na ...	mam *uh*·ler·gi·yi nuh ...
dairy produce	mléčné výrobky	*mlair*·chnair *vee*·rob·ki
gluten	lepek	*le*·pek
MSG	glutaman sodný	*glu*·tuh·muhn sod·nee
nuts	ořechy	*o*·rzhe·khi
seafood	plody moře	*plo*·di *mo*·rzhe

menu reader

boršč m	*borshch*	*beetroot soup*
bramboračka f	*bruhm-bo-ruhch-kuh*	*thick soup of potatoes & mushrooms*
bramborák m	*bruhm-bo-rak*	*potato cake*
čevapčiči n pl	*che-vuhp-chi-chi*	*fried or grilled minced veal, pork & mutton made into cone-like shapes*
drštky f pl	*drsht-ki*	*sliced tripe*
dušená roštěnka f	*du-she-na rosh-tyen-kuh*	*braised beef slices in sauce*
fazolová polévka f	*fuh-zo-lo-va po-lairf-kuh*	*bean soup*
guláš m	*gu-lash*	*thick, spicy stew, usually made with beef & potatoes*
gulášová polévka f	*gu-la-sho-va po-lairf-kuh*	*beef goulash soup*
houskové knedlíky m pl	*hohs-ko-vair kned-lee-ki*	*bread dumplings*
hovězí guláš n	*ho-vye-zee gu-lash*	*beef stew, sometimes served with dumplings*
hrachová polévka f	*hra-kho-va po-lairf-kuh*	*thick pea soup with bacon*
hranolky f pl	*hruh-nol-ki*	*French fries*
jablečný závin m	*yuh-blech-nee za-vin*	*apple strudel*
jelito n	*ye-li-to*	*black pudding*
karbanátek m	*kuhr-buh-na-tek*	*hamburger with breadcrumbs, egg, diced bread roll & onions*
klobása f	*klo-ba-suh*	*thick sausage*
koprová polévka f	*kop-ro-va po-lairf-kuh*	*dill & sour cream soup*

krokety f pl	*kro*-ke-ti	deep-fried mashed potato balls
kuřecí polévka s nudlemi f	*ku*-rzhe-tsee po-lairf-kuh s *nud*-le-mi	chicken noodle soup
kuře na paprice n	*ku*-rzhe nuh *puh*-pri-tse	chicken boiled in spicy paprika cream sauce
lečo n	*le*-cho	stewed onions, capsicums, tomatoes, eggs & sausage
míchaná vejce f pl	*mee*-khuh-na *vey*-tse	scrambled eggs
nudlová polévka f	*nud*-lo-va po-lairf-kuh	noodle soup made from chicken broth with vegetables
oplatka f	*o*-pluht-kuh	large paper-thin waffle
ovocné knedlíky m pl	*o*-vots-nair *kned*-lee-ki	fruit dumplings
palačinka f	*puh*-luh-chin-kuh	crepe • pancake
plněná paprika f	*pl*-nye-na *puh*-pri-kuh	capsicum stuffed with minced meat & rice, in tomato sauce
Pražská šunka f	*pruhzh*-ska *shun*-kuh	Prague ham – ham pickled in brine & spices & smoked over a fire
přírodní řízek m	*przhee*-rod-nyee *rzhee*-zek	pork or veal schnitzel without breadcrumbs
rizoto n	*ri*-zo-to	a mixture of pork, onions, peas & rice
ruské vejce n pl	*rus*-kair *vey*-tse	hard-boiled eggs & ham, topped with mayonnaise & caviar
rybí polévka f	*ri*-bee po-lairf-kuh	fish soup usually made with carp & some carrots, potatoes & peas
smažený květák s bramborem m	*smuh*-zhe-nee *kvye*-tak s *bruhm*-bo-rem	cauliflower florets fried in breadcrumbs & served with boiled potatoes & tartar sauce
svíčková na smetaně f	*sveech*-ko-va nuh *sme*-ta-nye	roast beef & dumplings in carrot cream sauce, topped with lemon, cranberries & whipped cream
tvarohový koláč m	*tvuh*-ro-ho-vee *ko*-lach	pastry with cottage cheese & raisins

emergencies

basics

Help!	Pomoc!	*po*·mots
Stop!	Zastav!	*zuhs*·tuhf
Go away!	Běžte pryč!	*byezh*·te prich
Thief!	Zloděj!	*zlo*·dyey
Fire!	Hoří!	*ho*·rzhee
Watch out!	Pozor!	*po*·zor

Call ...!	Zavolejte ...!	*zuh*·vo·ley·te ...
a doctor	lékaře	*lair*·kuh·rzhe
an ambulance	sanitku	*suh*·nit·ku
the police	policii	*po*·li·tsi·yi

It's an emergency.
To je naléhavý případ. — to ye *nuh*·lair·huh·vee *przhee*·puhd

Could you help me, please?
Můžete prosím pomoci? — *moo*·zhe·te *pro*·seem *po*·mo·tsi

Can I use the phone?
Mohu si zatelefonovat? — *mo*·hu si *zuh*·te·le·fo·no·vuht

I'm lost.
Zabloudil/Zabloudila jsem. m/f — *zuh*·bloh·dyil/*zuh*·bloh·dyi·luh ysem

Where are the toilets?
Kde jsou toalety? — gde ysoh *to*·uh·le·ti

police

Where's the police station?
Kde je policejní stanice? — gde ye *po*·li·tsey·nyee *stuh*·nyi·tse

I want to report an offence.
Chci nahlásit trestný čin. — khtsi *nuh*·hla·sit *trest*·nee chin

I have insurance.
Jsem pojištěný/pojištěná. m/f — ysem *po*·yish·tye·nee/*po*·yish·tye·na

I've been ...	... mě.	... mye
assaulted	Přepadli	*przhe*·puhd·li
raped	Znásilnili	*zna*·sil·nyi·li
robbed	Okradli	*o*·kruhd·li

I've lost my ...	Ztratil/Ztratila	ztruh·tyil/ztruh·tyi·luh
	jsem ... m/f	ysem ...
My ... was/were stolen.	Ukradli mě ...	u·kruhd·li mye ...
backpack	batoh	buh·tawh
credit card	kreditní kartu	kre·dit·nyee kuhr·tu
bag	zavazadlo	zuh·vuh·zuhd·lo
handbag	kabelku	kuh·bel·ku
jewellery	šperky	shper·ki
money	peníze	pe·nyee·ze
passport	pas	puhs
travellers cheques	cestovní šeky	tses·tov·nyee she·ki
wallet	peněženku	pe·nye·zhen·ku
I want to contact my ...	Potřebuji se obrátit na ...	pot·rzhe·bu·yi se o·bra·tyit nuh ...
consulate	můj konzulát	mooy kon·zu·lat
embassy	mé velvyslanectví	mair vel·vi·sluh·nets·tvee

health

medical needs

Where's the nearest ...?	Kde je nejbližší ...?	gde ye ney·blizh·shee ...
dentist	zubař	zu·buhrzh
doctor	lékař	lair·kuhrzh
hospital	nemocnice	ne·mots·nyi·tse
(night) pharmacist	(non-stop) lékárník	(non·stop) lair·kar·nyeek

I need a doctor (who speaks English).

Potřebuji (anglickomluvícího) — pot·rzhe·bu·yi (uhn·glits·kom·lu·vee·tsee·ho)
doktora. — dok·to·ruh

Could I see a female doctor?

Mohla bych být vyšetřená — mo·hluh bikh beet vi·shet·rzhe·na
lékařkou? — lair·kuhrzh·koh

I've run out of my medication.

Došly mi léky. — dosh·li mi lair·ki

symptoms, conditions & allergies

I'm sick.	Jsem nemocný/	ysem ne·mots·nee/
	nemocná. m/f	ne·mots·na
It hurts here.	Tady to bolí.	tuh·di to bo·lee
I have (a) …	Mám …	mam …

asthma	astma n	uhst·muh
bronchitis	zánět průdušek m	za·nyet proo·du·shek
constipation	zácpa f	zats·puh
cough n	kašel m	kuh·shel
diarrhoea	průjem m	proo·yem
fever	horečka f	ho·rech·kuh
headache	bolesti hlavy f	bo·les·tyi hluh·vi
heart condition	srdeční porucha f	sr·dech·nyee po·ru·khuh
nausea	nevolnost f	ne·vol·nost
pain n	bolest f	bo·lest
sore throat	bolest v krku f	bo·lest f kr·ku
toothache	bolení zubu n	bo·le·nyee zu·bu

I'm allergic	Jsem alergický/	ysem uh·ler·gits·kee/
to …	alergická na … m/f	uh·ler·gits·ka nuh …
antibiotics	antibiotika	uhn·ti·bi·o·ti·kuh
anti-inflammatories	protizánětlivé léky	pro·tyi·za·nyet·li·vair lair·ki
aspirin	aspirin	uhs·pi·rin
bees	včely	fche·li
codeine	kodein	ko·deyn
penicillin	penicilin	pe·ni·tsi·lin

antiseptic	antiseptický	uhn·ti·sep·tits·kee
	prostředek m	prost·rzhe·dek
bandage	obvaz m	ob·vuhz
condoms	prezervativy m pl	pre·zer·vuh·ti·vi
contraceptives	antikoncepce f	uhn·ti·kon·tsep·tse
diarrhoea medicine	lék na průjem m	lairk nuh proo·yem
insect repellent	prostředek na	pros·trzhe·dek nuh
	hubení hmyzu m	hu·be·nyee hmi·zu
laxatives	projímadla m pl	pro·yee·muhd·la
painkillers	prášky proti bolesti m pl	prash·ki pro·tyi bo·les·tyi
rehydration salts	iontový nápoj m	yon·to·vee na·poy
sleeping tablets	prášky na spaní m pl	prash·ki nuh spuh·nyee

english–czech dictionary

Czech nouns in this dictionary have their gender indicated by ⓜ (masculine), ⓕ (feminine) or ⓝ (neuter).
If it's a plural noun, you'll also see pl. Adjectives are given in the masculine form only. Words are also marked
as a (adjective), v (verb), sg (singular), pl (plural), inf (informal) or pol (polite) where necessary.

A

accident *nehoda* ⓕ ne·ho·duh
accommodation *ubytování* ⓝ
　u·bi·to·va·nyee
adaptor *adaptor* ⓜ uh·duhp·tor
address *adresa* ⓕ uh·dre·suh
after *po* po
air-conditioned *klimatizovaný* klí·muh·ti·zo·vuh·nee
airplane *letadlo* ⓝ le·tuhd·lo
airport *letiště* ⓝ le·tyish·tye
alcohol *alkohol* ⓜ uhl·ko·hol
all *a všichni* vshikh·nyi
allergy *alergie* ⓕ uh·ler·gi·ye
ambulance *ambulance* ⓕ uhm·bu·luhn·tse
and *a* uh
ankle *kotník* ⓜ kot·nyeek
arm *paže* ⓕ puh·zhe
ashtray *popelník* ⓜ po·pel·nyeek
ATM *bankomat* ⓜ buhn·ko·muht

B

baby *nemluvně* ⓝ nem·luv·nye
back (body) *záda* ⓝ za·duh
backpack *batoh* ⓜ buh·tawh
bad *špatný* shpuht·nee
bag *taška* ⓕ tuhsh·kuh
baggage claim *výdej zavazadel*
　vee·dey zuh·vuh·zuh·del
bank *banka* ⓕ buhn·kuh
bar *bar* ⓜ buhr
bathroom *koupelna* ⓕ koh·pel·nuh
battery *baterie* ⓕ buh·te·ri·ye
beautiful *krásný* kras·nee
bed *postel* ⓕ pos·tel
beer *pivo* ⓝ pí·vo
before *před* przhed
behind *za* zuh
bicycle *kolo* ⓝ ko·lo
big *velký* vel·kee
bill *účet* ⓜ oo·chet
black *černý* cher·nee

blanket *deka* ⓕ de·kuh
blood group *krevní skupina* ⓕ
　krev·nyee sku·pi·nuh
blue *modrý* mod·ree
book (make a reservation) v *objednat* ob·yed·nuht
bottle *láhev* ⓕ la·hef
bottle opener *otvírák na láhve* ⓜ
　ot·vee·rak nuh lah·ve
boy *chlapec* ⓜ khluh·pets
brakes (car) *brzdy* ⓕ pl brz·di
breakfast *snídaně* ⓕ snee·duh·nye
broken (faulty) *zlomený* zlo·me·nee
bus *autobus* ⓜ ow·to·bus
business *obchod* ⓜ op·khod
buy *koupit* koh·pit

C

café *kavárna* ⓕ kuh·var·nuh
camera *fotoaparát* ⓜ fo·to·uh·puh·rat
camp site *autokempink* ⓜ ow·to·kem·pink
cancel *zrušit* zru·shit
can opener *otvírák na konzervy* ⓜ
　ot·vee·rak nuh kon·zer·vi
car *auto* ⓝ ow·to
cash *hotovost* ⓕ ho·to·vost
cash (a cheque) v *inkasovat šek* in·kuh·so·vuht shek
cell phone *mobil* ⓜ mo·bil
centre *střed* ⓜ strzhed
change (money) v *vyměnit* vi·mye·nyit
cheap *levný* lev·nee
check (bill) *účet* ⓜ oo·chet
check-in *recepce* ⓕ re·tsep·tse
chest *hruď* ⓕ hrud'
child *dítě* ⓝ dye·tye
cigarette *cigareta* ⓕ tsi·guh·re·tuh
city *město* ⓝ myes·to
clean a *čistý* chis·tee
closed *zavřený* zuh·vrzhe·nee
coffee *káva* ⓕ ka·vuh
coins *mince* ⓕ min·tse
cold a *chladný* khluhd·nee
collect call *hovor na účet volaného* ⓜ
　ho·vor nuh oo·chet vo·luh·nair·ho

come *přijít* przhi-yeet
computer *počítač* ⓜ po-chee-tuhch
condom *kondom/prezervativ* ⓜ pre-zer-vuh-tif
contact lenses *kontaktní čočky* ① pl
    kon-tuhkt-nyee choch-ki
cook ∨ *vařit* vuh-rzhit
cost *cena* ① tse-nuh
credit card *kreditní karta* ①
    kre-dit-nyee kuhr-tuh
cup *šálek* ⓜ sha-lek
currency exchange *směnárna* ① smye-nar-nuh
customs (immigration) *celnice* ① tsel-ni-tse
Czech a *český* ches-kee
Czech (language) *čeština* ① chesh-tyi-nuh
Czech Republic *Česká republika* ①
    ches-ka re-pu-bli-kuh

D

dangerous *nebezpečný* ne-bez-pech-nee
date (time) *schůzka* ① skhooz-kuh
day *den* ⓜ den
delay *zpoždění* ① zpozh-dye-nyee
dentist *zubař/zubařka* ⓜ/① zu-buhrzh/zu-buhrzh-kuh
depart *odjet* od-yet
diaper *plenka* ① plairn-kuh
dictionary *slovník* ⓜ slov-nyeek
dinner *večeře* ① ve-che-rzhe
direct *přímý* przhee-mee
dirty *špinavý* shpi-nuh-vee
disabled *invalidní* in-vuh-lid-nyee
discount *sleva* ① sle-vuh
doctor *doktor/doktorka* ⓜ/① dok-tor/dok-tor-kuh
double bed *manželská postel* ① muhn-zhels-ka pos-tel
double room *dvoulůžkový pokoj* ⓜ
    dvoh-loozh-ko-vee po-koy
drink *nápoj* ⓜ na-poy
drive ∨ *řídit* rzhee-dyit
drivers licence *řidičský průkaz* ⓜ
    rzhi-dyich-skee proo-kuhz
drugs (illicit) *drogy* ① pl dro-gi
dummy (pacifier) *dudlík* ⓜ dud-leek

E

ear *ucho* ⓝ u-kho
east *východ* ⓜ vee-khod
eat *jíst* yeest
economy class *turistická třída* ① tu-ris-tits-ka trzhee-duh
electricity *elektřina* ① e-lek-trzhi-nuh
elevator *výtah* ⓜ vee-tuh
email *email* ⓔ ee-meyl

embassy *velvyslanectví* ⓝ vel-vi-sluh-nets-tvee
emergency *pohotovost* ① po-ho-to-vost
English (language) *angličtina* ① uhn-glich-tyi-nuh
entrance *vstup* ⓜ vstup
evening *večer* ⓜ ve-cher
exchange rate *směnný kurs* ⓜ smye-nee kurz
exit *východ* ⓜ vee-khod
expensive *drahý* druh-hee
express mail *expresní zásilka* ① eks-pres-nyee za-sil-kuh
eye *oko* ⓝ o-ko

F

far *daleko* duh-le-ko
fast *rychlý* rikh-lee
father *otec* ⓜ o-tets
film (camera) *film* ⓜ film
finger *prst* ⓜ prst
first-aid kit *lékárnička* ① lair-kar-nyich-kuh
first class *první třída* ① prv-nyee trzhee-duh
fish *ryba* ① ri-buh
food *jídlo* ⓝ yeed-lo
foot *chodidlo* ⓝ kho-dyid-lo
fork *vidlička* ① vid-lich-kuh
free (of charge) *bezplatný* bez-pluht-nee
friend *přítel/přítelkyně* ⓜ/①
    przhee-tel/przhee-tel-ki-nye
fruit *ovoce* ⓝ o-vo-tse
full *plný* pl-nee
funny *legrační* le-gruhch-nyee

G

gift *dar* ⓜ duhr
girl *dívka* ① dyeef-kuh
glass (drinking) *sklenička* ① skle-nyich-kuh
glasses *brýle* ① pl bree-le
go *jít* yeet
good *dobrý* do-bree
green *zelený* ze-le-nee
guide *průvodce* ⓜ proo-vod-tse

H

half *polovina* ① po-lo-vi-nuh
hand *ruka* ① ru-kuh
handbag *kabelka* ① kuh-bel-kuh
happy *šťastný* shtyast-nee
have *mít* meet
he *on* on
head *hlava* ① hluh-vuh
heart *srdce* ⓝ srd-tse

heat *horko* ⓝ hor-ko
heavy *těžký* tyezh-kee
help v *pomoci* po-mo-tsi
here *tady* tuh-di
high *vysoký* vi-so-kee
highway *dálnice* ⓕ dal-nyi-tse
hike v *trampovat* truhm-po-vuht
holiday *svátek* ⓜ sva-tek
homosexual *homosexuál* ⓜ ho-mo-sek-su-al
hospital *nemocnice* ⓕ ne-mots-nyi-tse
hot *horký* hor-kee
hotel *hotel* ⓜ ho-tel
hungry *hladový* hluh-do-vee
husband *manžel* ⓜ muhn-zhel

I

I *já* ya
identification (card) *osobní doklad* ⓕ
  o-sob-nyee dok-luhd
ill *nemocný* ne-mots-nee
important *důležitý* doo-le-zhi-tee
included *včetně* fchet-nye
injury *zranění* ⓝ zruh-nye-nyee
insurance *pojištění* ⓝ po-yish-tye-nyee
Internet *internet* ⓜ in-ter-net
interpreter *tlumočník/tlumočnice* ⓜ/ⓕ
  tlu-moch-nyeek/tlu-moch-nyi-tse

J

jewellery *šperky* ⓜ pl shper-ki
job *zaměstnání* ⓝ zuh-myest-na-nyee

K

key *klíč* ⓜ kleech
kilogram *kilogram* ⓜ ki-lo-gruhm
kitchen *kuchyň* ⓕ ku-khin'
knife *nůž* ⓜ noozh

L

laundry (place) *prádelna* ⓕ pra-del-nuh
lawyer *advokát/advokátka* ⓜ/ⓕ
  uhd-vo-kat/uhd-vo-kat-kuh
left (direction) *levý* le-vee
left-luggage office *úschovna zavazadel* ⓕ
  oos-khov-nuh zuh-vuh-zuh-del
leg *noha* ⓕ no-huh

lesbian *lesbička* ⓕ les-bich-kuh
less *menší* men-shee
letter (mail) *dopis* ⓜ do-pis
lift (elevator) *výtah* ⓜ vee-tah
light *světlo* ⓝ svyet-lo
like v *mít rád* meet rad
lock *zámek* ⓜ za-mek
long *dlouhý* dloh-hee
lost *ztracený* ztruh-tse-nee
lost-property office *ztráty a nálezy* ⓕ
  ztra-ti uh na-le-zi
love v *milovat* mi-lo-vuht
luggage *zavazadlo* ⓝ zuh-vuh-zuhd-lo
lunch *oběd* ⓜ o-byed

M

mail *pošta* ⓕ posh-tuh
man *muž* ⓜ muzh
map (of country) *mapa* ⓕ muh-puh
map (of town) *plán* ⓜ plan
market *trh* ⓜ trh
matches *zápalky* ⓕ pl za-puhl-ki
meat *maso* ⓝ muh-so
medicine *lék* ⓜ laik
menu *jídelní lístek* ⓜ yee-del-nyee lees-tek
message *zpráva* ⓕ zpra-vuh
milk *mléko* ⓝ mlair-ko
minute *minuta* ⓕ mi-nu-tuh
mobile phone *mobil* ⓜ mo-bil
money *peníze* ⓜ pl pe-nyee-ze
month *měsíc* ⓜ mye-seets
morning *ráno* ⓝ ra-no
mother *matka* ⓕ muht-kuh
motorcycle *motorka* ⓕ mo-tor-kuh
motorway *dálnice* ⓕ dal-nyi-tse
mouth *ústa* ⓝ oos-tuh
music *hudba* ⓕ hud-buh

N

name *jméno* ⓝ ymair-no
napkin *ubrousek* ⓜ u-broh-sek
nappy *plenka* ⓕ plen-kuh
near *blízko* bleez-ko
neck *krk* ⓜ krk
new *nový* no-vee
news *zprávy* ⓕ pl zpra-vi
newspaper *noviny* ⓕ pl no-vi-ni
night *noc* ⓕ nots
no *ne* ne

noisy *hlučný* hluch-nee
nonsmoking *nekuřácký* ne-ku-rzhats-kee
north *sever* m̂ se-ver
nose *nos* m̂ nos
now *teď* ted'
number *číslo* n̂ chees-lo

O

oil (engine) *olej* m̂ o-ley
old *starý* stuh-ree
one-way ticket *jednoduchá jízdenka* f̂
  yed-no-du-kha yeez-den-kuh
open a *otevřený* o-tev-rzhe-nee
outside *venku* ven-ku

P

package *balík* m̂ buh-leek
paper *papír* m̂ puh-peer
park (car) v *parkovat* puhr-ko-vuht
passport *pas* m̂ puhs
pay *platit* pluh-tyit
pen *propiska* f̂ pro-pis-kuh
petrol *benzín* m̂ ben-zeen
pharmacy *lékárna* f̂ lair-kar-nuh
phonecard *telefonní karta* f̂
  te-le-fo-nyee kuhr-tuh
photo *fotka* f̂ fot-kuh
plate *talíř* m̂ tuh-leerzh
police *policie* f̂ po-li-tsi-ye
postcard *pohled* m̂ po-hled
post office *pošta* f̂ posh-tuh
pregnant *těhotná* tye-hot-na
price *cena* f̂ tse-nuh

Q

quiet *tichý* tyi khee

R

rain *déšť* m̂ dairsht'
razor *břitva* f̂ brzhit-vuh
receipt *stvrzenka* f̂ stvr-zen-kuh
red *červený* cher-ve-nee
refund *vrácení peněz* n̂ vruh-tse-nyee pe-nyez
registered mail *doporučená zásilka* f̂
  do-po-ru-che-na za-sil-kuh
rent v *pronajmout* pro-nai-moht

repair v *opravit* o-pruh-vit
reservation *rezervace* f̂ re-zer-vuh-tse
restaurant *restaurace* f̂ res-tow-ruh-tse
return v *vrátit se* vra-tyit se
return ticket *zpáteční jízdenka* f̂
  zpa-tech-nyee yeez-den-kuh
right (direction) *pravý* pruh-vee
road *silnice* f̂ sil-nyi-tse
room *pokoj* m̂ po-koy

S

safe a *bezpečný* bez-pech-nee
sanitary napkins *dámské vložky* f̂ pl
  dams-kair vlozh-ki
seat *místo* n̂ mees-to
send *poslat* pos-luht
service station *benzínová pumpa* f̂
  ben-zee-no-va pum-puh
sex *pohlaví* n̂ po hluh-vee
shampoo *šampon* m̂ shuhm-pon
share (a dorm) *spolubývat* spo-lu-o-bee-vuht
shaving cream *pěna na holení* f̂
  pye-nuh nuh ho-le-nyee
she *ona* o-nuh
sheet (bed) *prostěradlo* n̂ pros-tye-ruhd-lo
shirt *košile* f̂ ko-shi-le
shoes *boty* f̂ pl bo-ti
shop *obchod* m̂ op-khod
short *krátký* krat-kee
shower *sprcha* f̂ spr-khuh
single room *jednolůžkový pokoj* m̂
  yed-no-loozh-ko-vee po-koy
skin *kůže* f̂ koo-zhe
skirt *sukně* f̂ suk-nye
sleep v *spát* spat
slowly *pomalu* po-muh lu
small *malý* muh-lee
smoke (cigarettes) v *kouřit* koh-rzhit
soap *mýdlo* n̂ meed-lo
some *několik* nye-ko-lik
soon *brzy* br-zi
south *jih* m̂ yih
souvenir shop *obchod se suvenýry* m̂
  op-khod se su-ve-nee-ri
speak *říci* rzhee-tsi
spoon *lžíce* f̂ lzhee-tse
stamp *známka* f̂ znam-kuh
station (train) *nádraží* n̂ na-druh-zhee
stomach *žaludek* m̂ zhuh-lu-dek

stop v *zastavit* zuhs-tuh-vit
stop (bus) *zastávka* ① zuhs-taf-kuh
street *ulice* ① u-li-tse
student *student/studentka* ⑩/①
    stu-dent/stu-dent-kuh
sun *slunce* ① slun-tse
sunscreen *opalovací krém* ⑩ o-puh-lo-vuh-tsee krairm
swim v *plavat* pluh-vuht

T

tampons *tampon* ⑩ tuhm-pon
taxi *taxík* ⑩ tuhk-seek
teaspoon *lžička* ① lzhich-kuh
teeth *zuby* ⑩ pl zu-bi
telephone *telefon* te-le-fon
television *televize* ① te-le-vi-ze
temperature (weather) *teplota* ① te-plo-tuh
tent *stan* ⑩ stuhn
that (one) *tamten* tuhm-ten
they *oni* o-nyi
thirsty *žíznivý* zheez-nyi-vee
this (one) *tenhle* ten-hle
throat *hrdlo* ⑪ hrd-lo
ticket *vstupenka* ① fstu-pen-kuh
time *čas* ⑩ chuhs
tired *unavený* u-nuh-ve-nee
tissues *kosmetické kapesníčky* ⑩ pl
    kos-me-tits-kair kuh-pes-neech-ki
today *dnes* dnes
toilet *toaleta* ① to-uh-le-tuh
tomorrow *zítra* zeet-ruh
tonight *dnes večer* dnes ve-cher
toothbrush *zubní kartáček* ⑩ zub-nyee kuhr-ta-chek
toothpaste *zubní pasta* ① zub-nyee puhs-tuh
torch (flashlight) *baterka* ① buh-ter-kuh
tour *okružní jízda* ① o-kruzh-nyee yeez-duh
tourist office *turistická informační kancelář* ①
    tu-ris-tits-ka in-for-muhch-nyee kuhn-tse-larzh
towel *ručník* ⑩ ruch-nyeek
train *vlak* ⑩ vluhk
translate *přeložit* przhe-lo-zhit
travel agency *cestovní kancelář* ①
    tses-tov-nyee kuhn-tse-larzh
travellers cheque *cestovní šek* ⑩ tses-tov-nyee shek
trousers *kalhoty* ① pl kuhl-ho-ti
twin beds *dvoupostel* ① dvoh-pos-tel
tyre *pneumatika* ① pne-u-muh-ti-kuh

U

underwear *spodní prádlo* ⑪ spod-nyee prad-lo
urgent *naléhavý* nuh-lair-huh-vee

V

vacant *volný* vol-nee
vacation (from school) *prázdniny* ① prazd-nyi-ni
vacation (from work) *dovolená* ① do-vo-le-na
vegetable *zelenina* ① ze-le-nyi-nuh
vegetarian a *vegetariánský* ve-ge-tuh-ri-yans-kee

W

waiter/waitress *číšník/číšnice* ⑩/①
    cheesh-nyeek/cheesh-nyi-tse
wallet *peněženka* ① pe-nye-zhen-ka
walk v *jít* yeet
warm a *teplý* tep-lee
wash (something) *umýt* u-meet
watch *hodinky* ① pl ho-dyin-ki
water *voda* ① vo-duh
we *my* mi
weekend *víkend* ⑩ vee-kend
west *západ* ⑩ za-puhd
wheelchair *invalidní vozík* ⑩ in-vuh-lid-nyee vo-zeek
when *kdy* gdi
where *kde* gde
white *bílý* bee-lee
who *kdo* gdo
why *proč* proch
wife *manželka* ① muhn-zhel-kuh
window *okno* ⑪ ok-no
wine *víno* ⑪ vee-no
with *s* s
without *bez* bez
woman *žena* ① zhe-nuh
write *psát* p-sat

Y

yellow *žlutý* zhlu-tee
yes *ano* uh-no
yesterday *včera* fche-ruh
you sg inf *ty* ti
you sg pol&pl *vy* vi

German

german alphabet

A a a	*B b* be	*C c* tse	*D d* de	*E e* e
F f ef	*G g* ge	*H h* ha	*I i* i	*J j* yot
K k ka	*L l* el	*M m* em	*N n* en	*O o* o
P p pe	*Q q* ku	*R r* er	*S s* es	*T t* te
U u u	*V v* fau	*W w* ve	*X x* iks	*Y y* ewp·si·lon
Z z tset				

███ german

introduction

Romantic, flowing, literary ... not usually how German (*Deutsch* doytsh) is described, but maybe it's time to reconsider. After all, this is the language that's played a major role in the history of Europe and remains one of the most widely spoken languages on the continent. It's taught throughout the world and chances are you're already familiar with a number of German words that have entered English – *kindergarten*, *kitsch* and *hamburger*, for example, are all of German origin.

German is spoken by around 100 million people, and is the official language of Germany, Austria and Liechtenstein, as well as one of the official languages of Belgium, Switzerland and Luxembourg. German didn't spread across the rest of the world with the same force as English, Spanish or French. Germany only became a unified nation in 1871 and never established itself as a colonial power. After the reunification of East and West Germany, however, German has become more important in global politics and economics. Its role in science has long been recognised and German literature lays claim to some of the most famous written works ever printed. Just think of the enormous influence of Goethe, Nietzsche, Freud and Einstein.

German is usually divided into two forms – Low German (*Plattdeutsch* plat-doytsh) and High German (*Hochdeutsch* hokh-doytsh). Low German is an umbrella term used for the dialects spoken in Northern Germany. High German is considered the standard form and is understood throughout German-speaking communities, from the Swiss Alps to the cosy cafés of Vienna; it's also the form used in this phrasebook.

Both German and English belong to the West Germanic language family along with a number of other languages including Dutch and Yiddish. The primary reason why German and English have grown apart is that the Normans, on invading England in 1066, brought with them a large number of non-Germanic words. As well as the recognisable words, the grammar of German will also make sense to an English speaker. Even with a slight grasp of German grammar, you'll still manage to get your point across. On the other hand, German tends to join words together (while English uses a number of separate words) to express a single notion. You shouldn't be intimidated by this though - after a while you'll be able to tell parts of words and recognising 'the Football World Cup qualifying match' hidden within *Fussballweltmeisterschaftsqualifikationsspiel* won't be a problem at all!

pronunciation

vowel sounds

German vowels can be short or long, which influences the meaning of words. They're pronounced crisply and distinctly, so *Tee* (tea) is tey, not *tey*-ee.

symbol	english equivalent	german example	transliteration
a	run	*hat*	hat
aa	father	*habe*	*haa*-be
ai	aisle	*mein*	main
air	fair	*Bär*	bair
aw	saw	*Boot*	bawt
e	bet	*Männer*	*me*-ner
ee	see	*fliegen*	*flee*-gen
eu	nurse	*schön*	sheun
ew	ee pronounced with rounded lips	*zurück*	tsu-*rewk*
ey	as in 'bet', but longer	*leben*	*ley*-ben
i	hit	*mit*	mit
o	pot	*Koffer*	*ko*-fer
oo	zoo	*Schuhe*	*shoo*-e
ow	now	*Haus*	hows
oy	toy	*Leute, Häuser*	*loy*-te, *hoy*-zer
u	put	*unter*	*un*-ter

word stress

Almost all German words are pronounced with stress on the first syllable. While this is a handy rule of thumb, you can always rely on the coloured pronunciation guides, which show the stressed syllables in italics.

consonant sounds

All German consonant sounds exist in English except for the kh and r sounds. The kh sound is generally pronounced at the back of the throat, like the 'ch' in 'Bach' or the Scottish 'loch'. The r sound is pronounced at the back of the throat, almost like saying g, but with some friction, a bit like gargling.

symbol	english equivalent	german example	transliteration
b	**bed**	*Bett*	bet
ch	**cheat**	*Tschüss*	chews
d	**dog**	*dein*	dain
f	**fat**	*vier*	feer
g	**go**	*gehen*	*gey*·en
h	**hat**	*helfen*	*hel*·fen
k	**kit**	*kein*	kain
kh	**loch**	*ich*	ikh
l	**lot**	*laut*	lowt
m	**man**	*Mann*	man
n	**not**	*nein*	nain
ng	**ring**	*singen*	*zing*·en
p	**pet**	*Preis*	prais
r	**run** (throaty)	*Reise*	*rai*·ze
s	**sun**	*heiß*	hais
sh	**shot**	*schön*	sheun
t	**top**	*Tag*	taak
ts	**hits**	*Zeit*	tsait
v	**very**	*wohnen*	*vaw*·nen
y	**yes**	*ja*	yaa
z	**zero**	*sitzen*	*zi*·tsen
zh	**pleasure**	*Garage*	ga·*raa*·zhe

pronunciation – GERMAN

tools

language difficulties

Do you speak English?
Sprechen Sie Englisch? — shpre·khen zee *eng*·lish

Do you understand?
Verstehen Sie? — fer·*shtey*·en zee

I (don't) understand.
Ich verstehe (nicht). — ikh fer·*shtey*·e (nikht)

What does (Kugel) mean?
Was bedeutet (Kugel)? — vas be·*doy*·tet (*koo*·gel)

How do you ...?	*Wie ...?*	vee ...
pronounce this	*spricht man dieses Wort aus*	shprikht man *dee*·zes vort ows
write (*Schweiz*)	*schreibt man (Schweiz)*	shraipt man (shvaits)

Could you please ...?	*Könnten Sie ...?*	*keun*·ten zee ...
repeat that	*das bitte wiederholen*	das *bi*·te vee·der·*haw*·len
speak more slowly	*bitte langsamer sprechen*	*bi*·te *lang*·za·mer shpre·khen
write it down	*das bitte aufschreiben*	das *bi*·te *owf*·shrai·ben

essentials

Yes.	*Ja.*	yaa
No.	*Nein.*	nain
Please.	*Bitte.*	*bi*·te
Thank you.	*Danke.*	*dang*·ke
Thank you very much.	*Vielen Dank.*	*fee*·len dangk
You're welcome.	*Bitte.*	*bi*·te
Excuse me.	*Entschuldigung.*	ent·*shul*·di·gung
Sorry.	*Entschuldigung.*	ent·*shul*·di·gung

54

numbers

0	*null*	nul		16	*sechzehn*	*zeks·tseyn*		
1	*eins*	ains		17	*siebzehn*	*zeep·tseyn*		
2	*zwei*	tsvai		18	*achtzehn*	*akht·tseyn*		
3	*drei*	drai		19	*neunzehn*	*noyn·tseyn*		
4	*vier*	feer		20	*zwanzig*	*tsvan·tsikh*		
5	*fünf*	fewnf		21	*einundzwanzig*	*ain·unt·tsvan·tsikh*		
6	*sechs*	zeks		22	*zweiundzwanzig*	*tsvai·unt·tsvan·tsikh*		
7	*sieben*	*zee·ben*		30	*dreißig*	*drai·tsikh*		
8	*acht*	akht		40	*vierzig*	*feer·tsikh*		
9	*neun*	noyn		50	*fünfzig*	*fewnf·tsikh*		
10	*zehn*	tseyn		60	*sechzig*	*zekh·tsikh*		
11	*elf*	elf		70	*siebzig*	*zeep·tsikh*		
12	*zwölf*	zveulf		80	*achtzig*	*akht·tsikh*		
13	*dreizehn*	*drai·tseyn*		90	*neunzig*	*noyn·tsikh*		
14	*vierzehn*	*feer·tseyn*		100	*hundert*	*hun·dert*		
15	*fünfzehn*	*fewnf·tseyn*		1000	*tausend*	*tow·sent*		

time & dates

What time is it?	*Wie spät ist es?*	vee shpeyt ist es
It's one o'clock.	*Es ist ein Uhr.*	es ist ain oor
It's (10) o'clock.	*Es ist (zehn) Uhr.*	es ist (tseyn) oor
Quarter past (one).	*Viertel nach (eins).*	*fir·tel* naakh (ains)
Half past (one).	*Halb (zwei).* (lit: half two)	halp (tsvai)
Quarter to (one).	*Viertel vor (eins).*	*fir·tel* fawr (ains)
At what time ...?	*Um wie viel Uhr ...?*	um vee feel oor ...
At ...	*Um ...*	um ...
am	*vormittags*	*fawr·mi·taaks*
pm (midday–6pm)	*nachmittags*	*naakh·mi·taaks*
pm (6pm–midnight)	*abends*	*aa·bents*
Monday	*Montag*	*mawn·taak*
Tuesday	*Dienstag*	*deens·taak*
Wednesday	*Mittwoch*	*mit·vokh*
Thursday	*Donnerstag*	*do·ners·taak*
Friday	*Freitag*	*frai·taak*
Saturday	*Samstag*	*zams·taak*
Sunday	*Sonntag*	*zon·taak*

January	Januar	yan·u·aar
February	Februar	fey·bru·aar
March	März	merts
April	April	a·pril
May	Mai	mai
June	Juni	yoo·ni
July	Juli	yoo·li
August	August	ow·gust
September	September	zep·tem·ber
October	Oktober	ok·taw·ber
November	November	no·vem·ber
December	Dezember	de·tsem·ber

What date is it today?
Der Wievielte ist heute? — dair vee·feel·te ist hoy·te

It's (18 October).
Heute ist (der achtzehnte Oktober). — hoy·te ist dair (akh·tseyn·te ok·taw·ber)

| since (May) | seit (Mai) | zait (mai) |
| until (June) | bis (Juni) | bis (yoo·ni) |

yesterday	gestern	ges·tern
today	heute	hoy·te
tonight	heute Abend	hoy·te aa·bent
tomorrow	morgen	mor·gen

last ...		
night	vergangene Nacht	fer·gang·e·ne nakht
week	letzte Woche	lets·te vo·khe
month	letzten Monat	lets·ten maw·nat
year	letztes Jahr	lets·tes yaar

next ...		
week	nächste Woche	neykhs·te vo·khe
month	nächsten Monat	neykhs·ten maw·nat
year	nächstes Jahr	neykhs·tes yaar

yesterday/	gestern/	ges·tern/
tomorrow ...	morgen ...	mor·gen ...
morning	Morgen	mor·gen
afternoon	Nachmittag	naakh·mi·taak
evening	Abend	aa·bent

weather

What's the weather like?	Wie ist das Wetter?	vee ist das *ve*·ter

It's ...

cloudy	*Es ist wolkig.*	es ist *vol*·kikh
cold	*Es ist kalt.*	es ist kalt
hot	*Es ist heiß.*	es ist hais
raining	*Es regnet.*	es *reyg*·net
snowing	*Es schneit.*	es shnait
sunny	*Es ist sonnig.*	es ist *zo*·nikh
warm	*Es ist warm.*	es ist varm
windy	*Es ist windig.*	es ist *vin*·dikh

spring	*Frühling* m	*frew*·ling
summer	*Sommer* m	*zo*·mer
autumn	*Herbst* m	herpst
winter	*Winter* m	*vin*·ter

border crossing

I'm here ...	Ich bin hier ...	ikh bin heer ...
in transit	*auf der Durchreise*	owf dair *durkh*·rai·ze
on business	*auf Geschäftsreise*	owf ge·*shefts*·rai·ze
on holiday	*im Urlaub*	im *oor*·lowp

I'm here for ...	Ich bin hier für ...	ikh bin heer fewr ...
(10) days	*(zehn) Tage*	(tseyn) *taa*·ge
(three) weeks	*(drei) Wochen*	(drai) *vo*·khen
(two) months	*(zwei) Monate*	(tsvai) *maw*·na·te

I'm going to (Salzburg).
Ich gehe nach (Salzburg).   ikh *gey*·e nakh *zalts*·boorg

I'm staying at the (Hotel Park).
Ich wohne im (Hotel Park).   ikh *vaw*·ne im (ho·*tel* park)

I have nothing to declare.
Ich habe nichts zu verzollen.   ikh *haa*·be nikhts tsoo fer·*tso*·len

I have something to declare.
Ich habe etwas zu verzollen.   ikh *haa*·be *et*·vas tsoo fer·*tso*·len

That's (not) mine.
Das ist (nicht) meins.   das ist (nikht) mains

transport

tickets & luggage

Where can I buy a ticket?
Wo kann ich eine Fahrkarte kaufen?   vaw kan ikh *ai*·ne *faar*·kar·te *kow*·fen

Do I need to book a seat?
Muss ich einen Platz   mus ikh *ai*·nen plats
reservieren lassen?   re·zer·*vee*·ren *la*·sen

One ...ticket to	*Einen ... nach*	*ai*·nen ... naakh
(Berlin), please.	*(Berlin), bitte.*	(ber·*leen*) *bi*·te
one-way	*einfache Fahrkarte*	*ain*·fa·khe *faar*·kar·te
return	*Rückfahrkarte*	*rewk*·faar·kar·te

I'd like to ...	*Ich möchte meine*	ikh *meukh*·te *mai*·ne
my ticket, please.	*Fahrkarte bitte ...*	*faar*·kar·te *bi*·te ...
cancel	*zurückgeben*	tsu·*rewk*·gey·ben
change	*ändern lassen*	*en*·dern *la*·sen
collect	*abholen*	ab·*ho*·len
confirm	*bestätigen lassen*	be·*shtey*·ti·gen *la*·sen

I'd like a ...	*Ich hätte gern*	ikh *he*·te gern
seat, please.	*einen ...*	*ai*·nen ...
nonsmoking	*Nichtraucherplatz*	*nikht*·row·kher·plats
smoking	*Raucherplatz*	*row*·kher·plats

How much is it?
Was kostet das?   vas *kos*·tet das

Is there air conditioning?
Gibt es eine Klimaanlage?   gipt es *ai*·ne *klee*·ma·an·*laa*·ge

Is there a toilet?
Gibt es eine Toilette?   gipt es *ai*·ne to·a·*le*·te

How long does the trip take?
Wie lange dauert die Fahrt?   vee *lang*·e *dow*·ert dee faart

Is it a direct route?
Ist es eine direkte Verbindung?   ist es *ai*·ne di·*rek*·te fer·*bin*·dung

I'd like a luggage locker.
Ich hätte gern ein Gepäckschließfach.   ikh *he*·te gern ain ge·*pek*·shlees·fakh

My luggage has been ...	Mein Gepäck ist ...	main ge·*pek* ist ...
damaged	*beschädigt*	be·*shey*·dikht
lost	*verloren gegangen*	fer·*law*·ren ge·*gang*·en
stolen	*gestohlen worden*	ge·*shtaw*·len *vor*·den

getting around

Where does flight (D4) arrive?
Wo ist die Ankunft des Fluges (D4)?   vaw ist dee *an*·kunft des *floo*·ges (de feer)

Where does flight (D4) depart?
Wo ist die der Abflug des Fluges (D4)?   vaw ist dair *ab*·flug des *floo*·ges (de feer)

Where's the ...?	Wo ist ...?	vaw ist ...
arrivalls hall	*Ankunftshalle*	*an*·kunfts·*ha*·le
departures hall	*Abflughalle*	*ab*·flug·*ha*·le

Is this the ...	Fährt ...	fairt ...
to (Hamburg)?	*nach (Hamburg)?*	nakh (*ham*·burg)
boat	*das Boot*	das bawt
bus	*der Bus*	dair bus
plane	*das Flugzeug*	das *flook*·tsoyk
train	*der Zug*	dair tsook

What time's	Wann fährt der	van fairt dair
the ... bus?	... Bus?	... bus
first	*erste*	*ers*·te
last	*letzte*	*lets*·te
next	*nächste*	*neykhs*·te

At what time does it leave?
Wann fährt es ab?   van fairt es ap

At what time does it arrive?
Wann kommt es an?   van komt es an

How long will it be delayed?
Wie viel Verspätung wird es haben?   vee feel fer·*shpey*·tung virt es *haa*·ben

What station/stop is this?
Welcher Bahnhof/Halt ist das?   *vel*·kher *baan*·hawf/halt ist das

What's the next station/stop?
Welches ist der nächste   *vel*·khes ist dair *neykhs*·te
Bahnhof/Halt?   *baan*·hawf/halt

Does it stop at (Freiburg)?
Hält es in (Freiburg)?   helt *es* in (*frai*·boorg)

Please tell me when we get to (Kiel).
Könnten Sie mir bitte sagen,   *keun*·ten zee meer *bi*·te *zaa*·gen
wann wir in (Kiel) ankommen?   van veer in (keel) *an*·ko·men

How long do we stop here?
Wie lange halten wir hier?   vee *lan*·ge *hal*·ten veer heer

Is this seat available?
Ist dieser Platz frei?   ist *dee*·zer plats frai

That's my seat.
Dieses ist mein Platz.   *dee*·zes ist main plats

I'd like a taxi ...   *Ich hätte gern*   ikh *he*·te gern
     ein Taxi für ...   ain *tak*·si fewr ...
   at (9am)   *(neun Uhr vormittags)*   (noyn oor *fawr*·mi·taaks)
   now   *sofort*   zo·*fort*
   tomorrow   *morgen*   *mor*·gen

Is this taxi available?
Ist dieses Taxi frei?   ist *dee*·zes *tak*·si frai

How much is it to ...?
Was kostet es bis ...?   vas *kos*·tet es bis ...

Please put the meter on.
Schalten Sie bitte den Taxameter ein.   *shal*·ten zee *bi*·te deyn tak·sa·*mey*·ter ain

Please take me to (this address).
Bitte bringen Sie mich zu   *bi*·te *bring*·en zee mikh tsoo
(dieser Adresse).   (*dee*·zer a·*dre*·se)

Please ...   *Bitte ...*   *bi*·te ...
   slow down   *fahren Sie langsamer*   *faa*·ren zee *lang*·za·mer
   stop here   *halten Sie hier*   *hal*·ten zee heer
   wait here   *warten Sie hier*   *var*·ten zee heer

car, motorbike & bicycle hire

I'd like to hire a ...	*Ich möchte ... mieten.*	ikh *meukh*·te ... *mee*·ten
bicycle	*ein Fahrrad*	ain *faar*·raat
car	*ein Auto*	ain *ow*·to
motorbike	*ein Motorrad*	ain *maw*·tor·raat
with ...	*mit ...*	mit ...
a driver	*Fahrer*	*faa*·rer
air conditioning	*Klimaanlage*	*klee*·ma·an·*laa*·ge
How much for ... hire?	*Wie viel kostet es pro ...?*	vee feel *kos*·tet es praw ...
hourly	*Stunde*	*shtun*·de
daily	*Tag*	taak
weekly	*Woche*	*vo*·khe
air	*Luft* f	luft
oil	*Öl* n	eul
petrol	*Benzin* n	ben·*tseen*
tyres	*Reifen* m pl	*rai*·fen

I need a mechanic.
Ich brauche einen Mechaniker.　　ikh *brow*·khe *ai*·nen me·*khaa*·ni·ker

I've run out of petrol.
Ich habe kein Benzin mehr.　　ikh *haa*·be kain ben·*tseen* mair

I have a flat tyre.
Ich habe eine Reifenpanne.　　ikh *haa*·be *ai*·ne *rai*·fen·pa·ne

directions

Where's the ...?	*Wo ist ...?*	vaw ist ...
bank	*die Bank*	dee bangk
city centre	*die Innenstadt*	*i*·nen·shtat
hotel	*das Hotel*	das ho·*tel*
market	*der Markt*	dair markt
police station	*das Polizeirevier*	das po·li·*tsai*·re·veer
post office	*das Postamt*	das *post*·amt
public toilet	*die öffentliche Toilette*	dee *eu*·fent·li·khe to·a·*le*·te
tourist office	*das Fremden-verkehrsbüro*	das *frem*·den-fer·kairs·bew·*raw*

Is this the road to (Frankfurt)?
Führt diese Straße — fewrt dee·ze shtraa·se
nach (Frankfurt)? — naakh (frank·foort)

Can you show me (on the map)?
Können Sie es mir — keu·nen zee es meer
(auf der Karte) zeigen? — (owf dair kar·te) tsai·gen

What's the address?
Wie ist die Adresse? — vee ist dee a·dre·se

How far is it?
Wie weit ist es? — vee vait ist es

How do I get there?
Wie kann ich da hinkommen? — vee kan ikh daa hin·ko·men

Turn ...	*Biegen Sie ... ab.*	bee·gen zee ... ap
at the corner	*an der Ecke*	an dair e·ke
at the traffic lights	*bei der Ampel*	bai dair am·pel
left/right	*links/rechts*	lingks/rekhts

It's ...	*Es ist ...*	es ist ...
behind ...	*hinter ...*	hin·ter ...
far away	*weit weg*	vait vek
here	*hier*	heer
in front of ...	*vor ...*	fawr ...
left	*links*	lingks
near (to ...)	*nahe (zu ...)*	naa·e (zoo ...)
next to ...	*neben ...*	ney·ben ...
on the corner	*an der Ecke*	an dair e·ke
opposite ...	*gegenüber ...*	gey·gen·ew·ber ...
right	*rechts*	rekhts
straight ahead	*geradeaus*	ge·raa·de·ows
there	*dort*	dort

north	*Norden* m	nor·den
south	*Süden* m	zew·den
east	*Osten* m	os·ten
west	*Westen* m	ves·ten

by bus	*mit dem Bus*	mit deym bus
by taxi	*mit dem Taxi*	mit deym tak·si
by train	*mit dem Zug*	mit deym tsook
on foot	*zu Fuß*	tsoo foos

Eingang/Ausgang	*ain*·gang/*ows*·gang	**Entrance/Exit**
Offen/Geschlossen	*o*·fen/ge·*shlo*·sen	**Open/Closed**
Zimmer Frei	*tsi*·mer frai	**Rooms Available**
Ausgebucht	*ows*·ge·bukht	**No Vacancies**
Auskunft	*ows*·kunft	**Information**
Polizeirevier	po·li·*tsai*·re·veer	**Police Station**
Verboten	fer·*baw*·ten	**Prohibited**
Toiletten/WC	to·a·*le*·ten/vee·*tsee*	**Toilets**
Herren	*hair*·en	**Men**
Damen	*daa*·men	**Women**
Heiß/Kalt	hais/kalt	**Hot/Cold**

accommodation

finding accommodation

Where's a/an ...?	*Wo ist ...?*	vaw ist ...
camping ground	*ein Campingplatz*	ain *kem*·ping·plats
guesthouse	*eine Pension*	*ai*·ne paang·*zyawn*
hotel	*ein Hotel*	ain ho·*tel*
inn	*ein Gasthof*	ain *gast*·hawf
youth hostel	*eine Jugendherberge*	*ai*·ne yoo·gent·her·ber·ge
Can you recommend somewhere ...?	*Können Sie etwas ... empfehlen?*	*keu*·nen zee *et*·vas ... emp·*fey*·len
cheap	*Billiges*	*bi*·li·ges
good	*Gutes*	*goo*·tes
luxurious	*Luxuriöses*	luk·su·ri·*eu*·ses
nearby	*in der Nähe*	in dair *ney*·e

I'd like to book a room, please.
Ich möchte bitte ein
Zimmer reservieren.
ikh *meukh*·te *bi*·te ain
tsi·mer re·zer·*vee*·ren

I have a reservation.
Ich habe eine Reservierung.
ikh *haa*·be *ai*·ne re·zer·*vee*·rung

My name's ...
Mein Name ist ...
main *naa*·me ist ...

Do you have a ... room?	Haben Sie ein ...?	haa·ben zee ain ...
single	Einzelzimmer	ain·tsel·tsi·mer
double	Doppelzimmer mit	do·pel·tsi·mer mit
	einem Doppelbett	ai·nem do·pel·bet
twin	Doppelzimmer mit	do·pel·tsi·mer mit
	zwei Einzelbetten	tsvai ain·tsel·be·ten

Can I pay by ...?	Nehmen Sie ...?	ney·men zee ...
credit card	Kreditkarten	kre·deet·kar·ten
travellers cheque	Reisescheks	rai·ze·sheks

How much is it per ...?	Wie viel kostet es pro ...?	vee feel kos·tet es praw ...
night	Nacht	nakht
person	Person	per·zawn

I'd like to stay for (two) nights.
Ich möchte für (zwei)   ikh meukh·te fewr (tsvai)
Nächte bleiben.   nekh·te blai·ben

From (July 2) to (July 6).
Vom (zweiten Juli) bis zum   vom (tsvai·ten yoo·li) bis tsum
(sechsten Juli).   (zeks·ten yoo·li)

Can I see it?
Kann ich es sehen?   kan ikh es zey·en

Am I allowed to camp here?
Kann ich hier zelten?   kan ikh heer tsel·ten

Is there a camp site nearby?
Gibt es in der Nähe einen Zeltplatz?   gipt es in dair ney·e ai·nen tselt·plats

requests & queries

When/Where is breakfast served?
Wann/Wo gibt es Frühstück?   van/vaw gipt es frew·shtewk

Please wake me at (seven).
Bitte wecken Sie mich   bi·te ve·ken zee mikh
um (sieben) Uhr.   um (zee·ben) oor

Could I have my key, please?
Könnte ich bitte meinen Schlüssel   keun·te ikh bi·te mai·nen shlew·sel
haben?   haa·ben

Can I get another (blanket)?
Kann ich noch (eine Decke) bekommen?   kan ikh nokh (ai·ne de·ke) be·ko·men

Is there a/an ...?	Haben Sie ...?	haa·ben zee ...
elevator	einen Aufzug	ai·nen owf·tsook
safe	einen Safe	ai·nen sayf

The room is too ...	Es ist zu ...	es ist tsoo ...
expensive	teuer	toy·er
noisy	laut	lowt
small	klein	klain

The ... doesn't work.	... funktioniert nicht.	... fungk·tsyo·neert nikht
air conditioning	Die Klimaanlage	dee klee·ma·an·laa·ge
fan	Der Ventilator	dair ven·ti·laa·tor
toilet	Die Toilette	dee to·a·le·te

This ... isn't clean.	Dieses ... ist nicht sauber.	dee·zes ... ist nikht zow·ber
pillow	Kopfkissen	kopf·ki·sen
sheet	Bettlaken	bet·laa·ken
towel	Handtuch	hant·tookh

checking out

What time is checkout?
Wann muss ich auschecken? van mus ikh *ows*·che·ken

Can I leave my luggage here?
Kann ich meine Taschen hier lassen? kan ikh *mai*·ne *ta*·shen heer *la*·sen

Could I have my ..., please?	Könnte ich bitte ... haben?	keun·te ikh bi·te ... haa·ben
deposit	meine Anzahlung	mai·ne an·tsaa·lung
passport	meinen Pass	mai·nen pas
valuables	meine Wertsachen	mai·ne vert·za·khen

communications & banking

the internet

Where's the local Internet café?
Wo ist hier ein Internet-café? vaw ist heer ain *in*·ter·net·ka·fey

How much is it per hour?
Was kostet es pro Stunde? vas *kos*·tet es praw *shtun*·de

I'd like to ...	Ich möchte ...	ikh *meukh*·te ...
check my email	*meine E-Mails checken*	*mai*·ne *ee*·mayls *che*·ken
get Internet access	*Internetzugang haben*	*in*·ter·net·tsoo·gang *haa*·ben
use a printer	*einen Drucker benutzen*	*ai*·nen *dru*·ker be·*nu*·tsen
use a scanner	*einen Scanner benutzen*	*ai*·nen *ske*·ner be·*nu*·tsen

mobile/cell phone

I'd like a ...	Ich hätte gern ...	ikh *he*·te gern ...
mobile/cell phone for hire	*ein Miethandy*	ain *meet*·hen·di
SIM card for your network	*eine SIM-Karte für Ihr Netz*	*ai*·ne *zim*·kar·te fewr eer nets

What are the rates?
Wie hoch sind die Gebühren? — vee hawkh zint dee ge·*bew*·ren

telephone

What's your phone number?
Wie ist Ihre Telefonnummer? — vee ist *ee*·re te·le·*fawn*·nu·mer

The number is ...
Die Nummer ist ... — dee *nu*·mer ist ...

Where's the nearest public phone?
Wo ist das nächste öffentliche Telefon? — vaw ist das *neykhs*·te *eu*·fent·li·khe te·le·*fawn*

I'd like to buy a phonecard.
Ich möchte eine Telefonkarte kaufen. — ikh *meukh*·te *ai*·ne te·le·*fawn*·kar·te *kow*·fen

I want to ...	Ich möchte ...	ikh *meukh*·te ...
call (Singapore)	*(nach Singapur) telefonieren*	(naakh *zing*·a·poor) te·le·fo·*nee*·ren
make a local call	*ein Ortsgespräch machen*	ain *awrts*·ge·shpreykh *ma*·khen
reverse the charges	*ein R-Gespräch führen*	ain *air*·ge·shpreykh *few*·ren

How much does ... cost?	Wie viel kostet ...?	vee feel *kos*·tet ...
a (three)-minute	*ein (drei)-minutiges*	ain (*drai*)·mi·*noo*·ti·ges
call	*Gespräch*	ge·*shpreykh*
each extra	*jede zusätzliche*	*yey*·de tsoo·*zeyts*·li·khe
minute	*Minute*	mi·*noo*·te

It's (one euro) per (minute).
(Ein Euro) für (eine Minute).   (ain *oy*·ro) fewr (*ai*·ne mi·*noo*·te)

post office

I want to send a ...	*Ich möchte ... senden.*	ikh *meukh*·te ... *zen*·den
fax	*ein Fax*	ain faks
letter	*einen Brief*	*ai*·nen breef
parcel	*ein Paket*	ain pa·*keyt*
postcard	*eine Postkarte*	*ai*·ne *post*·kar·te

I want to buy a/an ...	*Ich möchte ... kaufen.*	ikh *meukh*·te ... *kow*·fen
envelope	*einen Umschlag*	*ai*·nen *um*·shlaak
stamp	*eine Briefmarke*	*ai*·ne *breef*·mar·ke

Please send it	*Bitte schicken Sie das*	*bi*·te *shi*·ken zee das
(to Australia) by ...	*(nach Australien) per ...*	(nakh ows·*traa*·li·en) per ...
airmail	*Luftpost*	*luft*·post
express mail	*Expresspost*	eks·*pres*·post
registered mail	*Einschreiben*	*ain*·shrai·ben
surface mail	*Landbeförderung*	*lant*·be·feur·de·rung

Is there any mail for me?   *Ist Post für mich da?*   ist post fewr mikh da

bank

Where's a/an ...?	*Wo ist ...?*	vaw ist ...
ATM	*der Geldautomat*	dair gelt·ow·to·maat
foreign exchange	*die Geldwechselstube*	dee gelt·vek·sel·shtoo·be
office		

I'd like to ...	Ich möchte ...	ikh *meukh*·te ...
Where can I ...?	Wo kann ich ...?	vaw kan ikh ...
arrange a transfer	einen Transfer tätigen	ai·nen trans·*fer* tey·ti·gen
cash a cheque	einen Scheck einlösen	ai·nen shek *ain*·leu·zen
change a travellers cheque	einen Reisescheck einlösen	ai·nen *rai*·ze·shek *ain*·leu·zen
change money	Geld umtauschen	gelt *um*·tow·shen
get a cash advance	eine Barauszahlung	ai·ne *baar*·ows·tsaa·lung
withdraw money	Geld abheben	gelt *ap*·hey·ben

What's the ...?	Wie ...?	vee ...
charge for that	hoch sind die Gebühren dafür	hawkh zint dee ge·*bew*·ren da·*fewr*
exchange rate	ist der Wechselkurs	ist dair *vek*·sel·kurs

It's ...	Das ...	das ...
(12) euros	kostet (zwölf) euro	*kos*·tet (zveulf) *oy*·ro
free	ist umsonst	ist um·*zonst*

What time does the bank open?
Wann macht die Bank auf? — van makht dee bangk owf

Has my money arrived yet?
Ist mein Geld schon angekommen? — ist main gelt shawn *an*·ge·ko·men

sightseeing

getting in

What time does it open/close?
Wann macht es auf/zu? — van makht es owf/tsoo

What's the admission charge?
Was kostet der Eintritt? — vas *kos*·tet dair *ain*·trit

Is there a discount for children/students?
Gibt es eine Ermäßigung für Kinder/Studenten? — gipt es ai·ne er·*mey*·si·gung fewr *kin*·der/shtu·*den*·ten

I'd like a ...	Ich hätte gern ...	ikh *he*·te gern ...
catalogue	einen Katalog	*ai*·nen ka·*ta*·lawg
guide	einen Reiseführer	*ai*·nen *rai*·ze·few·rer
local map	eine Karte von hier	*ai*·ne *kar*·te fon heer

I'd like to see ...	Ich möchte ... sehen.	ikh *meukh*·te ... *zey*·en
What's that?	Was ist das?	vas ist das
Can I take a photo?	Kann ich fotografieren?	kan ikh fo·to·gra·*fee*·ren

tours

When's the next ...?	Wann ist der/die nächste ...? m/f	van ist dair/dee *neykhs*·te ...
day trip	Tagesausflug m	*taa*·ges·ows·flook
tour	Tour f	toor

Is ... included?	Ist ... inbegriffen?	ist ... *in*·be·gri·fen
accommodation	die Unterkunft	dee *un*·ter·kunft
the admission charge	der Eintritt	dair *ain*·trit
food	das Essen	das *e*·sen
transport	die Beförderung	dee be·*feur*·de·rung

How long is the tour?
Wie lange dauert die Führung?   vee *lang*·e *dow*·ert dee *few*·rung

What time should we be back?
Wann sollen wir zurück sein?   van *zo*·len veer tsu·*rewk* zain

---

sightseeing

castle	Burg f	burk
cathedral	Dom m	dawm
church	Kirche f	*kir*·khe
main square	Hauptplatz m	*howpt*·plats
monastery	Kloster n	*klaws*·ter
monument	Denkmal n	*dengk*·maal
museum	Museum n	mu·*zey*·um
old city	Altstadt f	*alt*·stat
palace	Schloss n	shlos
ruins	Ruinen f pl	ru·*ee*·nen
stadium	Stadion n	*shtaa*·di·on
statues	Statuen f pl	*shtaa*·tu·e

shopping

enquiries

Where's a ...?	Wo ist ...?	vaw ist ...
bank	die Bank	dee bangk
bookshop	die Buchhandlung	dee *bookh*-hand-lung
camera shop	das Fotogeschäft	das fo-to-ge-*sheft*
department store	das Warenhaus	das *vaa*-ren-hows
grocery store	der Lebensmittelladen	dair *ley*-bens-mi-tel-laa-den
market	der Markt	dair markt
newsagency	der Zeitungshändler	dair *tsai*-tungks-hen-dler
supermarket	der Supermarkt	dair *zoo*-per-markt

Where can I buy (a padlock)?
Wo kann ich (ein Vorhängeschloss) kaufen?
vaw kan ikh (ain *fawr*-heng-e-shlos) *kow*-fen

I'm looking for ...
Ich suche nach ...
ikh *zoo*-khe nakh ...

Can I look at it?
Können Sie es mir zeigen?
keu-nen zee es meer *tsai*-gen

Do you have any others?
Haben Sie noch andere?
haa-ben zee nokh *an*-de-re

Does it have a guarantee?
Gibt es darauf Garantie?
gipt es da-*rowf* ga-ran-*tee*

Can I have it sent overseas?
Kann ich es ins Ausland verschicken lassen?
kan ikh es ins *ows*-lant fer-*shi*-ken *la*-sen

Can I have my ... repaired?
Kann ich mein ... reparieren lassen?
kan ikh main ... re-pa-*ree*-ren *la*-sen

It's faulty.
Es ist fehlerhaft.
es ist *fey*-ler-haft

I'd like ..., please.	Ich möchte bitte ...	ikh *meukh*·te *bi*·te ...
a bag	eine Tüte	*ai*·ne *tew*·te
a refund	mein Geld	main gelt
	zurückhaben	tsu·*rewk*·haa·ben
to return this	dieses zurückgeben	*dee*·zes tsu·*rewk*·gey·ben

paying

How much is it?
Wie viel kostet das?   vee feel *kos*·tet das

Can you write down the price?
Können Sie den Preis aufschreiben?   *keu*·nen zee deyn prais *owf*·shrai·ben

That's too expensive.
Das ist zu teuer.   das ist tsoo *toy*·er

Can you lower the price?
Können Sie mit dem Preis   *keu*·nen zee mit dem prais
heruntergehen?   he·*run*·ter·gey·en

I'll give you (five) euros.
Ich gebe Ihnen (fünf) euro.   ikh *gey*·be *ee*·nen (fewnf) *oy*·ro

There's a mistake in the bill.
Da ist ein Fehler in der Rechnung.   daa ist ain *fey*·ler in dair *rekh*·nung

Do you accept ...?	Nehmen Sie ...?	*ney*·men zee ...
credit cards	Kreditkarten	kre·*deet*·kar·ten
debit cards	Debitkarten	*dey*·bit·kar·ten
travellers cheques	Reiseschecks	*rai*·ze·sheks

I'd like ..., please.	Ich möchte bitte ...	ikh *meukh*·te *bi*·te ...
a receipt	eine Quittung	*ai*·ne *kvi*·tung
my change	mein Wechselgeld	main *vek*·sel·gelt

clothes & shoes

Can I try it on?	Kann ich es anprobieren?	kan ikh es *an*·pro·bee·ren
My size is (40).	Ich habe Größe (vierzig).	ikh *haa*·be *greu*·se (*feer*·tsikh)
It doesn't fit.	Es passt nicht.	es past nikht

small	klein	klain
medium	mittelgroß	*mi*·tel·graws
large	groß	graws

I'd like a ...	Ich hätte gern ...	ikh *he*·te gern ...
newspaper	eine Zeitung	*ai*·ne *tsai*·tung
(in English)	(auf Englisch)	(owf *eng*·lish)
pen	einen Kugelschreiber	*ai*·nen *koo*·gel·shrai·ber

Is there an English-language bookshop?

| Gibt es einen Buchladen | gipt es *ai*·nen *bookh*·laa·den |
| für englische Bücher? | fewr *eng*·li·she *bew*·kher |

I'm looking for something by (Herman Hesse).

| Ich suche nach etwas von | ikh *zoo*·khe nakh *et*·vas fon |
| (Herman Hesse). | (*her*·man *he*·se) |

Can I listen to this?

| Kann ich mir das anhören? | kan ikh meer das *an*·heu·ren |

Can you ...?	Können Sie ...?	*keu*·nen zee ...
burn a CD from	eine CD von meiner	*ai*·ne tse de von *mai*·ner
my memory card	Speicherkarte brennen	*shpai*·kher·*kar*·te *bre*·nen
develop this film	diesen Film entwickeln	*dee*·zen film ent·*vi*·keln
load my film	mir den Film einlegen	meer deyn film *ain*·ley·gen

I need a ... film	Ich brauche einen	ikh *brow*·khe *ai*·nen
for this camera.	... für diese Kamera.	... fewr *dee*·ze *ka*·me·ra
APS	APS-Film	aa·pey·*es*·film
B&W	Schwarzweißfilm	shvarts·*vais*·film
colour	Farbfilm	*farp*·film
slide	Diafilm	*dee*·a·film
(200) speed	(zweihundert)-	(*tsvai*·hun·dert)·
	ASA-Film	*aa*·za·film

| When will it be ready? | Wann ist er fertig? | van ist air *fer*·tikh |

meeting people

greetings, goodbyes & introductions

Hello. (Austria)	*Servus.*	*zer*-vus
Hello. (Germany)	*Guten Tag.*	*goo*-ten taak
Hello. (Switzerland)	*Grüezi.*	*grew*-e-tsi
Hi.	*Hallo.*	*ha*-lo
Good night.	*Gute Nacht.*	*goo*-te nakht
Goodbye.	*Auf Wiedersehen.*	owf *vee*-der-zey-en
Bye.	*Tschüss/Tschau.*	chews/chow
See you later.	*Bis später.*	bis *shpey*-ter

Mr	*Herr*	her
Mrs	*Frau*	frow
Miss	*Fräulein*	*froy*-lain

How are you?	*Wie geht es Ihnen?*	vee geyt es *ee*-nen
Fine. And you?	*Danke, gut. Und Ihnen?*	*dang*-ke goot unt *ee*-nen
What's your name?	*Wie ist Ihr Name?*	vee ist eer *naa*-me
My name is …	*Mein Name ist …*	main *naa*-me ist …
I'm pleased to meet you.	*Angenehm.*	*an*-ge-neym

This is my …	*Das ist mein/meine …* m/f	das ist main/*mai*-ne …
brother	*Bruder*	*broo*-der
daughter	*Tochter*	*tokh*-ter
father	*Vater*	*faa*-ter
friend	*Freund/Freundin* m/f	froynt/*froyn*-din
husband	*Mann*	man
mother	*Mutter*	*mu*-ter
partner (intimate)	*Partner/Partnerin* m/f	*part*-ner/*part*-ne-rin
sister	*Schwester*	*shves*-ter
son	*Sohn*	zawn
wife	*Frau*	frow

Here's my …	*Hier ist meine …*	heer ist *mai*-ne …
What's your …?	*Wie ist Ihre …?*	vee ist *ee*-re …
address	*Adresse*	a-*dre*-se
email address	*E-mail-Adresse*	ee-mayl-a-*dre*-se
fax number	*Faxnummer*	*faks*-nu-mer
phone number	*Telefonnummer*	te-le-*fawn*-nu-mer

What's your occupation?	Als was arbeiten Sie? pol	als vas *ar*·bai·ten zee
	Als was arbeitest du? inf	als vas *ar*·bai·test doo
I'm a/an ...	Ich bin ein/eine ... m/f	ikh bin ain/*ai*·ne ...
artist	Künstler/Künstlerin m/f	*kewnst*·ler/*kewnst*·le·rin
business person	Geschäftsmann m	ge·*shefts*·man
	Geschäftsfrau f	ge·*shefts*·frow
farmer	Bauer/Bäuerin m/f	*bow*·er/*boy*·e·rin
manual worker	Arbeiter/Arbeiterin m/f	*ar*·bai·ter/*ar*·bai·te·rin
office worker	Büroangestellte m&f	bew·*raw*·an·ge·shtel·te
scientist	Wissenschaftler m	*vi*·sen·shaft·ler
	Wissenschaftlerin f	*vi*·sen·shaft·le·rin
student	Student/Studentin m/f	shtu·*dent*/shtu·*den*·tin

background

Where are you from?	Woher kommen Sie? pol	*vaw*·hair *ko*·men zee
	Woher kommst du? inf	*vaw*·hair komst doo
I'm from ...	Ich komme aus ...	ikh *ko*·me ows ...
Australia	Australien	ows·*traa*·li·en
Canada	Kanada	*ka*·na·daa
England	England	*eng*·lant
New Zealand	Neuseeland	noy·*zey*·lant
the USA	den USA	deyn oo·es·*aa*
Are you married?	Sind Sie verheiratet? pol	zint zee fer·*hai*·ra·tet
	Bist du verheiratet? inf	bist doo fer·*hai*·ra·tet
I'm married.	Ich bin verheiratet.	ikh bin fer·*hai*·ra·tet
I'm single.	Ich bin ledig.	ikh bin *ley*·dikh

age

How old ...?	Wie alt ...?	vee alt ...
are you	sind Sie pol	zint zee
	bist du inf	bist doo
is your daughter	ist Ihre Tochter pol	ist *ee*·re *tokh*·ter
is your son	ist Ihr Sohn pol	ist eer zawn
I'm ... years old.	Ich bin ... Jahre alt.	ikh bin ... *yaa*·re alt
He/She is ... years old.	Er/Sie ist ... Jahre alt.	air/zee ist ... *yaa*·re alt

feelings

I'm (not) ...	Ich bin (nicht) ...	ikh bin (nikht) ...
Are you ...?	Sind Sie ...? pol	zint zee ...
	Bist du ...? inf	bist doo ...
happy	glücklich	glewk-likh
sad	traurig	trow-rikh
I'm (not) ...	Ich habe (kein) ...	ikh haa-be (kain) ...
Are you ...?	Haben Sie ...? pol	haa-ben zee ...
	Hast du ...? inf	hast doo ...
hungry	Hunger	hung-er
thirsty	Durst	durst
I'm (not) ...	Mir ist (nicht) ...	meer ist (nikht) ...
Are you ...?	Ist Ihnen/dir ...? pol/inf	ist ee-nen/deer ...
cold	kalt	kalt
hot	heiß	hais

entertainment

going out

Where can I find ...?	Wo sind die ...?	vaw zint dee ...
clubs	Klubs	klups
gay venues	Schwulen- und	shvoo-len unt
	Lesbenkneipen	les-ben-knai-pen
pubs	Kneipen	knai-pen
I feel like going	Ich hätte Lust,	ikh he-te lust
to a/the ...	... zu gehen.	... tsoo gey-en
concert	zum Konzert	tsoom kon-tsert
movies	ins Kino	ins kee-no
party	zu eine Party	tsoo ai-ne par-ti
restaurant	in ein Restaurant	in ain res-to-rang
theatre	ins Theater	ins te-aa-ter

interests

Do you like ...?	*Magst du ...?* inf	maakst doo ...
I (don't) like ...	*Ich mag (keine/ keinen) ...* m/f	ikh maak (*kai*·ne/ *kai*·nen) ...
art	*Kunst* f	kunst
sport	*Sport* m	shport
I (don't) like ...	*Ich ... (nicht) gern.*	ikh ... (nikht) gern
cooking	*koche*	*ko*·khe
reading	*lese*	*ley*·ze
travelling	*reise*	*rai*·ze
Do you like to dance?		
Tanzt du gern? inf		tantst doo gern
Do you like music?		
Hörst du gern Musik? inf		heurst doo gern mu·*zeek*

food & drink

finding a place to eat

Can you recommend a ...?	*Können Sie ... empfehlen?*	*keu*·nen zee ... emp·*fey*·len
bar	*eine Kneipe*	*ai*·ne *knai*·pe
café	*ein Café*	ain ka·*fey*
restaurant	*ein Restaurant*	ain res·to·*rang*
I'd like ..., please.	*Ich hätte gern ..., bitte.*	ikh *he*·te gern ... *bi*·te
a table for (five)	*einen Tisch für (fünf) Personen*	*ai*·nen tish fewr (fewnf) per·*zaw*·nen
the (non)smoking section	*einen (Nicht-) rauchertisch*	*ai*·nen (nikht·) *row*·kher·tish

ordering food

breakfast	*Frühstück* n	*frew*·shtewk
lunch	*Mittagessen* n	*mi*·taak·e·sen
dinner	*Abendessen* n	*aa*·bent·e·sen
snack	*Snack* m	snek

What would you recommend?

Was empfehlen Sie?		vas emp·*fey*·len zee

I'd like (the) ..., please.	*Bitte bringen Sie ...*	*bi*·te *bring*·en zee ...
bill	*die Rechnung*	dee *rekh*·nung
drink list	*die Getränkekarte*	dee ge·*treng*·ke·kar·te
menu	*die Speisekarte*	dee *shpai*·ze·kar·te
that dish	*dieses Gericht*	*dee*·zes ge·*rikht*

drinks

(cup of) coffee ...	*(eine Tasse) Kaffee ...*	(*ai*·ne *ta*·se) *ka*·fey ...
(cup of) tea ...	*(eine Tasse) Tee ...*	(*ai*·ne *ta*·se) tey ...
with milk	*mit Milch*	mit milkh
without sugar	*ohne Zucker*	*aw*·ne *tsu*·ker
(orange) juice	*(Orangen)Saft* m	(o·*rang*·zhen·)zaft
mineral water	*Mineralwasser* n	mi·ne·*raal*·va·ser
soft drink	*Softdrink* m	*soft*·dringk
(boiled) water	*(heißes) Wasser* n	(*hai*·ses) *va*·ser

in the bar

I'll have ...	*Ich hätte gern ...*	ikh *he*·te gern ...
I'll buy you a drink.	*Ich gebe dir einen aus.* inf	ikh *gey*·be deer *ai*·nen ows
What would you like?	*Was möchtest du?* inf	vas *meukh*·test doo
Cheers!	*Prost!*	prawst
brandy	*Weinbrand* m	*vain*·brant
cognac	*Kognak* m	*ko*·nyak
cocktail	*Cocktail* m	*kok*·tayl
a shot of (whisky)	*einen (Whisky)*	*ai*·nen (*vis*·ki)
a bottle of ...	*eine Flasche ...*	*ai*·ne *fla*·she ...
a glass of ...	*ein Glas ...*	ain glaas ...
red wine	*Rotwein*	*rawt*·vain
sparkling wine	*Sekt*	zekt
white wine	*Weißwein*	*vais*·vain
a ... of beer	*... Bier*	... beer
bottle	*eine Flasche*	*ai*·ne *fla*·she
glass	*ein Glas*	ain glaas

self-catering

What's the local speciality?
Was ist eine örtliche Spezialität?   vas ist *ai*·ne *eurt*·li·khe shpe·tsya·li·*teyt*

What's that?
Was ist das?   vas ist das

How much is (a kilo of cheese)?
Was kostet (ein Kilo Käse)?   vas *kos*·tet (ain *kee*·lo *key*·ze)

I'd like …	Ich möchte …	ikh *meukh*·te …
(100) grams	(hundert) Gramm	(hun·dert) gram
(two) kilos	(zwei) Kilo	(tsvai) *kee*·lo
(three) pieces	(drei) Stück	(drai) shtewk
(six) slices	(sechs) Scheiben	(zeks) *shai*·ben

Less.	Weniger.	*vey*·ni·ger
Enough.	Genug.	ge·*nook*
More.	Mehr.	mair

special diets & allergies

Is there a vegetarian restaurant near here?
Gibt es ein vegetarisches   gipt es ain vege·*tar*·ish·shes
Restaurant hier in der Nähe?   res·to·*rang* heer in dair *ney*·e

Do you have vegetarian food?
Haben Sie vegetarisches Essen?   *haa*·ben zee ve·ge·*taa*·ri·shes *e*·sen

Could you prepare a meal without …?	Können Sie ein Gericht ohne … zubereiten?	*keu*·nen zee ain ge·*rikht aw*·ne … *tsoo*·be·rai·ten
butter	Butter	*bu*·ter
eggs	Eiern	*ai*·ern
meat stock	Fleischbrühe	*flaish*·brew·e

I'm allergic to …	Ich bin allergisch gegen …	ikh bin a·*lair*·gish *gey*·gen …
dairy produce	Milchprodukte	*milkh*·pro·duk·te
gluten	Gluten	*gloo*·ten
MSG	Natrium-glutamat	*naa*·tri·um·glu·ta·maat
nuts	Nüsse	*new*·se
seafood	Meeresfrüchte	*mair*·res·frewkh·te

menu reader

Bayrisch Kraut n	*bai*-rish krowt	shredded cabbage cooked with sliced apples, wine & sugar
Berliner m	ber-*lee*-ner	jam doughnut
Cervelatwurst f	ser-ve-*laat*-vurst	spicy pork & beef sausage
Erdäpfelgulasch n	*ert*-ep-fel-goo-lash	spicy sausage & potato stew
gekochter Schinken m	ge-*kokh*-ter *shing*-ken	cooked ham
Graupensuppe f	*grow*-pen-zu-pe	barley soup
Greyerzer m	*grai*-er-tser	a smooth, rich cheese
Grießklößchensuppe f	*grees*-kleus-khen-zu-pe	soup with semolina dumplings
Gröstl n	greustl	grated fried potatoes with meat
Grünkohl mit Pinkel m	*grewn*-kawl mit *ping*-kel	cabbage with sausages
Holsteiner Schnitzel n	*hol*-shtai-ner *shni*-tsel	veal schnitzel with fried egg & seafood
Husarenfleisch n	hu-*zaa*-ren-flaish	braised beef, veal & pork fillets with sweet peppers, onions & sour cream
Hutzelbrot n	*hu*-tsel-brawt	bread made of prunes & other dried fruit
Kaiserschmarren m	*kai*-zer-shmar-ren	pancakes with raisins, fruit compote or chocolate sauce
Kaisersemmeln f pl	*kai*-zer-ze-meln	Austrian bread rolls
Katenwurst f	*kaa*-ten-vurst	country-style smoked sausage
Königsuppe f	*keu*-ni-gin-zu-pe	creamy chicken soup
Königstorte f	*keu*-niks-tor-te	rum-flavoured fruit cake
Krautsalat m	*krowt*-za-laat	coleslaw
Leipziger Allerlei n	*laip*-tsi-ger *a*-ler-lai	mixed vegetable stew
Linzer Torte f	*lin*-tser *tor*-te	latticed tart with jam topping

Nudelauflauf m	*noo-del-owf-lowf*	*pasta casserole*
Obatzter m	*aw-bats-ter*	*Bavarian soft cheese mousse*
Ochsenschwanzsuppe f	*ok-sen-shvants-zu-pe*	*oxtail soup*
Palatschinken m	*pa-lat-shing-ken*	*pancakes filled with jam or cheese*
Rollmops m	*rol-mops*	*pickled herring fillet rolled around chopped onions or gherkins*
Sauerbraten m	*zow-er-braa-ten*	*marinated roasted beef served with a sour cream sauce*
Sauerkraut n	*zow-er-krowt*	*pickled cabbage*
Schafskäse m	*shaafs-key-ze*	*sheep's milk feta*
Schmorbraten m	*shmawr-braa-ten*	*beef pot roast*
Schnitzel n	*shni-tsel*	*pork, veal or chicken breast rolled in breadcrumbs & fried*
Strammer Max m	*shtra-mer maks*	*ham, sausage or pork sandwich, served with fried eggs & onions*
Streichkäse m	*shtraikh-key-ze*	*any kind of soft cheese spread*
Streuselkuchen m	*shtroy-zel-koo-khen*	*coffee cake topped with cinnamon*
Strudel m	*shtroo-del*	*loaf-shaped pastry with a sweet or savoury filling*
Tascherl n	*ta-sherl*	*pastry with meat, cheese or jam*
Voressen n	*fawr-e-sen*	*meat stew*
Weinkraut n	*vain-krowt*	*white cabbage, braised with apples & simmered in wine*
Wiener Schnitzel n	*vee-ner shni-tsel*	*crumbed veal schnitzel*
Wiener Würstchen n	*vee-ner vewrst-khen*	*frankfurter (sausage)*
Zwetschgendatschi m	*tsvetsh-gen-dat-shi*	*damson plum tart*
Zwiebelsuppe f	*tsvee-bel-zu-pe*	*onion soup*
Zwiebelwurst f	*tsvee-bel-vurst*	*liver & onion sausage*

emergencies

basics

Help!	Hilfe!	hil·fe
Stop!	Halt!	halt
Go away!	Gehen Sie weg!	gey·en zee vek
Thief!	Dieb!	deeb
Fire!	Feuer!	foy·er
Watch out!	Vorsicht!	foi·zikht
Call ...!	Rufen Sie ...!	roo·fen zee ...
a doctor	einen Arzt	ai·nen artst
an ambulance	einen Krankenwagen	ai·nen krang·ken·vaa·gen
the police	die Polizei	dee po·li·tsai

It's an emergency!
Es ist ein Notfall!   es ist ain *nawt*·fal

Could you help me, please?
Könnten Sie mir bitte helfen?   *keun*·ten zee meer *bi*·te *hel*·fen

I have to use the telephone.
Ich muss das Telefon benutzen.   ikh mus das te·le·*fawn* be·*nu*·tsen

I'm lost.
Ich habe mich verirrt.   ikh *haa*·be mikh fer·*irt*

Where are the toilets?
Wo ist die Toilette?   vo ist dee to·a·*le*·te

police

Where's the police station?
Wo ist das Polizeirevier?   vaw ist das po·li·*tsai*·re·veer

I want to report an offence.
Ich möchte eine Straftat melden.   ikh *meukh*·te *ai*·ne *shtraaf*·taat *mel*·den

I have insurance.
Ich bin versichert.   ikh bin fer·*zi*·khert

I've been ...	Ich bin ... worden.	ikh bin ... *vor*·den
assaulted	angegriffen	*an*·ge·gri·fen
raped	vergewaltigt	fer·ge·*val*·tikht
robbed	bestohlen	be·*shtaw*·len

I've lost my...	Ich habe ... verloren.	ikh *haa*·be ... fer·*law*·ren
My ... was/	Man hat mir ...	man hat meer ...
were stolen.	gestohlen.	ge·*shtaw*·len
backpack	meinen Rucksack	*mai*·nen *ruk*·zak
bags	meine Reisetaschen	*mai*·ne *rai*·ze·ta·shen
credit card	meine Kreditkarte	*mai*·ne kre·*deet*·kar·te
handbag	meine Handtasche	*mai*·ne *hant*·ta·she
jewellery	meinen Schmuck	*mai*·nen shmuk
money	mein Geld	main gelt
passport	meinen Pass	*mai*·nen pas
travellers cheques	meine Reiseschecks	*mai*·ne *rai*·ze·sheks
wallet	meine Brieftasche	*mai*·ne *breef*·ta·she

I want to contact	Ich mochte mich mit	ikh *meukh*·te mikh mit
my ...	... in Verbindung setzen.	... in fer·*bin*·dung *ze*·tsen
consulate	meinem Konsulat	*mai*·nem kon·zu·*laat*
embassy	meiner Botschaft	*mai*·ner *bawt*·shaft

health

medical needs

Where's the	Wo ist der/die/das	vaw ist dair/dee/das
nearest ...?	nächste ...? m/f/n	*neykhs*·te ...
dentist	Zahnarzt m	*tsaan*·artst
doctor	Arzt m	artst
hospital	Krankenhaus n	*krang*·ken·hows
(night) pharmacist	(Nacht)Apotheke f	(nakht·)a·po·*tey*·ke

I need a doctor (who speaks English).
Ich brauche einen Arzt — ikh *brow*·khe *ai*·nen artst
(der Englisch spricht). — (dair *eng*·lish shprikht)

Could I see a female doctor?
Könnte ich von einer — *keun*·te ikh fon *ai*·ner
Ärztin behandelt werden? — *erts*·tin be·*han*·delt *ver*·den

I've run out of my medication.
Ich habe keine — ikh *haa*·be *kai*·ne
Medikamente mehr. — me·di·ka·*men*·te mair

symptoms, conditions & allergies

I'm sick.	Ich bin krank.	ikh bin krangk
It hurts here.	Es tut hier weh.	es toot heer vey

I have (a) ...	Ich habe ...	ikh haa·be ...
asthma	Asthma	ast·ma
bronchitis	Bronchitis	bron·khee·tis
constipation	Verstopfung	fer·shtop·fung
cough	Husten	hoos·ten
diarrhoea	Durchfall	durkh·fal
fever	Fieber	tee·ber
headache	Kopfschmerzen	kopf·shmer·tsen
heart condition	Herzbeschwerden	herts·be·shver·den
nausea	Übelkeit	ew·bel·kait
pain	Schmerzen	shmer·tsen
sore throat	Halsschmerzen	hals·shmer·tsen
toothache	Zahnschmerzen	tsaan·shmer·tsen

I'm allergic to ...	Ich bin allergisch gegen ...	ikh bin a·lair·gish gey·gen ...
antibiotics	Antibiotika	an·ti·bi·aw·ti·ka
anti-inflammatories	entzündungs-hemmende Mittel	en·tsewn·dungks-he·men·de mi·tel
aspirin	Aspirin	as·pi·reen
bees	Bienen	bee·nen
codeine	Kodein	ko·de·een
penicillin	Penizillin	pe·ni·tsi·leen

antiseptic	Antiseptikum n	an·ti·zep·ti·kum
bandage	Verband m	fer·bant
condoms	Kondom n	kon·dawm
contraceptives	Verhütungsmittel n	fer·hew·tungks·mi·tel
diarrhoea medicine	Mittel gegen Durchfall n	mi·tel gey·gen durkh·fal
insect repellent	Insektenschutzmittel n	in·zek·ten·shuts·mi·tel
laxatives	Abführmittel n	ap·fewr·mi·tel
painkillers	Schmerzmittel n	shmerts·mi·tel
rehydration salts	Kochsalzlösung n	kokh·zalts·leu·zung
sleeping tablets	Schlaftabletten f pl	shlaaf·ta·ble·ten

english–german dictionary

German nouns in this dictionary have their gender indicated by ⓜ (masculine), ⓕ (feminine) or ⓝ (neuter). If it's a plural noun, you'll also see pl. Words are also marked as n (noun), a (adjective), v (verb) sg (singular), pl (plural), inf (informal) and pol (polite) where necessary.

A

accident *Unfall* ⓜ un-fal
accommodation *Unterkunft* ⓕ un-ter-kunft
adaptor *Adapter* ⓜ a-dap-ter
address *Adresse* ⓕ a-dre-se
after *nach* naakh
air-conditioned *mit Klimaanlage* ⓕ
  mit klee-ma-an-laa-ge
airplane *Flugzeug* ⓝ flook-tsoyk
airport *Flughafen* ⓜ flook-haa-fen
alcohol *Alkohol* ⓜ al-ko-hawl
all a *alle* a-le
allergy *Allergie* ⓕ a-lair-gee
ambulance *Krankenwagen* ⓜ krang-ken-vaa-gen
and *und* unt
ankle *Knöchel* ⓜ kneu-khel
arm *Arm* ⓜ arm
ashtray *Aschenbecher* ⓜ a-shen-be-kher
ATM *Geldautomat* ⓜ gelt-ow-to-maat
Austria *Österreich* ⓝ eus-ter-raikh

B

baby *Baby* ⓝ bay-bi
back (body) *Rücken* ⓜ rew-ken
backpack *Rucksack* ⓜ ruk-zak
bad *schlecht* shlekht
bag *Tasche* ⓕ ta-she
baggage claim *Gepäckausgabe* ⓕ ge-pek-ows-gaa-be
bank *Bank* ⓕ bangk
bar *Lokal* ⓝ lo-kaal
bathroom *Badezimmer* ⓝ baa-de-tsi-mer
battery *Batterie* ⓕ ba-te-ree
beautiful *schön* sheun
bed *Bett* ⓝ bet
beer *Bier* ⓝ beer
before *vor* fawr
behind *hinter* hin-ter
Belgium ⓝ *Belgien* bel-gi-en

bicycle *Fahrrad* ⓝ faar-raat
big *groß* graws
bill *Rechnung* ⓕ rekh-nung
black *schwarz* shvarts
blanket *Decke* ⓕ de-ke
blood group *Blutgruppe* ⓕ bloot-gru-pe
blue *blau* blow
book (make a reservation) v *buchen* boo-khen
bottle *Flasche* ⓕ fla-she
bottle opener *Flaschenöffner* ⓜ fla-shen-euf-ner
boy *Junge* ⓜ yung-e
brakes (car) *Bremsen* ⓕ pl brem-zen
breakfast *Frühstück* ⓝ frew-shtewk
broken (faulty) *kaputt* ka-put
bus *Bus* ⓜ bus
business *Geschäft* ⓝ ge-sheft
buy *kaufen* kow-fen

C

café *Café* ⓝ ka-fey
camera *Kamera* ⓕ ka-me-ra
camp site *Zeltplatz* ⓜ tselt-plats
cancel *stornieren* shtor-nee-ren
can opener *Dosenöffner* ⓜ daw-zen-euf-ner
car *Auto* ⓝ ow-to
cash *Bargeld* ⓝ baar-gelt
cash (a cheque) v *(einen Scheck) einlösen*
  (ai-nen shek) ain-leu-zen
cell phone *Handy* ⓝ hen-di
centre *Zentrum* ⓝ tsen-trum
change (money) v *wechseln* vek-seln
cheap *billig* bi-likh
check (bill) *Rechnung* ⓕ rekh-nung
check-in *Abfertigungsschalter* ⓜ
  ap-fer-ti-gungks-shal-ter
chest *Brustkorb* ⓜ brust-korp
child *Kind* ⓝ kint
cigarette *Zigarette* ⓕ tsi-ga-re-te
city *Stadt* ⓕ shtat
clean a *sauber* zow-ber

losed *geschlossen* ge-shlo-sen
offee *Kaffee* m ka-fey
oins *Münzen* f pl mewn-tsen
old a *kalt* kalt
ollect call *R-Gespräch* n air-ge-shpreykh
ome *kommen* ko-men
omputer *Computer* m kom-pyoo-ter
ondom *Kondom* n kon-dawm
ontact lenses *Kontaktlinsen* f pl kon-takt-lin-zen
ook v *kochen* ko-khen
ost *Preis* m prais
redit card *Kreditkarte* f kre-deet-kar-te
up *Tasse* f ta-se
urrency exchange *Geldwechsel* m gelt-vek-sel
ustoms (immigration) *Zoll* m tsol

D

angerous *gefährlich* ge-fair-likh
ate (time) *Datum* n daa-tum
ay *Tag* m taak
elay n *Verspätung* f fer-shpey-tung
entist *Zahnarzt/Zahnärztin* m/f tsaan-artst/tsaan-erts-tin
epart *abfahren* ap-faa-ren
iaper *Windel* f vin-del
ictionary *Wörterbuch* n veur-ter-bookh
inner *Abendessen* n aa-bent-e-sen
irect *direkt* di-rekt
irty *schmutzig* shmu-tsikh
isabled *behindert* be-hin-dert
iscount n *Rabatt* m ra-bat
octor *Arzt/Ärztin* m/f artst/erts-tin
ouble bed *Doppelbett* n do-pel-bet
ouble room *Doppelzimmer mit einem Doppelbett* n do-pel-tsi-mer mit ai-nem do-pel-bet
rink *Getränk* n ge-trengk
rive v *fahren* faa-ren
rivers licence *Führerschein* m few-rer-shain
rugs (illicit) *Droge* f draw-ge
ummy (pacifier) *Schnuller* m shnu-ler

E

ar *Ohr* n awr
ast *Osten* m os-ten
at *essen* e-sen
conomy class *Touristenklasse* f tu-ris-ten-kla-se
lectricity *Elektrizität* f e-lek-tri-tsi-teyt
levator *Lift* m lift

email *E-Mail* e-mayl
embassy *Botschaft* f bawt-shaft
emergency *Notfall* m nawt-fal
English (language) *Englisch* n eng-lish
entrance *Eingang* m ain-gang
evening *Abend* m aa-bent
exchange rate *Wechselkurs* m vek-sel-kurs
exit *Ausgang* m ows-gang
expensive *teuer* toy-er
express mail *Expresspost* f eks-pres-post
eye *Auge* n ow-ge

F

far *weit* vait
fast *schnell* shnel
father *Vater* m faa-ter
film (camera) *Film* m film
finger *Finger* m fing-er
first-aid kit *Verbandskasten* m fer-bants-kas-ten
first class *erste Klasse* f ers-te kla-se
fish *Fisch* m fish
food *Essen* n e-sen
foot *Fuß* m foos
free (of charge) *gratis* graa-tis
friend *Freund/Freundin* m/f froynt/froyn-din
fruit *Frucht* f frukht
full *voll* fol
funny *lustig* lus-tikh

G

German (language) *Deutsch* n doytsh
Germany *Deutschland* n doytsh-lant
gift *Geschenk* n ge-shengk
girl *Mädchen* n meyt-khen
glass (drinking) *Glas* n glaas
glasses *Brille* f bri-le
go *gehen* gey-en
good *gut* goot
green *grün* grewn
guide *Führer* m few-rer

H

half *Hälfte* f helf-te
hand *Hand* f hant
handbag *Handtasche* f hant-ta-she
happy *glücklich* glewk-likh

have *haben* haa-ben
he *er* air
head *Kopf* ⓜ kopf
heart *Herz* ⓝ herts
heat n *Hitze* ① hi-tse
heavy *schwer* shvair
help v *helfen* hel-fen
here *hier* heer
high *hoch* hawkh
highway *Autobahn* ① ow-to-baan
hike v *wandern* van-dern
holiday *Urlaub* ⓜ oor-lowp
homosexual *homosexuell* haw-mo-zek-su-el
hospital *Krankenhaus* ⓝ krang-ken-hows
hot *heiß* hais
hotel *Hotel* ⓝ ho-tel
hungry *hungrig* hung-rikh
husband *Ehemann* ⓜ ey-e-man

I

I *ich* ikh
identification (card) *Personalausweis* ⓜ
  per-zo-naal-ows-vais
ill *krank* krangk
important *wichtig* vikh-tikh
included *inbegriffen* in-be-gri-fen
injury *Verletzung* ① fer-le-tsung
insurance *Versicherung* ① fer-zi-khe-rung
Internet *Internet* ⓝ in-ter-net
interpreter *Dolmetscher/Dolmetscherin* ⓜ/①
  dol-met-sher/dol-met-she-rin

J

jewellery *Schmuck* ⓜ shmuk
job *Arbeitsstelle* ① ar-baits-shte-le

K

key *Schlüssel* ⓜ shlew-sel
kilogram *Kilogramm* ⓝ kee-lo-gram
kitchen *Küche* ① kew-khe
knife *Messer* ⓝ me-ser

L

laundry (place) *Waschküche* ① vash-kew-khe
lawyer *Rechtsanwalt/Rechtsanwältin* ⓜ/①
  rekhts-an-valt/rekhts-an-vel-tin

left (direction) *links* lingks
left-luggage office *Gepäckaufbewahrung* ①
  ge-pek-owf-be-vaa-rung
leg *Bein* ⓝ bain
lesbian *Lesbierin* ① les-bi-e-rin
less *weniger* vey-ni-ger
letter (mail) *Brief* ⓜ breef
lift (elevator) *Lift* ⓜ lift
light *Licht* ⓝ likht
like v *mögen* meu-gen
lock *Schloss* ⓝ shlos
long *lang* lang
lost *verloren* fer-law-ren
lost-property office *Fundbüro* ⓝ funt-bew-raw
love v *lieben* lee-ben
luggage *Gepäck* ⓝ ge-pek
lunch *Mittagessen* ⓝ mi-taak-e-sen

M

mail *Post* ① post
man *Mann* ⓜ man
map *Karte* ① kar-te
market *Markt* ⓜ markt
matches *Streichhölzer* ⓝ pl shtraikh-heul-tser
meat *Fleisch* ⓝ flaish
medicine *Medizin* ① me-di-tseen
menu *Speisekarte* ① shpai-ze-kar-te
message *Mitteilung* ① mi-tai-lung
milk *Milch* ① milkh
minute *Minute* ① mi-noo-te
mobile phone *Handy* ⓝ hen-di
money *Geld* ⓝ gelt
month *Monat* ⓜ maw-nat
morning *Morgen* ⓜ mor-gen
mother *Mutter* ① mu-ter
motorcycle *Motorrad* ⓝ maw-tor-raat
motorway *Autobahn* ① ow-to-baan
mouth *Mund* ⓜ munt
music *Musik* ① mu-zeek

N

name *Name* ⓜ naa-me
napkin *Serviette* ① zer-vye-te
nappy *Windel* ① vin-del
near *nahe* naa-e
neck *Hals* ⓜ hals
new *neu* noy
news *Nachrichten* ① pl naakh-rikh-ten

newspaper *Zeitung* ① *tsai*-tung
night *Nacht* ① nakht
no *nein* nain
noisy *laut* lowt
nonsmoking *Nichtraucher* nikht-row-kher
north *Norden* ⓜ *nor*-den
nose *Nase* ① *naa*-ze
now *jetzt* yetst
number *Zahl* ① tsaal

O

oil (engine) *Öl* ⓝ eul
old *alt* alt
one-way ticket *einfache Fahrkarte* ①
  ain-*fa*-khe *faar*-kar-te
open a *offen* o-fen
outside *draußen* drow-sen

P

package *Paket* ⓝ pa-*kcyt*
paper *Papier* ⓝ pa-*peer*
park (car) v *parken* *par*-ken
passport *(Reise)Pass* ⓜ (*rai*-ze-)pas
pay *bezahlen* be-*tsaa*-len
pen *Kugelschreiber* ⓜ *koo*-gel-shrai-ber
petrol *Benzin* ⓝ ben-*tseen*
pharmacy *Apotheke* ① a-po-*tey*-ke
phonecard *Telefonkarte* ① te-le-*fawn*-kar-te
photo *Foto* ⓝ *faw*-to
plate *Teller* ⓜ *te*-ler
police *Polizei* ① po-li-*tsai*
postcard *Postkarte* ① *post*-kar-te
post office *Postamt* ⓝ *post*-amt
pregnant *schwanger* *shvung*-er
price *Preis* ⓜ prais

Q

quiet *ruhig* roo-ikh

R

rain n *Regen* ⓜ *rey*-gen
razor *Rasierer* ⓜ ra-*zee*-rer
receipt *Quittung* ① *kvi*-tung
red *rot* rawt
refund *Rückzahlung* ① *rewk*-tsaa-lung
registered mail *Einschreiben* ⓝ *ain*-shrai-ben

rent v *mieten* *mee*-ten
repair v *reparieren* re-pa-*ree*-ren
reservation *Reservierung* ① re-zer-*vee*-rung
restaurant *Restaurant* ⓝ res-to-*raang*
return v *zurückkommen* tsu-*rewk*-ko-men
return ticket *Rückfahrkarte* ① *rewk*-faar-kar-te
right (direction) *rechts* rekhts
road *Straße* ① *shtraa*-se
room *Zimmer* ⓝ *tsi*-mer

S

safe a *sicher* *zi*-kher
sanitary napkin *Damenbinden* ① pl *daa*-men-bin-den
seat *Platz* ⓜ plats
send *senden* *zen*-den
service station *Tankstelle* ① *tangk*-shte-le
sex *Sex* ⓜ seks
shampoo *Shampoo* ⓝ *sham*-poo
share (a dorm) *teilen (mit)* *tai*-len (mit)
shaving cream *Rasiercreme* ① ra-*zeer*-kreym
she *sie* zee
sheet (bed) *Bettlaken* ⓝ *bet*-laa-ken
shirt *Hemd* ⓝ hemt
shoes *Schuhe* ⓝ pl *shoo*-e
shop n *Geschäft* ⓝ ge-*sheft*
short *kurz* kurts
shower *Dusche* ① *doo*-she
single room *Einzelzimmer* ⓝ *ain*-tsel-tsi-mer
skin *Haut* ① howt
skirt *Rock* ⓜ rok
sleep v *schlafen* *shlaa*-fen
slowly *langsam* *lang*-zaam
small *klein* klain
smoke (cigarettes) v *rauchen* *row*-khen
soap *Seife* ① *zai*-fe
some *einige* *ai*-ni-ge
soon *bald* balt
south *Süden* ⓜ *zew*-den
souvenir shop *Souvenirladen* ⓜ zu-ve-*neer*-laa-den
speak *sprechen* *shpre*-khen
spoon *Löffel* ⓜ *leu*-fel
stamp *Briefmarke* ① *breef*-mar-ke
stand-by ticket *Standby-Ticket* ⓝ stend-*bai*-ti-ket
station (train) *Bahnhof* ⓜ *baan*-hawf
stomach *Magen* ⓜ *maa*-gen
stop v *anhalten* *an*-hal-ten
stop (bus) *Bushaltestelle* ① *bus*-hal-te-shte-le
street *Straße* ① *shtraa*-se

student *Student/Studentin* ⓜ/ⓕ
  shtu-*dent*/shtu-*den*-tin
sun *Sonne* ⓕ zo-ne
sunscreen *Sonnencreme* ⓕ zo-nen-kreym
swim v *schwimmen* shvi-men
Switzerland *Schweiz* ⓕ shvaits

T

tampons *Tampons* ⓜ pl tam-pons
taxi *Taxi* ⓝ tak-si
teaspoon *Teelöffel* ⓜ tey-leu-fel
teeth *Zähne* ⓜ pl tsey-ne
telephone *Telefon* ⓝ te-le-fawn
television *Fernseher* ⓜ fern-zey-er
temperature (weather) *Temperatur* ⓕ tem-pe-ra-*toor*
tent *Zelt* ⓝ tselt
that (one) *jene* yey-ne
they *sie* zee
thirsty *durstig* durs-tikh
this (one) *diese* dee-ze
throat *Kehle* ⓕ key-le
ticket (transport) *Fahrkarte* ⓕ faar-kar-te
ticket (sightseeing) *Eintrittskarte* ⓕ ain-trits-kar-te
time *Zeit* ⓕ tsait
tired *müde* mew-de
tissues *Papiertaschentücher* ⓝ pl
  pa-*peer*-ta-shen-tew-kher
today *heute* hoy-te
toilet *Toilette* ⓕ to-a-*le*-te
tomorrow *morgen* mor-gen
tonight *heute Abend* hoy-te aa-bent
toothbrush *Zahnbürste* ⓕ tsaan-bewrs-te
toothpaste *Zahnpasta* ⓕ tsaan-pas-ta
torch (flashlight) *Taschenlampe* ⓕ ta-shen-lam-pe
tour *Tour* ⓕ toor
tourist office *Fremdenverkehrsbüro* ⓝ
  frem-den-fer-kairs-bew-raw
towel *Handtuch* ⓝ hant-tookh
train *Zug* ⓜ tsook
translate *übersetzen* ew-ber-ze-tsen
travel agency *Reisebüro* ⓝ rai-ze-bew-raw
travellers cheque *Reisescheck* ⓜ rai-ze-shek
trousers *Hose* ⓕ haw-ze
twin beds *zwei Einzelbetten* ⓝ pl tsvai ain-tsel-be-ten
tyre *Reifen* ⓜ rai-fen

U

underwear *Unterwäsche* ⓕ un-ter-ve-she
urgent *dringend* dring-ent

V

vacant *frei* frai
vacation *Ferien* pl fair-i-en
vegetable *Gemüse* ⓝ ge-mew-ze
vegetarian a *vegetarisch* ve-ge-taa-rish
visa *Visum* ⓝ vee-zum

W

waiter *Kellner/Kellnerin* ⓜ/ⓕ kel-ner/kel-ne-rin
walk v *gehen* gey-en
wallet *Brieftasche* ⓕ breef-ta-she
warm a *warm* varm
wash (something) *waschen* va-shen
watch ⓝ *Uhr* oor
water *Wasser* ⓝ va-ser
we *wir* veer
weekend *Wochenende* ⓝ vo-khen-en-de
west *Westen* ⓜ ves-ten
wheelchair *Rollstuhl* ⓜ rol-shtool
when *wann* van
where *wo* vaw
white *weiß* vais
who *wer* vair
why *warum* va-*rum*
wife *Ehefrau* ⓕ ey-e-frow
window *Fenster* ⓝ fens-ter
wine *Wein* ⓜ vain
with *mit* mit
without *ohne* aw-ne
woman *Frau* ⓕ frow
write *schreiben* shrai-ben

Y

yellow *gelb* gelp
yes *ja* yaa
yesterday *gestern* ges-tern
you sg inf *du* doo
you sg pol *Sie* zee
you pl *Sie* zee

Hungarian

hungarian alphabet

A a o	*Á á* a	*B b* bey	*C c* tsey	*Cs cs* chey	*D d* dey	*Dz dz* dzey	*Dzs dzs* jey
E e e	*É é* ey	*F f* ef	*G g* gey	*Gy gy* dyey	*H h* ha	*I i* i	*Í í* ee
J j yey	*K k* ka	*L l* el	*Ly ly* ey	*M m* em	*N n* en	*Ny ny* en'	*O o* aw
Ó ó āw	*Ö ö* eu	*Ő ő* ēü	*P p* pey	*Q q* ku	*R r* er	*S s* esh	*Sz sz* es
T t tey	*Ty ty* tyey	*U u* u	*Ú ú* ū	*Ü ü* ew	*Ű ű* ēw	*V v* vey	*W w* *du*-plo-vey
X x iks	*Y y* *ip*-sil-awn	*Z z* zey	*Zs zs* zhey				

hungarian

MAGYAR

introduction

Hungarian (*magyar mo·dyor*) is a unique language. Though distantly related to Finnish, it has no significant similarities to any other language in the world. If you have some background in European languages you'll be surprised at just how different Hungarian is. English actually has more in common with Russian and Sinhala (from Sri Lanka) than it does with Hungarian – even though words like *goulash*, *paprika* and *vampire* came to English from this language.

So how did such an unusual language end up in the heart of the European continent? The answer lies somewhere beyond the Ural mountains in western Siberia, where the nomadic ancestors of today's Hungarian speakers began a slow migration west about 2000 years ago. At some point in the journey the group began to split. One group turned towards Finland, while the other continued towards the Carpathian Basin, arriving in the late 9th century. Calling themselves Magyars (derived from the Finno-Ugric words for 'speak' and 'man') they cultivated and developed the occupied lands. By AD 1000 the Kingdom of Hungary was officially established. Along the way Hungarian acquired words from languages like Latin, Persian, Turkish and Bulgarian, yet overall changed remarkably little.

With more than 14.5 million speakers worldwide, Hungarian is nowadays the official language of Hungary and a minority language in the parts of Eastern Europe which belonged to the Austro-Hungarian Empire before World War I – Slovakia, Croatia, the northern Serbian province of Vojvodina and parts of Austria, Romania and the Ukraine.

Hungarian is a language rich in grammar and expression. These characteristics can be both alluring and intimidating. Word order in Hungarian is fairly free, and it has been argued that this stimulates creative or experimental thinking. Some believe that the flexibility of the tongue, combined with Hungary's linguistic isolation, has encouraged the culture's strong tradition of poetry and literature. For the same reason, however, the language is resistant to translation and much of the nation's literary heritage is still unavailable to English speakers. Another theory holds that Hungary's extraordinary number of great scientists is also attributable to the language's versatile nature. Still, Hungarian needn't be intimidating and you won't need to look very far to discover the beauty of the language. You may even find yourself unlocking the poet or scientist within!

pronunciation

The Hungarian language may seem daunting with its long words and many accent marks, but it's surprisingly easy to pronounce. Like English, Hungarian isn't always written the way it's pronounced, but just stick to the coloured phonetic guides that accompany each phrase or word and you can't go wrong.

vowel sounds

Hungarian vowels sounds are similar to those found in the English words listed in the table below. The symbol ¯ over a vowel, like ā, means you say it as a long vowel sound. The letter y is always pronounced as in 'yes'.

symbol	english equivalent	hungarian example	transliteration
a	fa**ther**	*hátizsák*	*ha*·ti·zhak
aw	**law** (but short)	*kor*	kawr
e	b**e**t	*zsebkés*	*zheb*·keysh
ee	s**ee**	*cím*	tseem
eu	h**er**	*zöld*	zeuld
ew	**ee** pronounced with rounded lips	*csütörtök*	*chew*·teur·teuk
ey	h**ey**	*én*	eyn
i	b**i**t	*rizs*	rizh
o	p**o**t	*gazda*	*gaz*·do
oy	t**oy**	*megfojt,* *komoly*	*meg*·foyt, *kaw*·moy
u	p**u**t	*utas*	*u*·tosh

word stress

Accent marks over vowels don't influence word stress, which always falls on the first syllable of the word. The stressed syllables in our coloured pronunciation guides are always in italics.

consonant sounds

Always pronounce y like the 'y' in 'yes'. We've also used the ' symbol to show this
y sound when it's attached to n, d, and t and at the end of a syllable. You'll also see
double consonants like bb, dd or tt — draw them out a little longer than you would
in English.

symbol	english equivalent	hungarian example	transliteration
b	bed	*bajusz*	*bo·yus*
ch	cheat	*család*	*cho·lad*
d	dog	*dervis*	*der·vish*
dy	during	*magyar*	*mo·dyor*
f	fat	*farok*	*fo·rawk*
g	go	*gallér, igen*	*gol·leyr, i·gen*
h	hat	*hát*	*hat*
j	joke	*dzsem, hogy*	*jem, hawj*
k	kit	*kacsa*	*ko·cho*
l	lot	*lakat*	*lo·kot*
m	man	*most*	*mawsht*
n	not	*nem*	*nem*
p	pet	*pamut*	*po·mut*
r	run (rolled)	*piros*	*pi·rawsh*
s	sun	*kolbász*	*kawl·bas*
sh	shot	*tojást*	*taw·yasht*
t	top	*tag*	*tog*
ty	tutor	*kártya*	*kar·tyo*
ts	hats	*koncert*	*kawn·tsert*
v	very	*vajon*	*vo·yawn*
y	yes	*hajó, melyik*	*ho·yáw, me·yik*
z	zero	*zab*	*zob*
zh	pleasure	*zsemle*	*zhem·le*
'	a slight y sound	*poggyász, hány*	*pawd'·dyas, han'*

tools

language difficulties

Do you speak English?
Beszél/Beszélsz angolul? pol/inf — be·seyl/be·seyls on·gaw·lul

Do you understand?
Érti/Érted? pol/inf — eyr·ti/eyr·ted

I (don't) understand.
(Nem) Értem. — (nem) eyr·tem

What does (lángos) mean?
Mit jelent az, hogy (lángos)? — mit ye·lent oz hawj (lan·gawsh)

How do you ...?	*Hogyan ...?*	haw·dyon ...
pronounce this	*mondja ki ezt*	mawnd·yo ki ezt
write (útlevél)	*írja azt, hogy (útlevél)*	eer·yo ozt hawj (ūt·le·veyl)

Could you please ...?	*..., kérem.*	... key·rem
repeat that	*Megismételné ezt*	meg·ish·mey·tel·ney ezt
speak more slowly	*Tudna lassabban beszélni*	tud·no losh·shob·bon be·seyl·ni
write it down	*Leírná*	le·eer·na

essentials

Yes.	*Igen.*	i·gen
No.	*Nem.*	nem
Please.	*Kérem/Kérlek.* pol/inf	key·rem/keyr·lek
Thank you (very much).	*(Nagyon) Köszönöm.*	(no·dyawn) keu·seu·neum
You're welcome.	*Szívesen.*	see·ve·shen
Excuse me.	*Elnézést kérek.*	el·ney·zeysht key·rek
Sorry.	*Sajnálom.*	shoy·na·lawm

numbers

0	*nulla*	nul·lo	16	*tizenhat*	ti·zen·hot
1	*egy*	ej	17	*tizenhét*	ti·zen·heyt
2	*kettő*	ket·tēū	18	*tizennyolc*	ti·zen·nyawlts
3	*három*	ha·rawm	19	*tizenkilenc*	ti·zen·ki·lents
4	*négy*	neyj	20	*húsz*	hüs
5	*öt*	eut	21	*huszonegy*	hu·sawn·ej
6	*hat*	hot	22	*huszonkettő*	hu·sawn·ket·tēū
7	*hét*	heyt	30	*harminc*	hor·mints
8	*nyolc*	nyawlts	40	*negyven*	nej·ven
9	*kilenc*	ki·lents	50	*ötven*	eut·ven
10	*tíz*	teez	60	*hatvan*	hot·von
11	*tizenegy*	ti·zen·ej	70	*hetven*	het·ven
12	*tizenkettő*	ti·zen·ket·tēū	80	*nyolcvan*	nyawlts·von
13	*tizenhárom*	ti·zen·ha·rawm	90	*kilencven*	ki·lents·ven
14	*tizennégy*	ti·zen·neyj	100	*száz*	saz
15	*tizenöt*	ti·zen·eut	1000	*ezer*	e·zer

time & dates

What time is it?	*Hány óra?*	han' āw·ra
It's one o'clock.	*(Egy) óra van.*	(ej) āw·ra von
It's (10) o'clock.	*(Tíz) óra van.*	(teez) āw·ra von
Quarter past (10).	*Negyed (tizenegy).*	ne·dyed (ti·zen·ej)
Half past (10).	*Fél (tizenegy).*	feyl (ti·zen·ej)
Quarter to (11).	*Háromnegyed (tizenegy).*	ha·rawm·ne·dyed (ti·zen·ej)
At what time ...?	*Hány órakor ...?*	han' āw·ro·kawr ...
At ...	*...kor.*	...·kawr
am (morning)	*délelőtt*	deyl·e·lēütt
pm (afternoon)	*délután*	deyl·u·tan
pm (evening)	*este*	esh·te
Monday	*hétfő*	heyt·fēū
Tuesday	*kedd*	kedd
Wednesday	*szerda*	ser·do
Thursday	*csütörtök*	chew·teur·teuk
Friday	*péntek*	peyn·tek
Saturday	*szombat*	sawm·bot
Sunday	*vasárnap*	vo·shar·nop

January	január	yo·nu·ar
February	február	feb·ru·ar
March	március	mar·tsi·ush
April	április	ap·ri·lish
May	május	ma·yush
June	június	yū·ni·ush
July	július	yū·li·ush
August	augusztus	o·u·gus·tush
September	szeptember	sep·tem·ber
October	október	awk·tāw·ber
November	november	naw·vem·ber
December	december	de·tsem·ber

What date is it today?
  Hányadika van ma?   ha·nyo·di·ko von mo
It's (18 October).
  (Október tizennyolcadika) van.   (awk·tāw·ber ti·zen·nyawl·tso·di·ko) von

since (May)	(május) óta	(ma·yush) āw·to
until (June)	(június)ig	(yū·ni·ush)·ig
yesterday	tegnap	teg·nop
last night	tegnap éjjel	hawl·nop ey·yel
today	ma	mo
tonight	ma este	mo esh·te
tomorrow	holnap	hawl·nop
last/next ...	a múlt/a jövő ...	o mült/o yeu·vēû ...
week	héten	hey·ten
month	hónapban	hāw·nop·bon
year	évben	eyv·ben
yesterday/tomorrow ...	tegnap/holnap ...	teg·nop/hawl·nop ...
morning	reggel	reg·gel
afternoon	délután	deyl·u·tan
evening	este	esh·te

weather

What's the weather like?	Milyen az idő?	mi·yen oz i·dēū

It's ...

cloudy	Az idő felhős.	oz i·dēū fel·hēūsh
cold	Az idő hideg.	oz i·dēū hi·deg
hot	Az idő nagyon meleg.	oz i·dēū no·dyawn me·leg
raining	Esik az eső.	e·shik oz e·shēū
snowing	Esik a hó.	e·shik o hāw
sunny	Az idő napos.	oz i·dēū no·pawsh
warm	Az idő meleg.	oz i·dēū me·leg
windy	Az idő szeles.	oz i·dēū se·lesh

spring	tavasz	to·vos
summer	nyár	nyar
autumn	ősz	ēūs
winter	tél	teyl

border crossing

I'm ...	... vagyok.	... vo·dyawk
in transit	Átutazóban	at·u·to·zāw·bon
on business	Üzleti úton	ewz·le·ti ū·tawn
on holiday	Szabadságon	so·bod·sha·gawn

I'm here for ...	... vagyok itt.	... vo·dyawk itt
(10) days	(Tíz) napig	(teez) no·pig
(two) months	(Két) hónapig	(keyt) hāw·no·pig
(three) weeks	(Három) hétig	(ha·rawm) hey·tig

I'm going to (Szeged).
(Szeged)re megyek. — (se·ged)·re me·dyek

I'm staying at (the Gellért Hotel).
A (Gellért)ben fogok lakni. — o (gel·leyrt)·ben faw·gawk lok·ni

I have nothing to declare.
Nincs elvámolnivalóm. — ninch el·va·mawl·ni·vo·lāwm

I have something to declare.
Van valami elvámolnivalóm. — von vo·lo·mi el·va·mawl·ni·vo·lāwm

That's (not) mine.
Az (nem) az enyém. — oz (nem) oz e·nyeym

tools – HUNGARIAN

transport

tickets & luggage

Where can I buy a ticket?
Hol kapok jegyet? — hawl *ko*-pawk ye-dyet

Do I need to book a seat?
Kell helyjegyet váltanom? — kell *he*-ye-dyet *val*-ta-nawm

One ... ticket to (Eger), please.	*Egy ... jegy (Eger)be.*	ej ... yej (e-ger)-be
one-way	*csak oda*	chok aw-do
return	*oda-vissza*	aw-do-vis-so

I'd like to ... my ticket, please.	*Szeretném ... a jegyemet.*	se-ret-neym ... o ye-dye-met
cancel	*törölni*	teu-reul-ni
change	*megváltoztatni*	meg-val-tawz-tot-ni
collect	*átvenni*	at-ven-ni
confirm	*megerősíteni*	meg-e-rēū-shee-te-ni

I'd like a ... seat, please.	*... helyet szeretnék.*	... he-yet se-ret-neyk
nonsmoking	*Nemdohányzó*	nem-daw-han'-zāw
smoking	*Dohányzó*	daw-han'-zāw

How much is it?
Mennyibe kerül? — men'-nyi-be ke-rewl

Is there air conditioning?
Van légkondicionálás? — von leyg-kawn-di-tsi-aw-na-lash

Is there a toilet?
Van vécé? — von vey-tsey

How long does the trip take?
Mennyi ideig tart az út? — men'-nyi i-de-ig tort oz üt

Is it a direct route?
Ez közvetlen járat? — ez keuz-vet-len ya-rot

My luggage has been ...	*A poggyászom ...*	o pawd'-dya-sawm ...
damaged	*megsérült*	meg-shey-rewlt
lost	*elveszett*	el-ve-sett

My luggage has been stolen.
Ellopták a poggyászomat.   el·lawp·tak o pawd'·dya·saw·mot

Where can I find a luggage locker?
Hol találok egy poggyász-   hawl to·la·lawk ej pawd'·dyas·
megőrző automatát?   meg·eūr·zēū o·u·taw·mo·tat

getting around

Where does flight (BA15) arrive?
Hova érkezik a (BA tizenötös)   haw·vo eyr·ke·zik a (bey o ti·zen·eu·teush)
számú járat?   sa·mü ya·rot

Where does flight (BA26) depart?
Honnan indul a (BA huszonhatos)   hawn·non in·dul a (bey o hu·sawn·ho·tawsh)
számú járat?   sa·mü ya·rot

Where's (the) ...?	*Hol van ...?*	hawl von ...
arrivals hall	*az érkezési csarnok*	oz eyr·ke·zey·shi chor·nawk
departures hall	*az indulási csarnok*	oz in·du·la·shi chor·nawk
duty-free shop	*a vámmentes üzlet*	o vam·men·tesh ewz·let
gate (five)	*az (ötös) kapu*	oz (eu·teush) ko·pu

Which ... goes	*Melyik ... megy*	me·yik ... mej
to (Budapest)?	*(Budapest)re?*	(bu·do·pesht)·re
boat	*hajó*	ho·yāw
bus	*busz*	bus
plane	*repülőgép*	re·pew·lēū·geyp
train	*vonat*	vaw·not

What time's the	*Mikor megy ... (busz)?*	mi·kawr mej ... (bus)
... (bus)?		
first	*az első*	oz el·shēū
last	*az utolsó*	oz u·tawl·shāw
next	*a következő*	o keu·vet·ke·zēū

At what time does it arrive/leave?
Mikor érkezik/indul?   mi·kawr eyr·kez·ik/in·dul

How long will it be delayed?
Mennyit késik?   men'·nyit key·shik

What station/stop is this?
Ez milyen állomás/megálló?   ez mi·yen al·law·mash/meg·al·lāw

What's the next station/stop?

Mi a következő állomás/megálló?		mi o *keu*·vet·ke·zēū *al*·law·mash/*meg*·al·lāw

Does it stop at (Visegrád)?

Megáll (Visegrád)on? meg·all (*vi*·she·grad)·on

Please tell me when we get to (Eger).

Kérem, szóljon, amikor *key*·rem *sāwl*·yawn o·mi·kawr
(Eger)be érünk. (e·ger)·be ey·rewnk

How long do we stop here?

Mennyi ideig állunk itt? men'·nyi *i*·de·ig *al*·lunk itt

Is this seat available?

Szabad ez a hely? so·bod ez o *he*·y

That's my seat.

Az az én helyem. oz oz eyn *he*·yem

I'd like a taxi ... Szeretnék egy taxit ... se·ret·neyk ej *tok*·sit ...
  at (9am) (reggel kilenc)re (*reg*·gel *ki*·lents)·re
  now most mawsht
  tomorrow holnapra *hawl*·nop·ro

Is this taxi available?

Szabad ez a taxi? so·bod ez o *tok*·si

How much is it to ...?

Mennyibe kerül ...ba? men'·nyi·be *ke*·rewl ...·bo

Please put the meter on.

Kérem, kapcsolja be az órát. *key*·rem *kop*·chawl·yo be oz *āw*·rat

Please take me to (this address).

Kérem, vigyen el (erre a címre). kay·rem *vi*·dyen el (*er*·re o *tseem*·re)

Please ... Kérem, ... *key*·rem ...
  slow down lassítson *losh*·sheet·shawn
  stop here álljon meg itt *all*·yawn meg itt
  here várjon itt *var*·yawn itt

car, motorbike & bicycle hire

I'd like to hire a ...	Szeretnék egy ... bérelni.	se·ret·neyk ej ... *bey*·rel·ni
bicycle	biciklit	*bi*·tsik·lit
car	autót	o·u·tāwt
motorbike	motort	*maw*·tawrt

with a driver	soförrel	shaw-fēūr-rel
with air conditioning	lég-kondicionálóval	leyg-kawn-di-tsi-aw-naw-láw-vol
with antifreeze	fagyállóval	fod'-al-láw-vol
with snow chains	hólánccal	háw-lant'-tsol

How much	Mennyibe kerül	men'-nyi-be ke-rewl
for ... hire?	a kölcsönzés ...?	o keul-cheun-zeysh ...
hourly	óránként	āw-ran-keynt
daily	egy napra	ej nop-ro
weekly	egy hétre	ej heyt-re

air	levegő	le-ve-gēū
oil	olaj	aw-lo-y
petrol	benzin	ben-zin
tyres	gumi	gu-mi

I need a mechanic.
Szükségem van egy — sewk-shey-gem von ej
autószerelőre. — o-u-tāw-se-re-lēū-re

I've run out of petrol.
Kifogyott a benzinem. — ki-faw-dyawtt o ben-zi-nem

I have a flat tyre.
Defektem van. — de-fek-tem von

directions

Where's the ...?	Hol van a ...?	hawl von o ...
bank	bank	bonk
city centre	városközpont	va-rawsh-keuz-pawnt
hotel	szálloda	sal-law-do
market	piac	pi-ots
police station	rendőrség	rend-ēūr-sheyg
post office	postahivatal	pawsh-to-hi-vo-tol
public toilet	nyilvános vécé	nyil-va-nawsh vey-tsey
tourist office	turistairoda	tu-rish-to-i-raw-do

Is this the road to (Sopron)?
Ez az út vezet (Sopron)ba? — ez oz üt ve-zet (shawp-rawn)-bo

Can you show me (on the map)?
Meg tudja mutatni nekem — meg tud-yo mu-tot-ni ne-kem
(a térképen)? — (o teyr-key-pen)

What's the address?
Mi a cím? — mi o tseem

How far is it?
Milyen messze van? — mi·yen mes·se von

How do I get there?
Hogyan jutok oda? — haw·dyon yu·tawk aw·do

Turn ...	Forduljon ...	fawr·dul·yawn ...
at the corner	a saroknál	o sho·rawk·nal
at the traffic lights	a közlekedési lámpánál	o keuz·le·ke·dey·shi lam·pa·nal
left/right	balra/jobbra	bol·ro/yawbb·ro

It's ...	... van.	... von
behind ...	... mögött	... meu·geutt
far away	Messze	mes·se
here	Itt	itt
in front of ...	... előtt	... e·lēütt
left	Balra	bol·ro
near ...	... közelében	... keu·ze·ley·ben
next to ...	... mellett	... mel·lett
on the corner	A sarkon	o shor·kawn
opposite ...	...val szemben	...vol sem·ben
right	Jobbra	yawbb·ro
straight ahead	Egyenesen előttünk	e·dye·ne·shen e·lēüt·tewnk
there	Ott	ott

by bus	busszal	bus·sol
by taxi	taxival	tok·si·vol
by train	vonattal	vaw·not·tol
on foot	gyalog	dyo·lawg

north	észak	ey·sok
south	dél	deyl
east	kelet	ke·let
west	nyugat	nyu·got

signs

Bejárat/Kijárat	*be·ya·rot/ki·ya·rot*	**Entrance/Exit**
Nyitva/Zárva	*nyit·vo/zar·vo*	**Open/Closed**
Van Üres Szoba	*von ew·resh saw·bo*	**Rooms Available**
Minden Szoba Foglalt	*min·den saw·bo fawg·lolt*	**No Vacancies**
Információ	*in·fawr·ma·tsi·āw*	**Information**
Rendőrség	*rend·ēūr·sheyg*	**Police Station**
Tilos	*ti·lawsh*	**Prohibited**
Mosdó	*mawsh·dāw*	**Toilets**
Férfiak	*feyr·fi·ok*	**Men**
Nők	*nēūk*	**Women**
Meleg/Hideg	*me·leg/hi·deg*	**Hot/Cold**

accommodation

finding accommodation

Where's a ...?	*Hol van egy ...?*	hawl von ej ...
camping ground	*kemping*	*kem*·ping
guesthouse	*panzió*	*pon*·zi·āw
hotel	*szálloda*	*sal*·law·do
youth hostel	*ifjúsági szálló*	*if*·yū·sha·gi *sal*·lāw
Can you recommend somewhere ...?	*Tud ajánlani egy ... helyet?*	tud o·yan·lo·ni ej ... *he*·yet
cheap	*olcsó*	*awl*·chāw
good	*jo*	yāw
nearby	*közeli*	*keu*·ze·li
I'd like to book a room, please.	*Szeretnék egy szobát foglalni.*	*se*·ret·neyk ej saw·bat *fawg*·lol·ni
I have a reservation.	*Van foglalásom.*	von *fawg*·lo·la·shawm
My name's ...	*A nevem ...*	o *ne*·vem ...
Do you have a ... room?	*Van Önnek kiadó egy ... szobája?*	von *eun*·nek *ki*·o·dāw ed' ... *saw*·ba·yo
single	*egyágyas*	*ej*·a·dyosh
double	*dupláágyas*	*dup*·lo·a·dyosh
twin	*kétágyas*	*keyt*·a·dyosh

How much is it per ...?	Mennyibe kerül egy ...?	men'·nyi·be ke·rewl ej ...
night	éjszakára	ey·so·ka·ro
person	főre	feü·re

Can I pay by ...?	Fizethetek ...?	fi·zet·he·tek ...
credit card	hitelkártyával	hi·tel·kar·tya·vol
travellers cheque	utazási csekkel	u·to·za·shi chek·kel

I'd like to stay for (three) nights.
(Három) éjszakára. (ha·rawm) ey·so·ka·ro

From (July 2) to (July 6).
(Július kettő)től (július hat)ig. (yū·li·ush ket·teü)·teül (yū·li·ush hot)·ig

Can I see it?
Megnézhetem? meg·neyz·he·tem

Am I allowed to camp here?
Táborozhatok itt? ta·baw·rawz·ho·tawk itt

Where can I find the camping ground?
Hol találom a kempinget? hawl to·la·lawm o kem·pin·get

requests & queries

When/Where is breakfast served?
Mikor/Hol van a reggeli? mi·kawr/hawl von o reg·ge·li

Please wake me at (seven).
Kérem, ébresszen fel (hét)kor. key·rem eyb·res·sen fel (heyt)·kawr

Could I have my key, please?
Megkaphatnám a kulcsomat, kérem? meg·kop·hot·nam o kul·chaw·mot key·rem

Can I get another (blanket)?
Kaphatok egy másik (takaró)t? kop·ho·tawk ej ma·shik (to·ko·rāw)t

Is there a/an ...?	Van Önöknél ...?	von eu·neuk·neyl ...
elevator	lift	lift
safe	széf	seyf

The room is too ...	Túl ...	tül ...
expensive	drága	dra·go
noisy	zajos	zo·yawsh
small	kicsi	ki·chi

The ... doesn't work.	A ... nem működik.	o ... nem *mēw*-keu-dik
air conditioning	légkondicionáló	*leyg*-kawn-di-tsi-aw-na-lāw
fan	ventilátor	*ven*-ti-la-tawr
toilet	vécé	*vey*-tsey

This ... isn't clean.	Ez a ... nem tiszta.	ez o ... nem *tis*-to
sheet	lepedő	*le*-pe-dēū
towel	törülköző	*teu*-rewl-keu-zēū

checking out

What time is checkout?
Mikor kell kijelentkezni?   *mi*-kawr kell *ki*-ye-lent-kez-ni

Can I leave my luggage here?
Itt hagyhatom a csomagjaimat?   itt *hoj*-ho-tawm o *chaw*-mog-yo-i-mot

Could I have	Visszakaphatnám	*vis*-so-kop-hot-nam
my .... please?	..., kérem?	... *key*-rem
deposit	a letétemet	o *le*-tey-te-met
passport	az útlevelemet	oz *ūt*-le-ve-le-met
valuables	az értékeimet	oz *eyr*-tey-ke-i-met

communications & banking

the internet

Where's the local Internet café?
Hol van a legközelebbi   hawl von o *leg*-keu-ze-leb-bi
internet kávézó?   *in*-ter-net *ka*-vey-zāw

How much is it per hour?
Mennyibe kerül óránként?   *men'*-nyi-be *ke*-rewl *āw*-ran-keynt

I'd like to check my email.
Szeretném megnézni az e-mailjeimet.   *se*-ret-neym *meg*-neyz-ni oz *ee*-meyl-ye-i-met

I'd like to ...	Szeretnék ...	*se*-ret-neyk ...
get Internet	rámenni az	*ra*-men-ni oz
access	internetre	*in*-ter-net-re
use a printer	használni egy	*hos*-nal-ni ej
	nyomtatót	*nyawm*-to-tāwt
use a scanner	használni egy	*hos*-nal-ni ej
	szkennert	*sken*-nert

mobile/cell phone

I'd like a ...	Szeretnék egy ...	se·ret·neyk ej ...
mobile/cell phone	mobiltelefont	maw·bil·te·le·fawnt
for hire	bérelni	bey·rel·ni
SIM card	SIM-kártyát	sim·kar·tyat
for your network	ennek a hálózatnak	en·nek o ha·lāw·zot·nok

| What are the rates? | Milyen díjak vannak? | mi·yen dee·yok von·nok |

telephone

What's your phone number?
Mi a telefonszáma/   mi o te·le·fawn·sa·ma/
telefonszámod? pol/inf   te·le·fawn·sa·mawd

The number is ...
A szám ...   o sam ...

Where's the nearest public phone?
Hol a legközelebbi   hawl o leg·keu·ze·leb·bi
nyilvános telefon?   nyil·va·nawsh te·le·fawn

I'd like to buy a phonecard.
Szeretnék telefonkártyát venni.   se·ret·neyk te·le·fawn·kar·tyat ven·ni

I want to make a reverse-charge call.
'R' beszélgetést szeretnék kérni.   er·be·seyl·ge·teysht se·ret·neyk keyr·ni

I want to ...	Szeretnék ...	se·ret·neyk ...
call (Singapore)	(Szingapúr)ba	(sin·go·pūr)·bo
	telefonálni	te·le·faw·nal·ni
make a local call	helyi telefon-	he·yi te·le·fawn·
	beszélgetést	be·seyl·ge·teysht
	folytatni	faw·y·tot·ni

How much	Mennyibe	men'·nyi·be
does ... cost?	kerül ...?	ke·rewl ...
a (three)-minute	egy (három)perces	ej (ha·rawm)·per·tsesh
call	beszélgetés	be·seyl·ge·teysh
each extra minute	minden további perc	min·den taw·vab·bi perts

(30) forints per (30) seconds.
(Harminc) másodpercenként   (hor·mints) ma·shawd·per·tsen·keynt
(harminc) forint.   (hor·mints) faw·rint

post office

I want to send a ...	... szeretnék küldeni.	... se·ret·neyk kewl·de·ni
fax	Faxot	fok·sawt
letter	Levelet	le·ve·let
parcel	Csomagot	chaw·mo·gawt
postcard	Képeslapot	key·pesh·lo·pawt

I want to buy a/an...	... szeretnék venni.	... se·ret·neyk ven·ni
envelope	Borítékot	baw·ree·tey·kawt
stamp	Bélyeget	bey·ye·get

Please send it to (Australia) by ...	Kérem, küldje ... (Ausztráliá)ba.	key·rem kewld·ye ... (o·ust·ra·li·a)·bo
airmail	légipostán	ley·gi·pawsh·tan
express mail	expresszel	eks·press·zel
registered mail	ajánlottan	o·yan·law·tton
surface mail	simán	shi·man

Is there any mail for me?	Van levelem?	von le·ve·lem

bank

Where's a/an ...?	Hol van egy ...?	hawl von ej ...
ATM	bankautomata	bonk·o·u·taw·mo·to
foreign exchange office	valutaváltó ügynökség	vo·lu·to·val·tāw ewj·neuk·sheyg

I'd like to ...	Szeretnék ...	se·ret·neyk ...
Where can I ...?	Hol tudok ...?	hawl tu·dawk ...
arrange a transfer	pénzt átutalni	peynzt at·u·tol·ni
cash a cheque	beváltani egy csekket	be·val·to·ni ej chek·ket
change a travellers cheque	beváltani egy utazási csekket	be·val·to·ni ej u·to·za·shi chek·ket
change money	pénzt váltani	peynzt val·to·ni
get a cash advance	készpénzelőleget felvenni	keys·peynz·e·leü·le·get fel·ven·ni
withdraw money	pénzt kivenni	peynzt ki·ven·ni

What's the ...?	Mennyi ...?	men'-nyi ...
charge for that	a díj	o dee-y
exchange rate	a valutaárfolyam	o vo-lu-to-ar-faw-yom

It's (100) euros.	(Száz) euró.	(saz) e-u-raw
It's (500) forints.	(Ötszáz) forint.	(eut-saz) faw-rint
It's free.	Ingyen van.	in-dyen von

What time does the bank open?
Mikor nyit a bank? — mi-kawr nyit o bonk

Has my money arrived yet?
Megérkezett már a pénzem? — meg-eyr-ke-zett mar o peyn-zem

sightseeing

getting in

What time does it open/close?
Mikor nyit/zár? — mi-kawr nyit/zar

What's the admission charge?
Mennyibe kerül a belépőjegy? — men'-nyi-be ke-rewl o be-ley-pēū-yej

Is there a discount for students/children?
*Van kedvezmény diákok/ — von ked-vez-meyn' di-a-kawk/
gyerekek számára?* — dye-re-kek sa-ma-ro

I'd like a ...	Szeretnék egy ...	se-ret-neyk ej ...
catalogue	katalógust	ko-to-lāw-gusht
guide	idegenvezetőt	i-de-gen-ve-ze-tēūt
local map	itteni térképet	it-te-ni teyr-key-pet

I'd like to see ...	Szeretnék látni ...	se-ret-neyk lat-ni ...
What's that?	Az mi?	oz mi
Can I take a photo?	Fényképezhetek?	feyn'-key-pez-he-tek

tours

When's the	Mikor van a	mi-kawr von o
next ...?	következő ...?	keu-vet-ke-zēū ...
day trip	egynapos kirándulás	ej-no-pawsh ki-ran-du-lash
tour	túra	tū-ro

sightseeing

castle	*vár*	var
cathedral	*székesegyház*	*sey*-kesh-ej-haz
church	*templom*	*temp*-lawm
main square	*fő tér*	feū ter
monastery	*kolostor*	*kaw*-lawsh-tawr
monument	*emlékmű*	*em*-leyk-mēw
museum	*múzeum*	*mū*-ze-um
old city	*óváros*	*ūw*-va-rawsh
palace	*palota*	*po*-law-to
ruins	*romok*	*raw*-mawk
stadium	*stadion*	*shto*-di-awn
statues	*szobrok*	*saw*-brawk

Is ... included?	*Benne van az árban ...?*	*ben*-ne von oz *ar*-bon ...
accommodation	*a szállás*	o *sal*-lash
the admission charge	*a belépőjegy*	o *be*-ley-pēū-yej
food	*az ennivaló*	oz *en*-ni-vo-lāw
transport	*a közlekedés*	o *keuz*-le-ke-deysh

How long is the tour?
Mennyi ideig tart a túra?   men'-nyi *i*-de-ig tort o *tū*-ra

What time should we be back?
Mikorra érünk vissza?   *mi*-kawr-ro ey-rewnk *vis*-so

shopping

enquiries

Where's a ...?	*Hol van egy ...?*	hawl von ej ...
bank	*bank*	bonk
bookshop	*könyvesbolt*	*keun'*-vesh-bawlt
camera shop	*fényképezőgép-bolt*	feyn'-*key*-pe-zēū-geyp-bawlt
department store	*áruház*	*a*-ru-haz
grocery store	*élelmiszerbolt*	*ey*-lel-mi-ser-bawlt
market	*piac*	*pi*-ots
newsagency	*újságárus*	*ū*-y-shag-a-rush
supermarket	*élelmiszeráruház*	*ey*-lel-mi-ser-a-ru-haz

Where can I buy (a padlock)?
Hol tudok venni (egy lakatot)? hawl *tu*·dawk *ven*·ni (ej *lo*·ko·tawt)

I'm looking for ...
Keresem a ... ke·re·shem o ...

Can I look at it?
Megnézhetem? *meg*·neyz·he·tem

Do you have any others?
Van másmilyen is? von *mash*·mi·yen ish

Does it have a guarantee?
Van rajta garancia? von *ro*·y·to *go*·ron·tsi·o

Can I have it sent overseas?
El lehet küldetni külföldre? el *le*·het *kewl*·det·ni *kewl*·feuld·re

Can I have my ... repaired?
Megjavíttathatnám itt ...? *meg*·yo·veet·tot·hot·nam itt ...

It's faulty.
Hibás. *hi*·bash

I'd like ..., please. *..., kérem.* ... key·rem
  a bag *Kaphatnék egy zacskót* kop·hot·neyk ej *zoch*·kāwt
  a refund *Vissza szeretném* *vis*·so se·ret·neym
   kapni a pénzemet kop·ni o *peyn*·ze·met
  to return this *Szeretném* se·ret·neym
   visszaadni ezt *vis*·so·od·ni ezt

paying

How much is it?
Mennyibe kerül? men'·nyi·be ke·rewl

Could you write down the price?
Le tudná írni az árat? le *tud*·na *eer*·ni oz *a*·rot

That's too expensive.
Ez túl drága. ez tül *dra*·go

Do you have something cheaper?
Van valami olcsóbb? von *vo*·lo·mi *awl*·chāwbb

I'll give you (500 forints).
Adok Önnek (ötszáz forintot). o·dawk *eun*·nek (*eut*·saz *faw*·rin·tawt)

There's a mistake in the bill.
Valami nem stimmel a számlával. *vo*·lo·mi nem *shtim*·mel o *sam*·la·vol

Do you accept ...?	Elfogadnak ...?	el·faw·god·nok ...
credit cards	hitelkártyát	hi·tel·kar·tyat
debit cards	bankkártyát	bonk·kar·tyat
travellers cheques	utazási csekket	u·to·za·shi chek·ket

I'd like ..., please.	..., kérem.	... key·rem
a receipt	Kaphatnék egy nyugtát	kop·hot·neyk ej nyug·tat
my change	Szeretném megkapni	se·ret·neym meg·kop·ni
	a visszajáró pénzt	o vis·so·ya·raw peynzt

clothes & shoes

Can I try it on?	Felpróbálhatom?	fel·praw·bal·ho·tawm
My size is (40).	A méretem	o mey·re·tem
	(negyvenes).	(nej·ve·nesh)
It doesn't fit.	Nem jó.	nem yaw

small	kicsi	ki·chi
medium	közepes	keu·ze·pesh
large	nagy	noj

books & music

I'd like a ...	Szeretnek egy ...	se·ret·neyk ej ...
newspaper	(angol)	(on·gawl)
(in English)	újságot	üy·sha·gawt
pen	tollat	tawl·lot

Is there an English-language bookshop?

| Van valahol egy angol | von vo·lo·hawl ej on·gawl |
| nyelvű könyvesbolt? | nyel·vēw keun'·vesh·bawlt |

I'm looking for something by (Zsuzsa Koncz).

| (Koncz Zsuzsá)tól | (konts zhu·zha)·tāwl |
| keresek valamit. | ke·re·shek vo·lo·mit |

Can I listen to this?

| Meghallgathatom ezt? | meg·holl·got·ho·tawm ezt |

photography

Can you transfer photos from my camera to CD?
Át tudják vinni a képeket   at *tud*·yak *vin*·ni o *key*·pe·ket
a fényképezőgépemről CD-re?   o feyn'·key·pe·zēū·gey·pem·rēül *tsey*·dey·re

Can you develop this film?
Elő tudják hívni ezt a filmet?   e·lēū *tud*·yak *heev*·ni ezt o *fil*·met

Can you load my film?
Bele tudják tenni a filmet   be·le *tud*·yak *ten*·ni o *fil*·met
a gépembe?   o *gey*·pem·be

I need a ... film for this camera.	... filmet szeretnék.	... fil·met se·ret·neyk
B&W	Fekete-fehér	fe·ke·te·fe·heyr
colour	Színes	see·nesh
slide	Dia	di·o
(200) speed	(Kétszáz)as fényérzékenységű	(keyt·saz)·osh feyn'·eyr·zey·ken'·shey·gēw

When will it be ready?   *Mikor lesz kész?*   *mi*·kawr les keys

meeting people

greetings, goodbyes & introductions

Hello.	Szervusz/Szervusztok. sg/pl	ser·vus/ser·vus·tawk
Hi.	Szia/Sziasztok. sg/pl	si·o/si·os·tawk
Good night.	Jó éjszakát.	yāw ey·y·so·kat
Goodbye.	Viszlát.	vis·lat
Bye.	Szia/Sziasztok. sg/pl	si·o/si·os·tawk
Mr	Úr	ür
Mrs	Asszony	os·sawn'
Miss	Kisasszony	kish·os·sawn'
How are you?	Hogy van/vagy? pol/inf	hawj von/voj
Fine. And you?	Jól. És Ön/te? pol/inf	yāwl eysh eun/te
What's your name?	Mi a neve/neved? pol/inf	mi o ne·ve/ne·ved
My name is ...	A nevem ...	o ne·vem ...
I'm pleased to meet you.	Örvendek.	eur·ven·dek

This is my ...	Ez ...	ez ...
boyfriend	a barátom	o bo·ra·tawm
brother (older)	a bátyám	o ba·tyam
brother (younger)	az öcsém	oz eu·cheym
daughter	a lányom	o la·nyawm
father	az apám	oz o·pam
friend	a barátom/barátnőm m/f	o bo·ra·tawm/bo·rat·nēūm
girlfriend	a barátnőm	o bo·rat·nēūm
husband	a férjem	o feyr·yem
mother	az anyám	oz o·nyam
partner (intimate)	a barátom/barátnőm m/f	o bo·ra·tawm/bo·rat·nēūm
sister (older)	a nővérem	o nēū·vey·rem
sister (younger)	a húgom	o hū·gawm
son	a fiam	o fi·om
wife	a feleségem	o fe·le·shey·gem

Here's my ...	Itt van ...	itt von ...
address	a címem	o tsee·mem
email address	az e-mail címem	oz ee·meyl tsee·mem
fax number	a faxszámom	o foks·sa·mawm
phone number	a telefonszámom	o te·le·fawn·sa·mawm

What's your ...?	Mi ...?	mi ...
address	a címe	o tsee·me
email address	az e-mail címe	oz ee·meyl tsee·me
fax number	a faxszáma	o foks·sa·ma
phone number	a telefonszáma	o te·le·fawn·sa·ma

occupations

What's your occupation?	Mi a foglalkozása/ foglalkozásod? pol/inf	mi o fawg·lol·kaw·za·sho/ fawg·lol·kaw·za·shawd
I'm a/an ...	... vagyok.	... vo·dyawk
artist	Művész	mēw·veys
businessperson	Üzletember m	ewz·let·em·ber
	Üzletasszony f	ewz·let·os·sawn'
farmer	Gazda	goz·do
office worker	Irodai dolgozó	i·raw·do·i dawl·gaw·zāw
scientist	Természettudós	ter·mey·set·tu·dāwsh
student	Diák	di·ak
tradesperson	Kereskedő	ke·resh·ke·dēū

background

Where are you from?	Ön honnan jön? pol	eun *hawn*-non yeun
	Te honnan jössz? inf	te *hawn*-non yeuss
I'm from ...	Én ... jövök.	eyn ... *yeu*-veuk
Australia	Ausztráliából	o-ust-ra-li-a-bāwl
Canada	Kanadából	ko-no-da-bāwl
England	Angliából	ong-li-a-bāwl
New Zealand	Új-Zélandból	ü-y-zey-lond-bāwl
the USA	USAból	u-sho-bāwl
Are you married? m	Nős?	nēüsh
Are you married? f	Férjnél van?	feyr-y-neyl von
I'm ...	... vagyok.	... vo-dyawk
married	Nős/Férjnél m/f	nēüsh/feyr-y-neyl
single	Egyedülálló	e-dye-dewl-al-lāw

age

How old are you?	Hány éves? pol	han' ey-vesh
	Hány éves vagy? inf	han' ey-vesh voj
How old are your children?	Hány évesek a gyerekei/gyerekeid? pol/inf	han' ey-ve-shek o dye-re-ke-i/dye-re-ke-id
I'm ... years old.	... éves vagyok.	... ey-vesh vo-dyawk
He/She is ... years old.	... éves.	... ey-vesh

feelings

Are you ...?	... vagy?	... voj
happy	Boldog	bawl-dawg
hungry	Éhes	ey-hesh
sad	Szomorú	saw-maw-rū
thirsty	Szomjas	sawm-yosh
I'm ...	... vagyok.	... vo-dyawk
I'm not ...	Nem vagyok ...	nem vo-dyawk ...
happy	boldog	bawl-dawg
hungry	éhes	ey-hesh
sad	szomorú	saw-maw-rū
thirsty	szomjas	sawm-yosh

Are you cold?	*Fázik/Fázol?* pol/inf	fa-zik/fa-zawl
I'm (not) cold.	*(Nem) Fázom.*	(nem) fa-zawm
Are you hot?	*Melege/Meleged van?* pol/inf	me-le-ge/me-le-ged von
I'm hot.	*Melegem van.*	me-le-gem von
I'm not hot.	*Nincs melegem.*	ninch me-le-gem

entertainment

going out

Where can I find ...?	*Hol találok ...?*	hawl to-la-lawk ...
clubs	*klubokat*	klu-baw-kot
gay venues	*meleg*	me-leg
	szórakozóhelyeket	sāw-ro-kaw-zāw-he-ye-ket
pubs	*pubokat*	po-baw-kot
I feel like going	*Szeretnék*	se-ret-neyk
to a/the ...	*elmenni egy ...*	el-men-ni ej ...
concert	*koncertre*	kawn-tsert-re
movies	*moziba*	maw-zi-bo
party	*partira*	por-ti-ro
restaurant	*étterembe*	eyt-te-rem-be
theatre	*színházba*	seen-haz-bo

interests

Do you like ...?	*Szereted ...?*	se-re-ted ...
I (don't) like ...	*(Nem) Szeretem ...*	(nem) se-re-tem ...
art	*a művészetet*	o mēw-vey-se-tet
movies	*a filmeket*	o fil-me-ket
sport	*a sportot*	o shpawr-tawt
Do you like ...?	*Szeretsz ...?*	se-rets ...
I (don't) like ...	*(Nem) Szeretek ...*	(nem) se-re-tek ...
cooking	*főzni*	fēūz-ni
nightclubs	*diszkóba járni*	dis-kāw-bo yar-ni
reading	*olvasni*	awl-vosh-ni
shopping	*vásárolni*	va-sha-rawl-ni
travelling	*utazni*	u-toz-ni

Do you ...?		
dance	*Táncolsz?*	tan·tsawls
go to concerts	*Jársz koncertre?*	yars kawn·tsert·re
listen to music	*Hallgatsz zenét?*	holl·gots ze·neyt

food & drink

finding a place to eat

Can you recommend a ...?	*Tud/Tudsz ajánlani egy ...?* pol/inf	tud/tuds o·yan·lo·ni ej ...
bar	*bárt*	bart
café	*kávézót*	ka·vey·zawt
restaurant	*éttermet*	eyt·ter·met
I'd like ...	*Szeretnék ...*	se·ret·neyk ...
a table for (five)	*egy asztalt (öt) személyre*	ej os·tolt (eut) se·mey·re
the (non)smoking section	*a (nem)dohányzó részben ülni*	o (nem·)daw·han'·zäw reys·ben ewl·ni

ordering food

breakfast	*reggeli*	reg·ge·li
lunch	*ebéd*	e·beyd
dinner	*vacsora*	vo·chaw·ro
snack	*snack*	snekk
today's special	*napi ajánlat*	no·pi oy·an·lot

How long is the wait?		
Mennyi ideig kell várni?		men·nyi i·de·ig kell vaar·ni

What would you recommend?		
Mit ajánlana?		mit o·yan·lo·no

I'd like (the) ...	*... szeretném.*	... se·ret·neym
bill	*A számlát*	o sam·lat
drink list	*Az itallapot*	oz i·tol·lo·pawt
menu	*Az étlapot*	oz eyt·lo·pawt
that dish	*Azt az ételt*	ozt oz ey·telt

drinks

(cup of) coffee ...	(csésze) kávé ...	(chey·se) ka·vey ...
(cup of) tea ...	(csésze) tea ...	(chey·se) te·o ...
with milk	tejjel	ey·yel
without sugar	cukor nélkül	tsu·kawr neyl·kewl
... mineral water	... ásványvíz	... ash·van'·veez
sparkling	szénsavas	seyn·sho·vosh
still	szénsavmentes	seyn·shov·men·tesh
orange juice	narancslé	no·ronch·ley
soft drink	üdítőital	ew·dee·teū·i·tal
(boiled) water	(forralt) víz	(fawr·rolt) veez

in the bar

I'll have ...	... kérek.	... key·rek
I'll buy you a drink.	Fizetek neked egy italt.	fi·ze·tek ne·ked ej i·tolt
What would you like?	Mit kérsz?	mit keyrs
Cheers! (to one person)	Egészségedre!	e·geys·shey·ged·re
Cheers! (to more than one person)	Egészségetekre!	e·geys·shey·ge·tek·re
brandy	brandy	bren·di
champagne	pezsgő	pezh·geū
cocktail	koktél	kawk·teyl
a bottle/glass of (beer)	egy üveg/pohár (sör)	ej ew·veg/paw·har (sheur)
a shot of (whisky)	egy kupica (whisky)	ej ku·pi·tso (vis·ki)
a bottle/glass of ... wine	egy üveg/pohár ... bor	ej ew·veg/paw·har ... bawr
red	vörös	veu·reush
sparkling	pezsgő	pezh·geū
white	fehér	fe·heyr

What's the local speciality?
   Mi az itteni specialitás?   mi oz *it·*te·ni *shpe·*tsi·o·li·tash

What's that?
   Az mi?   oz mi

How much is (a kilo of cheese)?
   Mennyibe kerül (egy kiló sajt)?   men'·nyi·be ke·rewl (ej *ki·*läw shoyt)

I'd like ...	*Kérek ...*	key·rek ...
200 grams	*húsz dekát*	hüs *de·*kat
a kilo	*egy kilót*	ej *ki·*läwt
a piece	*egy darabot*	ej *do·*ro·bawt
a slice	*egy szeletet*	ej *se·*le·tet

Less.	*Kevésbé.*	ke·veysh·bey
Enough.	*Elég.*	e·leyg
More.	*Több.*	teubb

Is there a vegetarian restaurant near here?
   Van a közelben   von o *keu·*zel·ben
   vegetáriánus étterem?   ve·ge·ta·ri·a·nush *eyt·*te·rem

Do you have vegetarian food?
   Vannak Önöknél   von·nok *eu·*neuk·neyl
   vegetáriánus ételek?   ve·ge·ta·ri·a·nush *ey·*te·lek

Could you prepare	*Tudna készíteni*	tud·no key·see·te·ni
a meal without ...?	*egy ételt ... nélkül?*	ej *ey·*telt ... *neyl·*kewl
butter	*vaj*	vo·y
eggs	*tojás*	*taw·*yash
meat stock	*húsleveskocka*	hüsh·le·vesh·kawts·ko

I'm allergic to ...	*Allergiás vagyok a ...*	ol·ler·gi·ash vo·dyawk o ...
dairy produce	*tejtermékekre*	te·y·ter·mey·kek·re
gluten	*sikérre*	shi·keyr·re
MSG	*monoszódium*	maw·naw·säw·di·um
	glutamátra	glu·to·mat·ro
nuts	*diófélékre*	di·äw·fey·leyk·re
seafood	*tenger gyümölcseire*	ten·ger yew·meul·che·i·re

bableves csülökkel	*bob·le·vesh chew·leuk·kel*	*bean soup with smoked pork*
csúsztatott palacsinta	*chüs·to·tawtt po·lo·chin·to*	*pancakes in a stack sprinkled with chocolate*
dobostorta	*daw·bawsh·tawr·to*	*sponge cake with chocolate cream, with a glazed sponge layer on top*
gombaleves	*gom·bo·le·vesh*	*mushroom & onion soup seasoned with paprika*
grenadírmas	*gre·no·deer·morsh*	*potatoes with sweet paprika, onion & pasta, served with sour gherkins*
gulyásleves	*gu·yash·le·vesh*	*beef soup with vegetables & pasta*
halászlé vegyes halból	*ho·las·ley ve·dyesh hol·bāwl*	*fish soup with onion, tomato & a dose of paprika*
hortobágyi ürügulyás	*hawr·taw·ba·dyi ew·rew·gu·yash*	*mutton stew*
kacsapecsenye	*ko·cho·pe·che·nye*	*roasted duck with apples, quinces & marjoram*
korhelyleves	*kawr·he·y·le·vesh*	*stew of smoked ham, sauerkraut & sliced sausage*
kürtőskalács	*kewr·tēüsh·ko·lach*	*dough wrapped around a roller, coated with honey & almonds or walnuts & roasted on a spit*
lángos	*lan·gawsh*	*deep-fried potato cakes topped with cabbage, ham, cheese or sour cream*
lecsó	*le·chāw*	*stewed tomatoes, peppers, onions & paprika*
lekváros szelet	*lek·va·rawsh se·let*	*sponge cake layered with strawberry jam*

májgaluska	*ma·y·go·lush·ko*	fried egg dumplings made from chicken, veal or pork livers
mákos tészta	*ma·kawsh teys·to*	sweet pasta with poppy seeds
meggyes rétes	*mej·dyesh rey·tesh*	cherry & walnut strudel
meggyleves	*mejj·le·vesh*	chilled soup with cherries, sour cream & red wine
palóc leves	*po·lāwts le·vesh*	soup made from cubed leg of mutton or beef & vegetables
paprikás	*pop·ri·kash*	veal, chicken or rabbit stew
pörkölt	*peur·keult*	diced meat stew with a paprika gravy
sonkás kocka	*shawn·kash kots·ko*	chopped ham mixed with sour cream & pasta, then baked
sonkával töltött gomba	*shawn·ka·vol teul·teutt gawm·bo*	mushrooms stuffed with smoked ham in cheese sauce & grilled
székely gulyás	*sey·ke·y gu·yash*	stew of sautéed pork, bacon, sauerkraut & sour cream
szilvás gombóc	*sil·vash gawm·bāwts*	boiled potato-based dumplings filled with pitted plums
tokány	*taw·kan'*	meat stewed in white wine, tomato paste & seasonings
töltött káposzta	*teul·teutt ka·paws·to*	cabbage leaves stuffed with rice & ground pork
töltött paprika	*teul·teutt pop·ri·ko*	capsicums stuffed with rice & ground pork
tűzdelt fácán	*tēwz·delt fa·tsan*	pheasant larded with smoked bacon & roasted in red wine gravy
vargabéles	*vor·go·bey·lesh*	layered pasta & dough topped with a custard-like mixture
zöldbabfőzelék	*zeuld·bob·fēü·ze·leyk*	cooked green beans with sour cream & seasonings

emergencies

basics

Help!	Segítség!	she-geet-sheyg
Stop!	Álljon meg!	all-yawn meg
Go away!	Menjen innen!	men-yen in-nen
Thief!	Tolvaj!	tawl-voy
Fire!	Tűz!	tëwz
Watch out!	Vigyázzon!	vi-dyaz-zawn
Call a doctor!	Hívjon orvost!	heev-yawn awr-vawsht
Call an ambulance!	Hívja a mentőket!	heev-yo o men-tëü-ket
Call the police!	Hívja a rendőrséget!	heev-yo o rend-ëür-shey-get

It's an emergency!
Sürgős esetről van szó.   shewr-gëüsh e-shet-rëül von sāw

Could you help me, please?
Tudna segíteni?   tud-no she-gee-te-ni

Can I use your phone?
Használhatom a telefonját?   hos-nal-ho-tawm o te-le-fawn-yat

I'm lost.
Eltévedtem.   el-tey-ved-tem

Where are the toilets?
Hol a vécé?   hawl o vey-tsey

police

Where's the police station?
Hol a rendőrség?   hawl o rend-ëür-sheyg

I want to report an offence.
Bűncselekményt szeretnék   bëwn-che-lek-meynyt se-ret-neyk
bejelenteni.   be-ye-len-te-ni

I have insurance.
Van biztosításom.   von biz-taw-shee-ta-shawm

I've been ...

assaulted	Megtámadtak.	meg-ta-mod-tok
raped	Megerőszakoltak.	meg-e-rëü-so-kawl-tok
robbed	Kiraboltak.	ki-ro-bawl-tok

I've lost my ...	Elvesztettem ...	el·ves·tet·tem ...
My ... was/were stolen.	Ellopták ...	el·lawp·tak ...
backpack	a hátizsákomat	o ha·ti·zha·kaw·mot
bags	a csomagjaimat	o chaw·mog·yo·i·mot
credit card	a hitelkártyámat	o hi·tel·kar·tya·mot
handbag	a kézitáskámat	o key·zi·tash·ka·mot
jewellery	az ékszereimet	oz eyk·se·re·i·met
money	a pénzemet	o peyn·ze·met
passport	az útlevelemet	oz üt·le·ve·le·met
travellers cheques	az utazási	oz u·to·za·shi
	csekkjeimet	chekk·ye·i·met
wallet	a tárcámat	o tar·tsa·mot

I want to contact my embassy/consulate.

*Kapcsolatba akarok lépni
a követségemmel/
konzulátusommal.*

kop·chaw·lot·bo o·ko·rawk leyp·ni
o keu·vet·shey·gem·mel/
kawn·zu·la·tu·shawm·mol

health

medical needs

Where's the nearest ...?	Hol a legközelebbi ...?	hawl o leg·keu·ze·leb·bi ...
dentist	fogorvos	fawg·awr·vawsh
doctor	orvos	awr·vawsh
hospital	kórház	kawr·haz
(night) pharmacist	(éjszaka nyitvatartó) gyógyszertár	(ey·so·ko nyit·vo·tor·täw) dyäwj·ser·tar

I need a doctor (who speaks English).

*(Angolul beszélő) Orvosra
van szükségem.*

(on·gaw·lul be·sey·leü) awr·vawsh·ro
von sewk·shey·gem

Could I see a female doctor?

Beszélhetnék egy orvosnővel?

be·seyl·het·neyk ej awr·vawsh·nëü·vel

I've run out of my medication.

Elfogyott az orvosságom.

el·faw·dyawtt oz awr·vawsh·sha·gawm

symptoms, conditions & allergies

I'm sick.	Rosszul vagyok.	raws·sul vo·dyawk
It hurts here.	Itt fáj.	itt fa·y

I have a ...

cough	Köhögök.	keu·heu·geuk
headache	Fáj a fejem.	fa·y o fe·yem
sore throat	Fáj a torkom.	fa·y o tawr·kawm
toothache	Fáj a fogam.	fa·y o faw·gom

I have (a) ... ... van. ... von

asthma	Asztmám	ost·mam
bronchitis	Hörghurutom	heurg·hu·rut·awm
constipation	Székrekedésem	seyk·re·ke·dey·shem
diarrhoea	Hasmenésem	hosh·me·ney·shem
fever	Lázam	la·zom
heart condition	Szívbetegségem	seev·be·teg·sheyg·em
nausea	Hányingerem	han'·in·ge·rem
pain	Fájdalmam	fay·dol·mom

I'm allergic to ... Allergiás vagyok ... ol·ler·gi·ash vo·dyawk ...

antibiotics	az antibiotikumokra	oz on·ti·bi·aw·ti·ku·mawk·ro
anti-inflammatories	a gyulladásgátlókra	o dyul·lo·dash·gat·lāwk·ro
aspirin	az aszpirinre	oz os·pi·rin·re
bees	a méhekre	o mey·hek·re
codeine	a kodeinre	o ko·de·in·re
penicillin	a penicillinre	o pe·ni·tsil·lin·re

antiseptic n	fertőzésgátló	fer·tēū·zeysh·gat·lāw
bandage	kötés	keu·teysh
condoms	óvszer	āwv·ser
contraceptives	fogamzásgátló	faw·gom·zash·gat·lāw
diarrhoea medicine	hasmenés gyógyszer	hosh·men·eysh dyāwd'·ser
insect repellent	rovarírtó	raw·vor·ir·tāw
laxatives	hashajtó	hosh·ho·y·tāw
painkillers	fájdalomcsillapító	fa·y·do·lawm·chil·lo·pee·tāw
rehydration salts	folyadékpótló sók	faw·yo·deyk·pāwt·lāw shāwk
sleeping tablets	altató	ol·to·tāw

english–hungarian dictionary

In this dictionary, words are marked as n (noun), a (adjective), v (verb), sg (singular), pl (plural), inf (informal) or pol (polite) where necessary.

A

accident *baleset* bol-e-shet
accommodation *szállás* sal-lash
adaptor *adapter* o-dop-ter
address n *cím* tseem
after *után* u-tan
air-conditioned *légkondicionált*
  leyg-kawn-di-tsi-aw-nalt
airplane *repülőgép* re-pew-léü-geyp
airport *repülőtér* re-pew-léü-teyr
alcohol *alkohol* ol-kaw-hawl
all *minden* min-den
allergy *allergia* ol-ler-gi-o
ambulance *mentő* men-téü
and *és* eysh
ankle *boka* baw-ko
arm *kar* kor
ashtray *hamutartó* ho-mu-tor-tàw
ATM *bankautomata* bonk-o-u-taw-mo-to

B

baby *baba* bo-bo
back (body) *hát* hat
backpack *hátizsák* ha-ti-zhak
bad *rossz* rawss
bag *táska* tash-ko
baggage claim *poggyászkiadó* pawd'-dyas-ki-o-dàw
bank *bank* bonk
bar *bár* bar
bathroom *fürdőszoba* fewr-déü-saw-bo
battery *elem* e-lem
beautiful *szép* seyp
bed *ágy* aj
beer *sör* sheur
before *előtt* e-léütt
behind *mögött* meu-geutt
bicycle *bicikli* bi-tsik-li
big *nagy* noj
bill *számla* sam-lo
black *fekete* fe-ke-te

B (continued)

blanket *takaró* to-ko-ràw
blood group *vércsoport* veyr-chaw-pawrt
blue *kék* keyk
boat (big) *hajó* ho-yàw
boat (small) *csónak* chàw-nok
book (make a reservation) v *lefoglal* le-fawg-lol
bottle *üveg* ew-veg
bottle opener *sörnyitó* sheur-nyi-tàw
boy *fiú* fi-ù
brake (car) *fék* feyk
breakfast *reggeli* reg-ge-li
broken (faulty) *hibás* hi-bash
bus *busz* bus
business *üzlet* ewz-let
buy *vesz* ves

C

café *kávézó* ka-vey-zàw
camera *fényképezőgép* feyn'-key-pe-zéü-geyp
camp site *táborhely* ta-bawr-he-y
cancel *töröl* teu-reul
can opener *konzervnyitó* kawn-zerv-nyi-tàw
car *autó* o-u-tàw
cash n *készpénz* keys-peynz
cash (a cheque) v *bevált csekket* be-valt chek-ket
cell phone *mobil telefon* maw-bil te-le-fawn
centre n *központ* keuz-pawnt
change (money) v *pénzt vált* peynzt valt
cheap *olcsó* awl-chàw
check (bill) *számla* sam-lo
check-in n *bejelentkezés* be-ye-lent-ke-zeysh
chest *mellkas* mell-kosh
child *gyerek* dye-rek
cigarette *cigaretta* tsi-go-ret-to
city *város* va-rawsh
clean a *tiszta* tis-to
closed *zárva* zar-vo
coffee *kávé* ka-vey
coins *pénzérmék* peynz-eyr-meyk
cold a *hideg* hi-deg
collect call *'R' beszélgetés* er-be-seyl-ge-teysh
come *jön* yeun

omputer *számítógép* sa-mee-tāw-geyp
ondom *óvszer* āwv-ser
ontact lenses *kontaktlencse* kawn-tokt-len-che
ook v *főz* feüz
ost n *ár* ar
redit card *hitelkártya* hi-tel-kar-tyo
up *csésze* chey-se
urrency exchange *valutaátváltás* vo-lu-to-at-val-tash
ustoms (immigration) *vám* vam

D

angerous *veszélyes* ve-sey-yesh
ate (time) *dátum* da-tum
ay *nap* nop
elay n *késés* key-sheysh
entist *fogorvos* fawg-awr-vawsh
epart *elutazik* el-u-to-zik
iaper *pelenka* pe-len-ko
ictionary *szótár* sāw-tar
inner *vacsora* vo-chaw-ro
irect *közvetlen* keuz-vet-len
irty *piszkos* pis-kawsh
isabled *mozgássérült* mawz-gash-shey-rewlt
iscount n *árengedmény* ar-en-ged-meyn'
octor *orvos* awr-vawsh
ouble bed *dupla ágy* dup-lo aj
ouble room *duplaágyas szoba* dup-lo-a-dyosh saw-bo
rink v *ital* i-tol
rive v *vezet* ve-zet
rivers licence *jogosítvány* yaw-gaw-sheet-van'
rug (illicit) *kábítószerek* ka-bee-tāw-se-rek
ummy (pacifier) *cumi* tsu-mi

E

ar *fül* fewl
ast *kelet* ke-let
at *eszik* e-sik
conomy class *turistaosztály* tu-rish-to-aws-ta-y
lectricity *villany* vil-lon'
levator *lift* lift
mail *e-mail* ee-meyl
mbassy *nagykövetség* noj-keu-vet-sheyg
mergency *vészhelyzet* veys-he-y-zet
nglish (language) *angol* on-gawl
ntrance *bejárat* be-ya-rot
vening *este* esh-te
xchange rate *átváltási árfolyam* at-val-ta-shi ar-faw-yom

exit n *kijárat* ki-ya-rot
expensive *drága* dra-go
express mail *expressz posta* eks-press pawsh-to
eye *szem* sem

F

far *messze* mes-se
fast *gyors* dyawrsh
father *apa* o-po
film (camera) *film* film
finger *ujj* u-y
first-aid kit *elsősegély-láda* el-shēū-she-gey-la-do
first class *első osztály* el-shēū aws-ta-y
fish n *hal* hol
food *ennivaló* en-ni-vo-lāw
foot *lábfej* lab-fe-y
fork *villa* vil-lo
free (of charge) *ingyenes* in-dye-nesh
friend (female) *barátnő* bo-rat-nēū
friend (male) *barát* bo-rat
fruit *gyümölcs* dyew-meulch
full *tele* te-le
funny *mulatságos* mu-lot-sha-gawsh

G

gift *ajándék* o-yan-deyk
girl *lány* lan'
glass (drinking) *üveg* ew-veg
glasses *szemüveg* sem-ew-veg
go *megy* mej
good *jó* yāw
green *zöld* zeuld
guide n *idegenvezető* i-de-gen-ve-ze-tēū

H

half n *fél* feyl
hand *kéz* keyz
handbag *kézitáska* key-zi-tash-ko
happy *boldog* bawl-dawg
have *van neki* von ne-ki
he *ő* ēū
head *fej* fe-y
heart *szív* seev
heat n *forróság* fawr-rāw-shag
heavy *nehéz* ne-heyz
help v *segít* she-geet
here *itt* itt

high *magas* mo-gosh
highway *országút* awr-sag-üt
hike v *kirándul* ki-ran-dul
holiday *szabadság* so-bod-shag
homosexual n *homoszexuális* haw-maw-sek-su-a-lish
hospital *kórház* kawr-haz
hot *forró* fawr-ráw
hotel *szálloda* sal-law-do
Hungarian (language) *magyar* mo-dyor
Hungary *Magyarország* mo-dyor-awr-sag
hungry *éhes* ey-hesh
husband *férj* feyr-y

I

I *én* eyn
identification (card) *személyi igazolvány*
    se-mey-yi i-go-zawl-van'
ill *beteg* be-teg
important *fontos* fawn-tawsh
included *beleértve* be-le-eyrt-ve
injury *sérülés* shey-rew-leysh
insurance *biztosítás* biz-taw-shee-tash
Internet *Internet* in-ter-net
interpreter *tolmács* tawl-mach

J

jewellery *ékszerek* eyk-se-rek
job *állás* al-lash

K

key *kulcs* kulch
kilogram *kilogramm* ki-láw-gromm
kitchen *konyha* kawn'-ho
knife *kés* keysh

L

laundry (place) *mosoda* maw-shaw-do
lawyer *jogász* yaw-gas
left (direction) *balra* bol-ro
left-luggage office *csomagmegőrző*
    chaw-mog-meg-éür-zéü
leg *láb* lab
lesbian n *leszbikus* les-bi-kush
less *kevésbé* ke-veysh-bey
letter (mail) *levél* le-veyl
lift (elevator) *lift* lift

light n *fény* feyn'
like v *szeret* se-ret
lock n *zár* zar
long *hosszú* haws-sü
lost *elveszett* el-ve-sett
lost-property office *talált tárgyak hivatala*
    to-lalt tar-dyok hi-vo-to-lo
love v *szeret* se-ret
luggage *poggyász* pawd'-dyas
lunch *ebéd* e-beyd

M

mail n *posta* pawsh-to
man *férfi* feyr-fi
map *térkép* teyr-keyp
market *piac* pi-ots
matches *gyufa* dyu-fo
meat *hús* hüsh
medicine *orvosság* awr-vawsh-shag
menu *étlap* eyt-lop
message *üzenet* ew-ze-net
milk *tej* te-y
minute *perc* perts
mobile phone *mobil telefon* maw-bil te-le-fawn
money *pénz* peynz
month *hónap* háw-nop
morning *reggel* reg-gel
mother *anya* o-nyo
motorcycle *motorbicikli* maw-tawr-bi-tsik-li
motorway *autópálya* o-u-táw-pa-yo
mouth *száj* sa-y
music *zene* ze-ne

N

name *keresztnév* ke-rest-neyv
napkin *szalvéta* sal-vey-to
nappy *pelenka* pe-len-ko
near *közelében* keu-ze-ley-ben
neck *nyak* nyok
new *új* ü-y
news *hírek* hee-rek
newspaper *újság* ü-y-shag
night *éjszaka* ey-so-ko
no *nem* nem
noisy *zajos* zo-yawsh
nonsmoking *nemdohányzó* nem-daw-han'-záw
north *észak* ey-sok
nose *orr* awrr
now *most* mawsht
number *szám* sam

O

l (engine) *olaj* aw-lo-y
d (person/thing) *öreg/régi* eu-reg/rey-gi
ne-way ticket *csak oda jegy* chok aw-do yej
pen a *nyitva* nyit-vo
utside *kint* kint

P

ackage *csomag* chaw-mog
aper *papír* po-peer
ark (a car) v *parkol* por kawl
assport *útlevél* üt-le-veyl
ay *fizet* fi-zet
etrol *benzin* ben-zin
harmacy *gyógyszertár* dyāwj-ser-tar
honecard *telefonkártya* te-le-fawn-kar-tyo
hoto *fénykép* feyn'-keyp
ate *tányér* ta-nyeyr
olice *rendőrség* rend-ëür-sheyg
ostcard *levelezőlap* le-ve-le-zëü-lop
ost office *postahivatal* pawsh-to-hi-vo-tol
regnant *terhes* ter-hesh
rice *ár* ar

Q

uiet *csendes* chen-desh

R

ain n *eső* e-shëü
azor *borotva* baw-rawt-vo
eceipt n *nyugta* nyug-to
ed *piros* pi-rawsh
efund n *visszatérítés* vis-so-tey-ree-teysh
egistered mail *ajánlott levél* o-yan-lawtt le-veyl
ent v *bérel* bey-rel
epair v *megjavít* meg-yo-veet
eservation *foglalás* fawg-lo-lash
estaurant *étterem* eyt-te-rem
eturn v *visszatér* vis-so-teyr
eturn ticket *oda-vissza jegy* aw-do-vis-so yej
ght (direction) *jobbra* yawbb-ro
oad *út* üt
oom *szoba* saw-bo

S

safe a *biztonságos* biz-tawn-sha-gawsh
sanitary napkin *egészségügyi törlőkendő*
e-geys-sheyg-ew-nyi teur-lëü-ken-dëü
seat *ülés* ew-leysh
send *küld* kewld
service station *benzinkút* ben-zin-küt
sex *szex* seks
shampoo *sampon* shom-pawn
share (a dorm) *ben/ban lakik* -ben/-ban lu-kik
shaving cream *borotvakrém* baw-rawt-vo-kreym
she *ő* ëü
sheet (bed) *lepedő* le-pe-dëü
shirt *ing* ing
shoes *cipők* tsi-pëük
shop n *üzlet* ewz-let
short *alacsony* o-lo-chawn'
shower *zuhany* zu-hon'
single room *egyágyas szoba* ej-a-dyosh saw-bo
skin *bőr* bëür
skirt *szoknya* sawk-nyo
sleep v *alszik* ol-sik
slowly *lassan* lash-shon
small *kicsi* ki-chi
smoke (cigarettes) v *dohányzik* daw-han'-zik
soap *szappan* sop-pon
some *néhány* ney-han'
soon *hamarosan* ho-mo-raw-shon
south *dél* deyl
souvenir shop *ajándékbolt* o-yan deyk-bawlt
speak *beszél* be-seyl
spoon *kanál* ko-nal
stamp n *bélyeg* bey-yeg
stand-by ticket *készenléti jegy* key-sen-ley-ti yej
station (train) *állomás* al-law-mash
stomach *gyomor* dyaw-mawr
stop v *abbahagy* ob-bo-hoj
stop (bus) n *megálló* meg-al-lāw
street *utca* ut-tso
student *diák* di-ak
sun *nap* nop
sunscreen *napolaj* nop-aw-lo-y
swim v *úszik* ü-sik

T

tampons *tampon* tom-pawn
taxi *taxi* tok-si
teaspoon *tedskanál* te-ash-ko-nal
teeth *fogak* faw-gok
telephone n *telefon* te-le-fawn

television *televízió* te-le-vee-zi-āw
temperature (weather) *hőmérséklet*
    hēū-meyr-sheyk-let
tent *sátor* sha-tawr
that (one) *az* oz
they *ők* ēūk
thirsty *szomjas* sawm-yosh
this (one) *ez* ez
throat *torok* taw-rawk
ticket *jegy* yej
time *idő* i-dēū
tired *fáradt* fa-rott
tissues *szövetek* seu-ve-tek
today *ma* mo
toilet *vécé* vey-tsey
tomorrow *holnap* hawl-nop
tonight *ma este* mo esh-te
toothbrush *fogkefe* fawg-ke-fe
toothpaste *fogkrém* fawg-kreym
torch (flashlight) *zseblámpa* zheb-lam-po
tour n *túra* tū-ro
tourist office *turistairoda* tu-rish-to-i-raw-do
towel *törülköző* teu-rewl-keu-zēū
train *vonat* vaw-not
translate *fordít* fawr-deet
travel agency *utazási iroda* u-to-za-shi i-raw-do
travellers cheque *utazási csekk* u-to-za-shi chekk
trousers *nadrág* nod-rag
twin beds *két ágy* keyt aj
tyre *autógumi* o-u-tāw-gu-mi

U

underwear *alsónemű* ol-shāw-ne-mēw
urgent *sürgős* shewr-gēūsh

V

vacant *üres* ew-resh
vacation *vakáció* vo-ka-tsi-āw

vegetable n *zöldség* zeuld-sheyg
vegetarian a *vegetáriánus* ve-ge-ta-ri-a-nush
visa *vízum* vee-zum

W

waiter *pincér* pin-tseyr
walk v *sétál* shey-tal
wallet *tárca* tar-tsa-mot
warm a *meleg* me-leg
wash (something) *megmos* meg-mawsh
watch n *óra* āw-ro
water *víz* veez
we *mi* mi
weekend *hétvége* heyt-vey-ge
west *nyugat* nyu-got
wheelchair *rokkantkocsi* rawk-kont-kaw-chi
when *mikor* mi-kawr
where *hol* hawl
white *fehér* fe-heyr
who *ki* ki
why *miért* mi-eyrt
wife *feleség* fe-le-sheyg
window *ablak* ob-lok
wine *bor* bawr
with *-val/-vel* -vol/-vel
without *nélkül* neyl-kewl
woman *nő* nēū
write *ír* eer

Y

yellow *sárga* shar-go
yes *igen* i-gen
yesterday *tegnap* teg-nop
you sg inf *te* te
you pl inf *ti* ti
you sg pol *Ön* eun
you pl pol *Önök* eu-neuk

U

Polish

polish alphabet

A a a	*Ą ą* om/on	*B b* be	*C c* tse	*Ć ć* che	*D d* de
E e e	*Ę ę* em/en	*F f* ef	*G g* gye	*H h* kha	*I i* ee
J j yot	*K k* ka	*L l* el	*Ł ł* ew	*M m* em	*N n* en
Ń ń en′	*O o* o	*Ó ó* oo	*P p* pe	*R r* er	*S s* es
Ś ś esh	*T t* te	*U u* oo	*W w* woo	*Y y* i	*Z z* zet
Ż ż zhet	*Ż ż* zhyet				

polish

POLSKI

introduction

Ask most English speakers what they know about Polish (*polski* pol-skee), the language which donated the words *horde*, *mazurka* and *vodka* to English, and they will most likely dismiss it as an unpronounceable language. Who could pronounce an apparently vowel-less word like *szczyt* shchit (peak), for example? To be put off by this unfairly gained reputation, however, would be to miss out on a rich and rewarding language. The mother tongue of Copernicus, Chopin, Marie Curie and Pope John Paul II has a fascinating and turbulent past and symbolises the resilience of the Polish people in the face of domination and adversity.

The Polish tribes who occupied the basins of the Oder and Vistula rivers in the 6th century AD spoke a range of West Slavic dialects, which over time evolved into Polish. The closest living relatives of Polish are Czech and Slovak which also belong to the wider West Slavic family of languages. The language reached the apex of its influence during the era of the Polish Lithuanian Commonwealth (1569–1795). The Commonwealth covered a swath of territory from what are now Poland and Lithuania through Belarus, Ukraine and Latvia and part of Western Russia. Polish became a lingua franca throughout much of Central and Eastern Europe at this time due to the political, cultural, scientific and military might of this power.

When Poland was wiped off the map of Europe from 1795 to 1918 after three successive partitions in the second half of the 18th century (when it was carved up between Russia, Austria and Prussia), the language suffered attempts at both Germanisation and Russification. Later, after WWII, Poland became a satellite state of the Soviet Union and the language came under the renewed influence of Russian. Polish showed impressive resistance in the face of this oppression. The language not only survived these onslaughts but enriched itself by borrowing many words from both Russian and German. The works of Poland's greatest literary figures who wrote in exile – the Romantic poet Adam Mickiewicz – and, during Communist rule, the Nobel Prize winner Czesław Miłosz – are testament to this fact.

Today, Poland is linguistically one of the most homogenous countries in Europe – over 95% of the population speaks Polish as their first language. There are significant Polish-speaking minorities in the western border areas of Ukraine, Belarus and in southern Lithuania, with smaller populations in other neighbouring countries.

pronunciation

vowel sounds

Polish vowels are generally prounounced short, giving them a 'clipped' quality.

symbol	english equivalent	polish example	transliteration
a	**run**	*tak*	tak
ai	**aisle**	*tutaj*	*too*-tai
e	**bet**	*bez*	bes
ee	**see**	*wino*	*vee*-no
ey	**hey**	*kolejka*	ko-*ley*-ka
i	**bit**	*czy*	chi
o	**pot**	*woda*	*vo*-da
oo	**zoo**	*zakupy, mój*	za-*koo*-pi, mooy
ow	**how**	*migdał*	*meeg*-dow
oy	**toy**	*ojciec*	*oy*-chets

Polish also has nasal vowels, pronounced as though you're trying to force the air out o
your nose rather than your mouth. Nasal vowels are indicated in written Polish by the
letters *ą* and *ę*. Depending upon the letters that follow these vowels, they're pronounce
with either an 'm' or an 'n' sound following the vowel.

symbol	english equivalent	polish example	transliteration
em	like the 'e' in 'get' plus	*wstęp*	fstemp
en	nasal consonant sound	*mięso*	*myen*-so
om	like the 'o' in 'not' plus	*kąpiel*	*kom*-pyel
on	nasal consonant sound	*wąsy*	*von*-si

word stress

In Polish, stress almost always falls on the second-last syllable. In our coloure
pronunciation guides, the stressed syllable is italicised.

consonant sounds

Most Polish consonant sounds are also found in English, with the exception of the kh sound (pronounced as in the Scottish word *loch*) and the rolled r sound.

symbol	english equivalent	polish example	transliteration
b	bed	*babka*	*bap*·ka
ch	cheat	*cień, czas, ćma*	chen', chas, chma
d	dog	*drobne*	*drob*·ne
f	fat	*fala*	*fa*·la
g	go	*garnek*	*gar*·nek
j	joke	*dzieci*	*je*·chee
k	kit	*kac*	kats
kh	loch	*chata, hałas*	*kha*·ta, *kha*·was
l	lot	*lato*	*la*·to
m	man	*malarz*	*ma*·lash
n	not	*nagle*	*na*·gle
p	pet	*palec*	*pa*·lets
r	run (rolled)	*róg*	roog
s	sun	*samolot*	sa·*mo*·lot
sh	shot	*siedem, śnieg, szlak*	*shye*·dem, shnyek, shlak
t	top	*targ*	tark
v	very	*widok*	*vee*·dok
w	win	*złoto*	*zwɔ*·to
y	yes	*zajęty*	za·*yen*·ti
z	zero	*zachód*	za·khoot
zh	pleasure	*zima, żart, rzeźba*	*zhee*·ma, zhart, *zhezh*·ba
'	a slight y sound	*kwiecień*	*kfye*·chen'

tools

language difficulties

Do you speak English?
Czy pan/pani mówi   chi pan/*pa*·nee *moo*·vee
po angielsku? m/f pol   po an·*gyel*·skoo

Do you understand?
Czy pan/pani rozumie? m/f pol   chi pan/*pa*·nee ro·*zoo*·mye

I (don't) understand.
(Nie) Rozumiem.   (nye) ro·*zoo*·myem

What does (*nieczynne*) mean?
Co to znaczy (nieczynne)?   tso to *zna*·chi (nye·*chi*·ne)

How do you ...?   *Jak się ...?*   yak shye ...
  pronounce this   *to wymawia*   to vi·*mav*·ya
  write (*pierogi*)   *pisze (pierogi)* *pee*·she (pye·*ro*·gee)

Could you please ...?   *Proszę ...*   *pro*·she ...
  repeat that   *to powtórzyć*   to po v·*too*·zhich
  speak more   *mówić trochę*   *moo*·veech tro·khe
  slowly   *wolniej*   *vol*·nyey
  write it down   *to napisać*   to na·*pee*·sach

---

essentials

Yes.	*Tak.*	tak
No.	*Nie.*	nye
Please.	*Proszę.*	*pro*·she
Thank you (very much).	*Dziękuję (bardzo).*	jyen·*koo*·ye (*bar*·dzo)
You're welcome.	*Proszę.*	*pro*·she
Excuse me.	*Przepraszam.*	pshe·*pra*·sham
Sorry.	*Przepraszam.*	pshe·*pra*·sham

0	zero	ze·ro	15	piętnaście	pyent·nash·chye
1	jeden m	ye·den	16	szesnaście	shes·nash·chye
	jedna f	yed·na	17	siedemnaście	shye·dem·nash·chye
	jedno n	yed·no	18	osiemnaście	o·shem·nash·chye
2	dwa m	dva	19	dziewiętnaście	jye·vyet·nash·chye
	dwie f	dvye	20	dwadzieścia	dva·jyesh·chya
	dwoje n	dvo·ye	21	dwadzieścia	dva·jyesh·chya
3	trzy	tshi		jeden	ye·den
4	cztery	chte·ri	22	dwadzieścia	dva·jyesh·chya
5	pięć	pyench		dwa	dva
6	sześć	sheshch	30	trzydzieści	tshi·jyesh·chee
7	siedem	shye·dem	40	czterdzieści	chter·jyesh·chee
8	osiem	o·shyem	50	pięćdziesiąt	pyen·jye·shont
9	dziewięć	jye·vyench	60	sześćdziesiąt	shesh·jye·shont
10	dziesięć	jye·shench	70	siedemdziesiąt	shye·dem·jye·shont
11	jedenaście	ye·de·nash·chye	80	osiemdziesiąt	o·shem·jye·shont
12	dwanaście	dva·nash·chye	90	dziewięćdziesiąt	jye·vyen·jye·shont
13	trzynaście	tshi·nash·chye	100	sto	sto
14	czternaście	chter·nash·chye	1000	tysiąc	ti·shonts

time & dates

What time is it?	Która jest godzina?	ktoo·ra yest go·jee·na
It's one o'clock.	Pierwsza.	pyerf·sha
It's (10) o'clock.	Jest (dziesiąta).	yest (jye·shon·ta)
Quarter past (10).	Piętnaście po (dziesiątej).	pyent·nash·chye po (jye·shon·tey)
Half past (10).	Wpół do (jedenastej).	fpoow do (ye·de·nas·tey)
Quarter to (11).	Za piętnaście (jedenasta).	za pyent·nash·chye (ye·de·nas·ta)
At what time ...?	O której godzinie ...?	o ktoo·rey go·jee·nye ...
At ...	O ...	o ...
in the morning	rano	ra·no
in the afternooon	po południu	po po·wood·nyoo
in the evening (6pm–10pm)	wieczorem	vye·cho·rem
at night (11pm–3am)	w nocy	v no·tsi

tools – POLISH

135

Monday	poniedziałek	po·nye·*jya*·wek
Tuesday	wtorek	*fto*·rek
Wednesday	środa	*shro*·da
Thursday	czwartek	*chfar*·tek
Friday	piątek	*pyon*·tek
Saturday	sobota	so·*bo*·ta
Sunday	niedziela	nye·*jye*·la

January	styczeń	*sti*·chen'
February	luty	*loo*·ti
March	marzec	*ma*·zhets
April	kwiecień	*kfye*·chen'
May	maj	mai
June	czerwiec	*cher*·vyets
July	lipiec	*lee*·pyets
August	sierpień	*shyer*·pyen'
September	wrzesień	*vzhe*·shyen'
October	październik	pazh·jyer·neek
November	listopad	lees·*to*·pat
December	grudzień	*groo*·jyen'

What date is it today?	Którego jest dzisiaj?	ktoo·*re*·go yest *jee*·shai
It's (18 October).	Jest (osiemnastego	yest (o·shem·nas·*te*·go
	października).	pazh·jyer·*nee*·ka)
last night	wczoraj wieczorem	*fcho*·rai vye·*cho*·rem
last/next ...	w zeszłym/przyszłym ...	v *zesh*·wim/*pshish*·wim ...
week	tygodniu	ti·*god*·nyoo
month	miesiącu	mye·*shon*·tsoo
year	roku	*ro*·koo
yesterday/	wczoraj/	*fcho*·rai/
tomorrow ...	jutro ...	*yoo*·tro ...
morning	rano	*ra*·no
afternoon	po południu	po po·*wood*·nyoo
evening	wieczorem	vye·*cho*·rem

weather

What's the weather like?	*Jaka jest pogoda?*	ya·ka yest po·go·da

It's ...

cloudy	*Jest pochmurnie.*	yest pokh·moor·nye
cold	*Jest zimno.*	yest zheem·no
hot	*Jest gorąco.*	yest go·ron·tso
raining	*Pada deszcz.*	pa·da deshch
snowing	*Pada śnieg.*	pa·da shnyeg
sunny	*Jest słonecznie.*	yest swo·nech·nye
warm	*Jest ciepło.*	yest chyep·wo
windy	*Jest wietrznic.*	yest vyetzh·nye
spring	*wiosna* f	vyos·na
summer	*lato* n	la·to
autumn	*jesień* f	ye·shyen'
winter	*zima* f	zhee·ma

border crossing

I'm ...	*Jestem ...*	yes·tem ...
in transit	*w tranzycie*	v tran·zi·chye
on business	*służbowo*	swoozh·bo·vo
on holiday	*na wakacjach*	na va·kats·yakh
I'm here for ...	*Będę tu przez ...*	ben·de too pshes ...
(10) days	*(dziesięć) dni*	(jye·shench) dnee
(three) weeks	*(trzy) tygodnie*	(tshi) ti·god·nye
(two) months	*(dwa) miesiące*	(dva) mye·shon·tse

I'm going to (Kraków).
Jadę do (Krakowa).   ya·de do (kra·ko·va)

I'm staying at the (Pod Różą Hotel).
Zatrzymuję się w (hotelu 'pod Różą').   za·tshi·moo·ye shye v (ho·te·loo pod roo·zhom)

I have nothing to declare.
Nie mam nic do zgłoszenia.   nye mam neets do zgwo·she·nya

I have something to declare.
Mam coś do zgłoszenia.   mam tsosh do zgwo·she·nya

That's (not) mine.
To (nie) jest moje.   to (nye) yest mo·ye

transport

tickets & luggage

Where can I buy a ticket?
Gdzie mogę kupić bilet?   gjye *mo*·ge *koo*·peech *bee*·let

Do I need to book a seat?
Czy muszę rezerwować?   chi *moo*·she re·zer·*vo*·vach

One ... ticket	*Proszę bilet ...*	*pro*·she *bee*·let ...
(to Katowice), please.	*(do Katowic).*	do (ka·*to*·veets)
one-way	*w jedną stronę*	v *yed*·nom *stro*·ne
return	*powrotny*	po·*vro*·tni

I'd like to ...	*Chcę ... mój bilet.*	khtse ... mooy *bee*·let
my ticket, please.		
cancel	*odwołać*	od·*vo*·wach
change	*zmienić*	*zmye*·neech
collect	*odebrać*	o·*de*·brach
confirm	*potwierdzić*	po·*tvyer*·jyeech

I'd like a ... seat,	*Proszę miejsce ...*	*pro*·she *myeys*·tse ...
please.		
nonsmoking	*dla niepalących*	dla nye·pa·*lon*·tsikh
smoking	*dla palących*	dla pa·*lon*·tsikh

How much is it?
Ile kosztuje?   ee·le kosh·*too*·ye

Is there air conditioning?
Czy jest tam klimatyzacja?   chi yest tam klee·ma·ti·*za*·tsya

Is there a toilet?
Czy jest tam toaleta?   chi yest tam to·a·*le*·ta

How long does the trip take?
Ile trwa podróż?   ee·le trfa *po*·droosh

Is it a direct route?
Czy to jest bezpośrednie połączenie?   chi to yest bes·po·*shred*·nye po·won·*che*·nye

Where can I find a luggage locker?
Gdzie jest schowek na bagaż?   gjye yest *skho*·vek na *ba*·gazh

My luggage	*Mój bagaż*	mooy *ba*·gazh
has been ...	*został ...*	*zos*·tow ...
damaged	*uszkodzony*	oosh·ko·*dzo*·ni
lost	*zagubiony*	za·goo·*byo*·ni
stolen	*skradziony*	skra·*jyo*·ni

getting around

Where does flight (LO125) arrive/depart?
Skąd przylatuje/odlatuje   skont pshi·la·*too*·ye/od·la·*too*·ye
lot (LO125)?   lot (el o sto dva·*jyesh*·chya pyench)

Where's (the) ...?	*Gdzie jest ...?*	gjye yest ...?
arrivals hall	*hala przylotów*	*kha*·la pshi·*lo*·toof
departures hall	*hala odlotów*	*kha*·la od·*lo*·toof
duty-free shop	*sklep wolnocłowy*	sklep vol·no·*tswo*·vi
gate (five)	*wejście*	*veysh*·chve
	(numer pięć)	(*noo*·mer pyench)

Is this the ...	*Czy to jest ...*	chi to yest ...
to (Wrocław)?	*do (Wrocławia)?*	do (vrots·*wa*·vya)
bus	*autobus*	ow·*to*·boos
plane	*samolot*	sa·*mo*·lot
train	*pociąg*	*po*·chonk

When's the ... bus?	*Kiedy jest ... autobus?*	*kye*·di yest ... ow·*to*·boos
first	*pierwszy*	*pyerf*·shi
last	*ostatni*	os·*tat*·nee
next	*następny*	nas·*temp*·ni

At what time does it arrive/leave?
O której godzinie przyjeżdża/   o *ktoo*·rey go·*jee*·nye pshi·*yezh*·ja/
odjeżdża?   ot·*yezh*·ja

How long will it be delayed?
Jakie będzie opóźnienie?   *ya*·kye *ben*·jye o·poozh·*nye*·nye

What's the next station?
Jaka jest następna stacja?   *ya*·ka yest nas·*temp*·na *sta*·tsya

What's the next stop?
Jaki jest następny przystanek?   *ya*·kee yest nas·*tem*·pni pshi·*sta*·nek

Does it stop at (Kalisz)?
Czy on się zatrzymuje w (Kaliszu)?   chi on shye za·tshi·*moo*·ye f (ka·*lee*·shoo)

Please tell me when we get to (Krynica).
Proszę mi powiedzieć gdy   pro·she mee po·*vye*·jyech gdi
dojedziemy do (Krynicy).   do·ye·*jye*·mi do (kri·*nee*·tsi)

How long do we stop here?
Na jak długo się tu zatrzymamy?   na yak *dwoo*·go shye too za·tshi·*ma*·mi

Is this seat available?
Czy to miejsce jest wolne?   chi to *myeys*·tse yest *vol*·ne

That's my seat.
To jest moje miejsce.   to yest *mo*·ye *myeys*·tse

I'd like a taxi ...	*Chcę zamówić*	khtse za·*moo*·veech
	taksówę na ...	tak·*soof*·ke na ...
now	*teraz*	*te*·ras
tomorrow	*jutro*	*yoo*·tro
at (9am)	*(dziewiątą rano)*	(jye·*vyon*·tom *ra*·no)

Is this taxi available?
Czy ta taksówka jest wolna?   chi ta tak·*soof*·ka yest *vol*·na

How much is it to (Szczecin)?
Ile kosztuje do (Szczecina)?   ee·le kosh·*too*·ye (do shche·*chee*·na)

Please put the meter on.
Proszę włączyć taksometr.   pro·she *vwon*·chich tak·*so*·metr

Please take me to (this address).
Proszę mnie zawieźć pod (ten adres).   pro·she mnye za·*vyeshch* pod (ten *ad*·res)

Please ...	*Proszę ...*	pro·she ...
slow down	*zwolnić*	*zvol*·neech
stop here	*się tu zatrzymać*	shye too za·*tshi*·mach
wait here	*tu zaczekać*	too za·*che*·kach

car, motorbike & bicycle hire

I'd like to hire a ...	*Chcę wypożyczyć ...*	khtse vi·po·*zhi*·chich ...
bicycle	*rower*	*ro*·ver
car	*samochód*	sa·*mo*·khoot
motorbike	*motocykl*	mo·*to*·tsikl

with ...	z ...	z ...
air conditioning	klimatyzacją	klee-ma-ti-*za*-tsyom
a driver	kierowcą	kye-*rof*-tsom
antifreeze	płynem nie	*pwi*-nem nye
	zamarzającym	za-mar-za-*yon*-tsim
snow chains	łańcuchami	wan'-tsoo-*kha*-mee
	śnieżnymi	shnezh-*ni*-mee

How much for	Ile kosztuje	*ee*-le kosh-*too*-ye
... hire?	wypożyczenie na ...?	vi-po-zhi-*che*-nye na ...
hourly	godzinę	go-*jee*-ne
daily	dzień	jyen'
weekly	tydzień	*ti*-jyen'

air	powietrze n	po-*vye*-tshe
oil	olej m	*o*-ley
petrol	benzyna f	ben-*zi*-na
tyre	opona f	o-*po*-na

I need a mechanic.
Potrzebuję mechanika.   po-tshe-*boo*-ye me-kha-*nee*-ka

I've run out of petrol.
Zabrakło mi benzyny.   za-*bra*-kwo mee ben-*zi*-ni

I have a flat tyre.
Złapałem/Złapałam gumę. m/f   zwa-*pa*-wem/zwa-*pa*-wam *goo*-me

directions

Where's the ...?	Gdzie jest ...?	gjye yest ...
bank	bank	bank
city centre	centrum miasta	*tsen*-troom *myas*-ta
hotel	hotel	*ho*-tel
market	targ	tark
police station	komisariat	ko-mee-*sar*-yat
	policji	po-*leets*-yee
post office	urząd pocztowy	*oo*-zhond poch-*to*-vi
public toilet	toaleta publiczna	to-a-*le*-ta poo-*bleech*-na
tourist office	biuro turystyczne	*byoo*-ro too-ris-*tich*-ne

Is this the road to (Malbork)?
Czy to jest droga do (Malborka)?   chi to yest *dro*-ga do (mal-*bor*-ka)

Can you show me (on the map)?
Czy może pan/pani — chi *mo*·zhe pan/*pa*·nee
mi pokazać (na mapie)? m/f — mee po·*ka*·zach (na *ma*·pye)

What's the address?
Jaki jest adres? — *ya*·kee yest *ad*·res

How far is it?
Jak daleko to jest? — yak da·*le*·ko to yest

How do I get there?
Jak tam mogę się dostać? — yak tam *mo*·ge shye *dos*·tach

Turn ...	*Proszę skręcić ...*	*pro*·she *skren*·cheech ...
at the corner	*na rogu*	na *ro*·goo
at the traffic lights	*na światłach*	na *shfyat*·wakh
left/right	*w lewo/prawo*	v *le*·vo/*pra*·vo

It's ...	*To jest ...*	to yest ...
behind ...	*za ...*	za ...
far away	*daleko*	da·*le*·ko
here	*tu*	too
in front of ...	*przed ...*	pshet ...
left	*po lewej*	po *le*·vey
near	*blisko*	*blees*·ko
next to ...	*obok ...*	*o*·bok ...
on the corner	*na rogu*	na *ro*·goo
opposite ...	*naprzeciwko ...*	nap·she·*cheef*·ko ...
right	*po prawej*	po *pra*·vey
straight ahead	*na wprost*	na fprost
there	*tam*	tam

by bus	*autobusem*	ow·to·*boo*·sem
by taxi	*taksówką*	tak·*soof*·kom
by train	*pociągiem*	po·*chon*·gyem
on foot	*pieszo*	*pye*·sho

north	*północ*	*poow*·nots
south	*południe*	po·*wood*·nye
east	*wschód*	fskhoot
west	*zachód*	*za*·khoot

Wjazd/Wyjazd	vyazd/*vi*-yazd	**Entrance/Exit**
Otwarte/Zamknięte	ot-*far*-te/zamk-*nyen*-te	**Open/Closed**
Wolne pokoje	*vol*-ne po-*ko*-ye	**Rooms Available**
Brak wolnych miejsc	brak *vol*-nikh myeysts	**No Vacancies**
Informacja	een-for-*ma*-tsya	**Information**
Komisariat policji	ko-mee-*sar*-yat po-*lee*-tsyee	**Police Station**
Zabroniony	za-bro-*nyo*-ni	**Prohibited**
Toalety	to-a-*le*-ti	**Toilets**
Męskie	*mens*-kye	**Men**
Damskie	*dams*-kye	**Women**
Zimna/Gorąca	*zheem*-na/go-*ron*-tsa	**Hot/Cold**

accommodation

finding accommodation

Where's a ...?	*Gdzie jest ...?*	gjye yest ...
camping ground	*kamping*	*kam*-peeng
guesthouse	*pokoje gościnne*	po-*ko*-ye gosh-*chee*-ne
hotel	*hotel*	*ho*-tel
youth hostel	*schronisko*	skhro-*nees*-ko
	młodzieżowe	mwo-jye-*zho*-ve

Can you recommend	*Czy może pan/pani*	chi *mo*-zhe pan/*pa*-nee
somewhere ...?	*polecić coś ...?* m/f	po-*le*-cheech tsosh ...
cheap	*taniego*	ta-*nye*-go
good	*dobrego*	do-*bre*-go
nearby	*coś w pobliżu*	tsosh f po-*blee*-zhoo

I'd like to book a room, please.
  Chcę zarezerwować pokój.   khtse za-re-zer-*vo*-vach po-kooy

I have a reservation.
  Mam rezerwację.   mam re-zer-*va*-tsye

My name's ...
  Nazywam się ...   na-*zi*-vam shye ...

Do you have a ... room?	*Czy jest pokój ...?*	chi yest *po*·kooy ...
single	*jednoosobowy*	yed·no·o·so·*bo*·vi
double	*z podwójnym*	z pod·*vooy*·nim
	łóżkiem	*woozh*·kyem
twin	*z dwoma łóżkami*	z *dvo*·ma wozh·*ka*·mee

How much is it per ...?	*Ile kosztuje za ...?*	ee·le kosh·*too*·ye za ...
night	*noc*	nots
person	*osobę*	o·*so*·be

Can I pay ...?	*Czy mogę zapłacić ...?*	chi *mo*·ge za·*pwa*·cheech ...
by credit card	*kartą kredytową*	*kar*·tom kre·di·*to*·vom
with a travellers	*czekami*	che·*ka*·mee
cheque	*podróżnymi*	po·droozh·*ni*·mee

For (three) nights/weeks.
Na (trzy) noce/tygodnie. na (tshi) *no*·tse/ti·*god*·nye

From (2 July) to (6 July).
Od (drugiego lipca) do od (droo·*gye*·go *leep*·tsa) do
(szóstego lipca). (shoos·*te*·go *leep*·tsa)

Can I see it?
Czy mogę go zobaczyć? chi *mo*·ge go zo·*ba*·chich

Am I allowed to I camp here?
Czy mogę się tutaj rozbić? chi *mo*·ge shye *too*·tai *roz*·beech

Where can I find the camping ground?
Gdzie jest pole kampingowe? gjye yest *po*·le kam·peen·*go*·ve

requests & queries

When's breakfast served?
O której jest śniadanie? o *ktoo*·rey yest shnya·*da*·nye

Where's breakfast served?
Gdzie jest śniadanie? gjye yest shnya·*da*·nye

Please wake me at (seven).
Proszę obudzić mnie o (siódmej). *pro*·she o·*boo*·jeech mnye o (*shyood*·mey)

Could I have my key, please?
Czy mogę prosić o klucz? chi *mo*·ge *pro*·sheech o klooch

Can I get another (blanket)?
Czy mogę prosić o jeszcze chi *mo*·ge *pro*·sheech o *yesh*·che
jeden (koc)? *ye*·den (kots)

144

Is there an elevator/a safe?
   Czy jest winda/sejf?   chi yest *veen*·da/seyf

This (towel) isn't clean.
   Ten (ręcznik) nie jest czysty.   ten (*rench*·neek) nye yest *chis*·ti

It's too ...	Jest zbyt ...	yest zbit ...
expensive	*drogi*	*dro*·gee
noisy	*głośny*	*gwosh*·ni
small	*mały*	*ma*·wi

The ... doesn't work.	... nie działa.	... nye *jya*·wa
air conditioner	*Klimatyzator*	klee·ma·ti·*za*·tor
fan	*Wentylator*	ven·ti·*la*·tor
toilet	*Ubikacja*	oo·bee·*kats*·ya

checking out

What time is checkout?
   O której godzinie   o *ktoo*·rey go·*jye*·nye
   muszę się wymeldować?   *moo*·she shye vi·mel·*do*·vach

Can I leave my luggage here?
   Czy mogę tu zostawić   chi *mo*·ge too zo·*sta*·veech
   moje bagaże?   *mo*·ye ba·*ga*·zhe

Could I have	Czy mogę prosić	chi *mo*·ge pro·sheech
my ..., please?	o mój/moje ...? sg/pl	o mooy/*mo*·ye ...
deposit	*depozyt* sg	de·*po*·zit
passport	*paszport* sg	*pash*·port
valuables	*kosztowności* pl	kosh·tov·*nosh*·chee

communications & banking

the internet

Where's the local Internet café?
   Gdzie jest kawiarnia internetowa?   gjye yest ka·*vyar*·nya een·ter·ne·*to*·va

How much is it per hour?
   Ile kosztuje za godzinę?   *ee*·le kosh·*too*·ye za go·*jee*·ne

I'd like to ...	Chciałem/Chciałam ... m/f	khchow·em/khchow·am ...
check my email	sprawdzić mój email	sprav·jeech mooy ee·mayl
get Internet access	podłączyć się do internetu	pod·won·chich shye do een·ter·ne·too
use a printer	użyć drukarki	oo·zhich droo·kar·kee
use a scanner	użyć skaner	oo·zhich ska·ner

mobile/cell phone

I'd like a ...	Chciałem/Chciałam ... m/f	khchow·em/khchow·am ...
mobile/cell phone for hire	wypożyczyć telefon komórkowy	vi·po·zhi·chich te·le·fon ko·moor·ko·vi
SIM card for your network	kartę SIM na waszą sieć	kar·te seem na va·shom shyech

What are the rates?	Jakie są stawki za rozmowy?	ya·kye som staf·kee za roz·mo·vi

telephone

What's your phone number?
Jaki jest pana/pani numer telefonu? m/f pol
ya·kee yest pa·na/pa·nee noo·mer te·le·fo·noo

The number is ...
Numer jest ...
noo·mer yest ...

Where's the nearest public phone?
Gdzie jest najbliższy telefon?
gjye yest nai·bleezh·shi te·le·fon

I'd like to buy a chip phonecard.
Chciałem/Chciałam kupić czipową kartę telefoniczną. m/f
khchow·em/khchow·am koo·peech chee·po·vom kar·te te·le·fo·neech·nom

I want to ...	Chciałem/Chciałam ... m/f	khchow·em/khchow·am ...
call (Singapore)	zadzwonić do (Singapuru)	zad·zvo·neech do (seen·ga·poo·roo)
make a local call	zadzwonić pod lokalny numer	zad·zvo·neech pod lo·kal·ni noo·mer
reverse the charges	zamówić rozmowę na koszt odbiorcy	za·moo·veech roz·mo·ve na kosht od·byor·tsi

How much does ... cost?	Ile kosztuje ...?	ee·le kosh·too·ye ...
a (three)-minute call	rozmowa (trzy) minutowa	roz·mo·va (tshi) mee·noo·to·va
each extra minute	każda dodatkowa minuta	kazh·da do·dat·ko·va mee·noo·ta
(Two złotys) per (30) seconds.	(Dwa złote) za (trzydzieści) sekund.	(dva zwo·te) za (tshi·jyesh·chee) se·koond

post office

I want to send a ...	Chciałem/Chciałam wysłać ... m/f	khchow·em/khchow·am vis·wach ...
fax	faks	faks
letter	list	leest
parcel	paczkę	pach·ke
postcard	pocztówkę	poch·toof·ke

I want to buy a/an ...	Chciałem/Chciałam kupić ... m/f	khchow·em/khchow·am koo·peech ...
envelope	kopertę	ko·per·te
stamp	znaczek	zna·chek

Please send it (to Australia) by ...	Proszę wysłać to ... (do Australii).	pro·she vis·wach to ... (do ows·tra·lyee)
airmail	pocztą lotniczą	poch·tom lot·nee·chom
express mail	pocztą ekspresową	poch·tom eks·pre·so·vom
registered mail	pocztą poleconą	poch·tom po·le·tso·nom
surface mail	pocztą lądową	poch·tom lon·do·vom

Is there any mail for me?	Czy jest dla mnie jakaś korespondencja?	chi yest dla mnye ya·kash ko·res·pon·den·tsya

bank

Where's a/an ...?	Gdzie jest ...?	gjye yest ...
ATM	bankomat	ban·ko·mat
foreign exchange office	kantor walut	kan·tor va·loot

I'd like to ...	Chciałem/Chciałam ... m/f	khchow-em/khchow-am ...
Where can I ...?	Gdzie mogę ...?	gjye mo-ge ...
cash a cheque	wymienić czek	vi-mye-neech chek
	na gotówkę	na go-toof-ke
change a travellers	wymienić czek	vi-mye-neech chek
cheque	podróżny	po-droozh-ni
change money	wymienić	vi-mye-neech
	pieniądze	pye-nyon-dze
get a cash	dostać zaliczkę	dos-tach za-leech-ke
advance	na moją kartę	na mo-yom kar-te
	kredytową	kre-di-to-vom
withdraw money	wypłacić	vi-pwa-cheech
	pieniądze	pye-nyon-dze
What's the ...?	Jaki/Jaka jest ...? m/f	ya-kee/ya-ka yest ...
charge for that	prowizja f	pro-veez-ya
exchange rate	kurs wymiany m	koors vi-mya-ni

It's (12) złotys.
To kosztuje (dwanaście) złotych.   to kosh-too-ye (dva-nash-chye) zwo-tikh

It's free.
Jest bezpłatny.   yest bes-pwat-ni

What time does the bank open?
W jakich godzinach   v ya-keekh go-jee-nakh
jest bank otwarty?   yest bank ot-far-ti

Has my money arrived yet?
Czy doszły już moje pieniądze?   chi dosh-wi yoosh mo-ye pye-nyon-dze

sightseeing

getting in

What time does it open/close?
O której godzinie jest   o ktoo-rey go-jee-nye yest
otwarte/zamknięte?   ot-far-te/zam-knyen-te

What's the admission charge?
Ile kosztuje wstęp?   ee-le kosh-too-ye fstemp

Is there a discount for students/children?

Czy jest zniżka dla — chi yest *zneezh*·ka dla
studentów/dzieci? — stoo·den·toof/*jye*·chee

I'd like to see ...

Chciałem/Chciałam obejrzeć ... m/f — khchow·em/khchow·am o·bey·zhech ...

What's that?

Co to jest? — tso to yest

Can I take a photo?

Czy mogę zrobić zdjęcie? — chi *mo*·ge *zro*·beech *zdyen*·chye

I'd like a ... — *Chciałem/Chciałam ...* m/f — khchow·em/khchow·am ...

catalogue	*broszurę*	bro·*shoo*·re
guide	*przewodnik*	pshe·*vod*·neek
local map	*mapę okolic*	*ma*·pe o·*ko*·leets

tours

When's the next ...? — *Kiedy jest następna ...?* — *kye*·di yest nas·*temp*·na ...

day trip	*wycieczka*	vi·*chyech*·ka
	jednodniowa	yed·no·*dnyo*·va
tour	*tura*	*too*·ra

Is ... included? — *Czy ... wliczone/a?* n&pl/f — chi ... vlee·*cho*·ne/na

accommodation	*noclegi są* pl	nots·*le*·gee som
the admission charge	*opłata za wstęp jest* f	o·*pwa*·ta za fstemp yest
food	*wyżywienie jest* n	vi·zhi·*vye*·nye yest

Is transport included?

Czy transport jest wliczony? — chi *trans*·port yest vlee·*cho*·ne

How long is the tour?

Jak długo trwa wycieczka? — yak *dwoo*·go trfa vi·*chyech*·ka

What time should we be back?

O której godzinie — o *ktoo*·rey go·*jee*·nye
powinniśmy wrócić? — po·vee·*neesh*·mi *vroo*·cheech

castle	zamek m	za-mek
cathedral	katedra f	ka-te-dra
church	kościół m	kosh-chyoow'
main square	rynek główny m	ri-nek gwoov-ni
monastery	klasztor m	klash-tor
monument	pomnik m	pom-neek
museum	muzeum n	moo-ze-oom
old city	stare miasto n	sta-re myas-to
palace	pałac m	pa-wats
ruins	ruiny f pl	roo-ee-ni
stadium	stadion m	sta-dyon
statue	pomnik m	pom-neek

shopping

enquiries

Where's a ...?	Gdzie jest ...?	gjye yest ...
bank	bank	bank
bookshop	księgarnia	kshyen-gar-nya
camera shop	sklep fotograficzny	sklep fo-to-gra-feech-ni
department store	dom towarowy	dom to-va-ro-vi
grocery store	sklep spożywczy	sklep spo-zhiv-chi
market	targ	tark
newsagency	kiosk	kyosk
supermarket	supermarket	soo-per-mar-ket

Where can I buy (a padlock)?
Gdzie mogę kupić (kłódkę)?   gjye mo-ge koo-peech (kwoot-ke)

I'm looking for ...
Szukam ...   shoo-kam

Can I look at it?
Czy mogę to zobaczyć?   chi mo-ge to zo-ba-chich

Do you have any others?
Czy są jakieś inne?   chi som ya-kyesh ee-ne

Does it have a guarantee?
Czy to ma gwarancję?   chi to ma gva-ran-tsye

Can I have it sent overseas?
Czy mogę to wysłać za granicę?   chi *mo*·ge to *vis*·wach za gra·*nee*·tse

Can I have my ... repaired?
Czy mogę tu oddać ... do naprawy?   chi *mo*·ge too *ot*·dach ... do na·*pra*·vi

It's faulty.
To jest wadliwe.   to yest vad·*lee*·ve

I'd like to return this, please.
Chciałem/Chciałam to zwrócić. m/f   khchow·em/khchow·am to zvroo·cheech

I'd like a ..., please.   *Proszę o ...*   pro·she o ...
    bag   *torbę*   *tor*·be
    refund   *zwrot pieniędzy*   zvrot pye·*nyen*·dzi

paying

How much is it?
Ile to kosztuje?   ee·le to kosh·*too*·ye

Can you write down the price?
Proszę napisać cenę.   pro·she na·*pee*·sach *tse*·ne

That's too expensive.
To jest za drogie.   to yest za *dro*·gye

What's your final price?
Jaka jest pana/pani   *ya*·ka yest *pa*·na/*pa*·nee
ostateczna cena? m/f   os·ta·*tech*·na *tse*·na

I'll give you (10 złotys).
Dam panu/pani (dziesięć złotych). m/f   dam *pa*·noo/*pa*·nee (*jye*·shench *zwo*·tikh)

There's a mistake in the bill.
Na czeku jest pomyłka.   na *che*·koo yest po·*miw*·ka

Do you accept ...?	*Czy mogę zapłacić ...?*	chi *mo*·ge za·*pwa*·cheech ...
credit cards	*kartą kredytową*	*kar*·tom kre·di·*to*·vom
debit cards	*kartą debetową*	*kar*·tom de·be·*to*·vom
travellers	*czekami*	che·*ka*·mee
cheques	*podróżnymi*	pod·roozh·*ni*·mee
I'd like ..., please.	*Proszę o ...*	pro·she o ...
a receipt	*rachunek*	ra·*khoo*·nek
my change	*moją resztę*	*mo*·yom *resh*·te

clothes & shoes

Can I try it on?	Czy mogę przymierzyć?	chi mo·ge pshi·mye·zhich
My size is (40).	Noszę rozmiar (czterdzieści).	no·she roz·myar (chter·jyesh·chee)
It doesn't fit.	Nie pasuje.	nye pa·soo·ye
large/medium/small	L/M/S	el·ke/em·ke/es·ke

books & music

I'd like a ...	Chciałem/Chciałam ... m/f	khchow·em/khchow·am ...
newspaper (in English)	gazetę (w języku angielskim)	ga·ze·te (v yen·zi·koo an·gyel·skeem)
pen	długopis	dwoo·go·pees

Is there an English-language bookshop?
Czy jest tu księgarnia angielska?　　chi yest too kshyen·gar·nya an·gyel·ska

I'm looking for something by (Górecki).
Szukam czegoś (Góreckiego).　　shoo·kam che·gosh (goo·rets·kye·go)

Can I listen to this?
Czy mogę tego posłuchać?　　chi mo·ge te·go pos·woo·khach

photography

Can you ...?	Czy może pan/pani ...? m/f	chi mo·zhe pan/pa·nee ...
develop this film	wywołać ten film	vi·vo·wach ten film
load my film	założyć film	za·wo·zhich film
transfer photos from my camera to CD	skopiować zdjęcia z mojego aparatu na płytę kompaktową	sko·pyo·vach zdyen·chya z mo·ye·go a·pa·ra·too na pwi·te kom·pak·to·vom

I need a/an ... film for this camera.	Potrzebuję film ... do tego aparatu.	po·tshe·boo·ye film ... do te·go a·pa·ra·too
APS	APS	a pe es
B&W	panchromatyczny	pan·khro·ma·tich·ni
colour	kolorowy	ko·lo·ro·vi
slide	do slajdów	do slai·doof
(200) speed	(dwieście) ASA	(dvyesh·chye) a·sa

When will it be ready? Na kiedy będzie gotowe?　　na kye·di ben·jye go·to·ve

meeting people

greetings, goodbyes & introductions

Hello/Hi.	*Cześć.*	cheshch
Good night.	*Dobranoc.*	do·*bra*·nots
Goodbye.	*Do widzenia.*	do vee·*dze*·nya
Bye.	*Pa.*	pa
See you later.	*Do zobaczenia.*	do zo·ba·*che*·nya
Mr/Mrs/Miss	*Pan/Pani/Panna*	pan/*pa*·nee/*pa*·na
How are you?	*Jak pan/pani*	yak pan/*pa*·nee
	się miewa? m/f pol	shye *mye*·va
	Jak się masz? inf	yak shye mash
Fine. And you?	*Dobrze. A pan/pani?* m/f pol	*dob*·zhe a pan/*pa*·nee
	Dobrze. A ty? inf	*dob*·zhe a ti
What's your name?	*Jak się pan/pani*	yak shye pan/*pa*·nee
	nazywa? m/f pol	na·*zi*·va
	Jakie się nazywasz? inf	yak shye na·*zi*·vash
My name is ...	*Nazywam się ...*	na·*zi*·vam shye ...
I'm pleased to	*Miło mi pana/panią*	*mee*·wo mee *pa*·na/*pa*·nyom
meet you.	*poznać.* m/f pol	*po*·znach
	Miło mi ciebie poznać. inf	*mee*·wo mee *chye*·bye *po*·znach
This is my ...	*To jest mój/moja ...* m/f	to yest mooy/*mo*·ya ...
boyfriend	*chłopak*	*khwo*·pak
brother	*brat*	brat
daughter	*córka*	*tsoor*·ka
father	*ojciec*	*oy*·chyets
friend	*przyjaciel* m	pzhi·*ya*·chyel
	przyjaciółka f	pzhi·*ya*·chyoow·ka
girlfriend	*dziewczyna*	jyev·*chi*·na
husband	*mąż*	monzh
mother	*matka*	*mat*·ka
partner (intimate)	*partner/partnerka* m/f	*part*·ner/*part*·ner·ka
sister	*siostra*	*shyos*·tra
son	*syn*	sin
wife	*żona*	*zho*·na

Here's my ...	*Tu jest mój ...*	too yest mooy ...
What's your ...?	*Jaki jest pana/*	ya·kee yest pa·na/
	pani ...? m/f pol	pa·nee ...
(email) address	*adres (emailowy)*	ad·res (e·mai·lo·vi)
fax number	*numer faksu*	noo·mer fak·soo
phone number	*numer telefonu*	noo·mer te·le·fo·noo

occupations

What's your	*Jaki jest pana/pani*	ya·kee yest pa·na/pa·nee
occupation?	*zawód?* m/f pol	za·vood
I'm a/an ...	*Jestem ...*	yes·tem ...
artist	*artystą/artystką* m/f	ar·tis·tom/ar·tist·kom
farmer	*rolnikiem* m&f	rol·nee·kyem
manual worker	*pracownikiem*	pra·tsov·nee·kyem
	fizycznym m&f	fee·zich·nim
office worker	*pracownikiem*	pra·tsov·nee·kyem
	biurowym m&f	byoo·ro·vim
scientist	*naukowcem* m&f	now·kov·tsem
tradesperson	*rzemieślnikiem* m&f	zhe·mye·shlnee·kyem

background

Where are you from?	*Skąd pan/pani jest?* m/f pol	skont pan/pa·nee yest
I'm from ...	*Jestem z ...*	yes·tem z ...
Australia	*Australii*	ow·stra·lyee
Canada	*Kanady*	ka·na·di
England	*Anglii*	ang·lee
New Zealand	*Nowej Zelandii*	no·vey ze·lan·dyee
the USA	*USA*	oo es a

Are you married? (to a man)
Czy jest pan żonaty? pol   chi yest pan zho·na·ti

Are you married? (to a woman)
Czy jest pani zamężna? pol   chi yest pa·nee za·menzh·na

I'm married.
Jestem żonaty/zamężna. m/f   yes·tem zho·na·ti/za·menzh·na

I'm single.
Jestem nieżonaty/niezamężna. m/f   nye·zho·na·ti/nye·za·menzh·na

age

How old is your ...?	Ile lat ma pana/ pani ...? m/f pol	ee·le lat ma pa·na/ pa·nee ...
daughter	córka	tsoor·ka
son	syn	sin
How old are you?	Ile pan/pani ma lat? m/f pol	ee·le pan/pa·nee ma lat
	Ile masz lat? inf	ee·le mash lat
I'm ... years old.	Mam ... lat.	mam ... lat
He/She is ... years old.	On/Ona ma ... lat.	on/o·na ma ... lat

feelings

I'm (not) ...	(Nie) Jestem ...	(nye) yes·tem ...
Are you ...?	Czy jest pan/pani ...? m/f pol	chi yest pan/pa·nee ...
cold	zmarznięty/a m/f	zmar·znyen·ti/a
happy	szczęśliwy/a m/f	shchen·shlee·vi/a
hungry	głodny/a m/f	gwod·ni/a
sad	smutny/a m/f	smoot·ni/a
thirsty	spragniony/a m/f	sprag·nyo·ni/a

entertainment

going out

Where can I find ...?	Gdzie mogę znaleźć ...?	gjye mo·ge zna·lezhch ...
clubs	kluby nocne	kloo·bi nots·ne
gay venues	kluby dla gejów	kloo·bi dla ge·yoof
pubs	puby	pa·bi
I feel like going to a/the ...	Mam ochotę pójść ...	mam o·kho·te pooyshch ...
concert	na koncert	na kon·tsert
movies	na film	na feelm
party	na imprezę	na eem·pre·ze
restaurant	do restauracji	do res·tow·ra·tsyee
theatre	na sztukę	na shtoo·ke

Do you like ...?	Czy lubisz ...? inf	chi *loo*·beesh ...
I like ...	Lubię ...	*loo*·bye ...
cooking	gotować	go·*to*·vach
movies	oglądać filmy	o·*glon*·dach *feel*·mi
reading	czytać	*chi*·tach
sport	sport	sport
travelling	podróżować	po·droo·*zho*·vach

Do you like art?	Czy lubisz sztukę? inf	chi *loo*·beesh *shtoo*·ke
I like art.	Lubię sztukę.	*loo*·bye *shtoo*·ke

Do you ...?	Czy ...? inf	chi ...
dance	tańczysz	*tan'*·chish
go to concerts	chodzisz na koncerty	*kho*·jeesh na *kon*·tser·ti
listen to music	słuchasz muzyki	*swoo*·khash moo·*zi*·kee

food & drink

finding a place to eat

Can you	Czy może pan/pani	chi *mo*·zhe pan/*pa*·nee
recommend a ...?	polecić ...? m/f	po·*le*·cheech ...
bar	bar	bar
café	kawiarnię	ka·*vyar*·nye
restaurant	restaurację	res·tow·*rats*·ye

I'd like ..., please.	Proszę ...	*pro*·she ...
a table for (five)	o stolik na (pięć) osób	o *sto*·leek na (pyench) o·soob
the (non)smoking section	dla (nie)palących	dla (nye·)pa·*lon*·tsikh

ordering food

breakfast	śniadanie n	shnya·*da*·nye
lunch	obiad m	*o*·byad
dinner	kolacja f	ko·*la*·tsya
snack	przekąska f	pshe·*kons*·ka

What would you recommend?

Co by pan polecił? m		tso bi pan po·*le*·cheew
Co by pani poleciła? f		tso bi *pa*·nee po·le·*chee*·wa

I'd like (the) ..., please. *Proszę ...*   *pro*·she ...

bill	o rachunek	o ra·*khoo*·nek
drink list	o spis napojów	o spees na·*po*·yoof
menu	o jadłospis	o ya·*dwo*·spees
that dish	to danie	to *da*·nye

drinks

(cup of) coffee ...	(filiżanka) kawy ...	(fee·lee·*zhan*·ka) *ka*·vi ...
(cup of) tea ...	(filiżanka) herbaty ...	(fee·lee·*zhan*·ka) her·*ba*·ti ...
with milk	z mlekiem	z *mle*·kyem
without sugar	bez cukru	bez *tsoo*·kroo
(orange) juice	sok (pomarańczowy) m	sok (po·ma·ran'·*cho*·vi)
soft drink	napój m	*na*·pooy
... water	woda ...	*vo*·da ...
hot	gorąca	go·*ron*·tsa
mineral	mineralna	mee·ne·*ral*·na

in the bar

I'll have ...	Proszę ...	*pro*·she ...
I'll buy you a drink.	Kupię ci drinka. inf	*koo*·pye chee *dreen*·ka
What would you like?	Co zamówić dla ciebie? inf	tso za·*moo*·veech dla *chye*·bye
Cheers!	Na zdrowie!	na *zdro*·vye
brandy	brandy m	*bren*·di
champagne	szampan m	*sham*·pan
a shot of (vodka)	kieliszek (wódki)	kye·*lee*·shek (*vood*·kee)
a bottle/glass of beer	butelka/szklanka piwa	boo·*tel*·ka/*shklan*·ka *pee*·va
a bottle/glass	butelka/kieliszek	boo·*tel*·ka/kye·*lee*·shek
of ... wine	wina ...	*vee*·na ...
red	czerwonego	cher·vo·*ne*·go
sparkling	musującego	moo·soo·yon·*tse*·go
white	białego	bya·*we*·go

self-catering

What's the local speciality?

Co jest miejscową specjalnością?		tso yest myeys·*tso*·vom spe·tsyal·*nosh*·chyom

What's that?

Co to jest?		tso to yest

How much (is a kilo of cheese)?

Ile kosztuje (kilogram sera)?		ee·le kosh·*too*·ye (kee·*lo*·gram *se*·ra)

I'd like ...	*Proszę ...*	*pro*·she ...
200 grams	*dwadzieścia deko*	dva·*jyesh*·chya *de*·ko
(two) kilos	*(dwa) kilo*	(dva) *kee*·lo
(three) pieces	*(trzy) kawałki*	(tshi) ka·*vow*·kee
(six) slices	*(sześć) plasterków*	(sheshch) plas·*ter*·koof

Less.	*Mniej.*	mney
Enough.	*Wystarczy.*	vis·*tar*·chi
More.	*Więcej.*	*vyen*·tsey

special diets & allergies

Is there a vegetarian restaurant near here?

Czy jest tu gdzieś restauracja wegetariańska?		chi yest too gjyesh res·tow·*ra*·tsya ve·ge·ta·*ryan*'·ska

Do you have vegetarian food?

Czy jest żywność wegetariańska?		chi yest *zhiv*·noshch ve·ge·tar·*yan*'·ska

Could you prepare a meal without ...?	*Czy można przygotować jedzenie bez ...?*	chi *mo*·zhna pshi·go·*to*·vach ye·*dze*·nye bes ...
butter	*masła*	*mas*·wa
eggs	*jajek*	*yai*·ek
meat stock	*wywaru mięsnego*	vi·*va*·roo myens·*ne*·go

I'm allergic to ...	*Mam uczulenie na ...*	mam oo·choo·*le*·nye na ...
dairy produce	*produkty mleczne*	pro·*dook*·ti *mlech*·ne
gluten	*gluten*	*gloo*·ten
MSG	*glutaminian sodu*	gloo·ta·*mee*·nyan *so*·doo
nuts	*orzechy*	o·*zhe*·khi
seafood	*owoce morza*	o·*vo*·tse *mo*·zha

barszcz biały m	barshch *bya*·wi	*thick sourish wheat & potato-starch soup with marjoram*
barszcz czerwony m	barshch cher·*vo*·ni	*beetroot soup with dumplings, hard-boiled egg slices or beans*
bigos m	*bee*·gos	*sauerkraut, cabbage & meat stew, simmered with mushrooms & prunes & flavoured with red wine*
bliny m pl	*blee*·ni	*small thick pancakes made from wheat or buckwheat flour & yeast*
budyń m	*boo*·din'	*milk-based cream dessert in a range of flavours (eg strawberry, vanilla or chocolate)*
chłodnik m	*khwod*·neek	*baby beetroot soup with yogurt & fresh vegetables, served cold*
ćwikła f	*chfeek*·wa	*boiled & grated beetroot with horseradish, served with roast or smoked meat & sausages*
drożdżówka f	drozh·*joof*·ka	*brioche (sweet yeast bun)*
flaczki m pl	*flach*·kee	*seasoned tripe & vegetables cooked in bouillon*
galareta f	ga·la·*re*·ta	*appetiser of meat or fish encased in aspic • sweet flavoured jelly*
gofry m pl	*go*·fri	*thick rectangular waffles served with toppings such as whipped cream, chocolate or jam*
golonka f	go·*lon*·ka	*boiled pigs' hocks served with sauerkraut or puréed yellow peas*
gołąbki m pl	go·*womb*·kee	*cabbage leaves stuffed with minced beef & rice*
grahamka f	gra·*kham*·ka	*small wholemeal roll*
grochówka f	gro·*khoof*·ka	*lentil soup*

jabłecznik m	ya-*bwech*-neek	apple strudel
kapuśniak m	ka-*poosh*-nyak	sauerkraut soup
kisiel m	*kee*-shyel	jelly-type dessert made with potato starch
klopsiki m pl	klop-*shee*-kee	meatballs made with ground beef, pork and/or veal
knedle m pl	*kned*-le	dumplings stuffed with plums, cherries or apples
kopytka n pl	ko-*pit*-ka	potato dumplings similar to gnocchi
łosoś wędzony m	*wo*-sosh ven-*dzo*-ni	smoked salmon
makowiec m	ma-*ko*-vyets	poppy-seed strudel
melba f	*mel*-ba	ice cream, fruit & whipped cream
mizeria f	mee-*zer*-ya	sliced cucumber in sour cream
naleśniki m pl	na-lesh-*nee*-kee	crèpes • pancakes
nóżki w galarecie n pl	*noosh*-kee v ga-la-*re*-chye	jellied pigs' knuckles
pierogi m pl	pye-*ro*-gee	ravioli-like dumplings made from noodle dough, usually stuffed with mincemeat, sauerkraut, mushroom, cheese & potato
rosół z makaronem m	*ro*-soow z ma-ka-*ro*-nem	bouillon with noodles
sałatka jarzynowa f	sa-*wat*-ka ya-zhi-*no*-va	salad made with potato, vegetables & mayonnaise
sernik m	*ser*-neek	cheesecake
szaszłyk m	*shash*-wik	shish kebab
śledź w śmietanie m	shlej v shmye-*ta*-nye	herring in sour cream
tatar m	*ta*-tar	minced sirloin served raw with onion, raw egg yolk & chopped dill cucumber
zapiekanka f	za-pye-*kan*-ka	half a bread roll filled with cheese & mushrooms, baked & served hot

emergencies

basics

Help!	*Na pomoc!*	na *po*·mots
Stop!	*Stój!*	stooy
Go away!	*Odejdź!*	o·deyj
Thief!	*Złodziej!*	zwo·jyey
Fire!	*Pożar!*	po·zhar
Watch out!	*Uważaj!*	oo·*va*·zhai
Call ...!	*Zadzwoń po ...!*	zad·zvon' po ...
a doctor	*lekarza*	le·*ka*·zha
an ambulance	*karetkę*	ka·*ret*·ke
the police	*policję*	po·*lee*·tsye

It's an emergency.
To nagły wypadek.   to *nag*·wi vi·*pa*·dek

Could you help me, please?
Czy może pan/pani mi pomóc? m/f   chi *mo*·zhe pan/*pa*·nee mee po·moots

Can I use the telephone?
Czy mogę użyć telefon?   chi *mo*·ge oo·zhich te·*le*·fon

I'm lost.
Zgubiłem/Zgubiłam się. m/f   zgoo·*bee*·wem/zgoo·*bee*·wam shye

Where are the toilets?
Gdzie są toalety?   gjye som to·a·*le*·ti

police

Where's the police station?
Gdzie jest posterunek policji?   gje yest pos·te·*roo*·nek po·*lee*·tsye

I want to report an offence.
Chciałem/Chciałam zgłosić   khchow·em/khchow·am zgwo·sheech
przestępstwo. m/f   pshe·*stemps*·tfo

I have insurance.
Mam ubezpieczenie.   mam oo·bes·pye·*che*·nye

I've been ...	Zostałem/Zostałam ... m/f	zo·stow·em/zo·stow·am ...
assaulted	napadnięty/a m/f	na·pad·nyen·ti/a
raped	zgwałcony/a m/f	zgvow·tso·ni/a
robbed	okradziony/a m/f	o·kra·jyo·ni/a

I've lost my ...	Zgubiłem/	zgoo·bee·wem/
	Zgubiłam ... m/f	zgoo·bee·wam ...
backpack	plecak	ple·tsak
bag	torbę	tor·be
credit card	kartę kredytową	kar·te kre·di·to·vom
handbag	torebkę	to·rep·ke
jewellery	biżuterię	bee·zhoo·ter·ye
money	pieniądze	pye·nyon·dze
passport	paszport	pash·port
wallet	portfel	port·fel

I want to contact my ...	Chcę się skontaktować z ...	khtse shye skon·tak·to·vach z ...
consulate	moim konsulatem	mo·yeem kon·soo·la·tem
embassy	moją ambasadą	mo·yom am·ba·sa·dom

health

medical needs

Where's the nearest ...?	Gdzie jest najbliższy/a ...? m/f	gjye yest nai·bleezh·shi/a ...
dentist	dentysta m	den·tis·ta
doctor	lekarz m	le·kash
hospital	szpital m	shpee·tal
(night) pharmacist	apteka (nocna) f	ap·te·ka (nots·na)

I need a doctor (who speaks English).
Szukam lekarza (który mówi po angielsku). — shoo·kam le·ka·zha (ktoo·ri moo·vee po an·gyel·skoo)

Could I see a female doctor?
Czy mogę się widzieć z lekarzem kobietą? — chi mo·ge shye vee·jyech z le·ka·zhem ko·bye·tom

I've run out of my medication.
Skończyły mi się lekarstwa. — skon·chi·wi mee shye le·kars·tfa

symptoms, conditions & allergies

I'm sick.	Jestem chory/a. m/f	yes·tem kho·ri/a
It hurts here.	Tutaj boli.	too·tai bo·lee
I have (a) ...	Mam ...	mam ...
asthma	astma f	ast·ma
constipation	zatwardzenie n	zat·far·dze·nye
cough	kaszel m	ka·shel
diarrhoea	rozwolnienie n	roz·vol·nye·nye
fever	gorączka f	go·ronch·ka
headache	ból głowy m	bool gwo·vi
heart condition	stan serca m	stan ser·tsa
nausea	mdłości pl	mdwosh·chee
pain	ból m	bool
sore throat	ból gardła m	bool gar·dwa
toothache	ból zęba m	bool zem·ba
I'm allergic to ...	Mam alergię na ...	mam a·ler·gye na ...
antibiotics	antybiotyki	an·ti·byo·ti·kee
anti-inflammatories	leki przeciwzapalne	le·kee pshe·cheef·za·pal·ne
aspirin	aspirynę	as·pee·ri·ne
bees	pszczoły	pshcho·wi
codeine	kodeinę	ko·de·ee·ne
penicillin	penicylinę	pe·nee·tsi·lee·ne
antiseptic	środki odkażające pl	shrod·kee od·ka·zha·yon·tse
bandage	bandaż m	ban·dash
condoms	kondom pl	kon·dom
contraceptives	środki	shrod·kee
	antykoncepcyjne pl	an·ti·kon·tsep·tsiy·ne
diarrhoea medicine	rozwolnienie	ros·vol·nye·nye
insect repellent	środek na owady m	shro·dek na o·va·di
laxatives	środek	shro·dek
	przeczyszczający m	pshe·chish·cha·yon·tsi
painkillers	środki	shrod·kee
	przeciwbólowe pl	pshe·cheef·boo·lo·ve
rehydration salts	sole fizjologiczne pl	so·le fee·zyo·lo·geech·ne
sleeping tablets	pigułki nasenne pl	pee·goow·kee na·se·ne

english–polish dictionary

Polish nouns in this dictionary have their gender indicated by ⓜ (masculine), ⓕ (feminine) or ⓝ (neuter).
If it's a plural noun, you'll also see pl. Adjectives are given in the masculine form only. Words are also marked
as a (adjective), v (verb), sg (singular), pl (plural), inf (informal) or pol (polite) where necessary.

A

accident *wypadek* ⓜ vi-*pa*-dek
accommodation *nocleg* ⓜ *nots*-leg
adaptor *zasilacz* ⓜ za-*shee*-lach
address *adres* ⓜ *a*-dres
after *po • za* po · za
air conditioning *klimatyzacja* ⓕ klee-ma-ti-*za*-tsya
airplane *samolot* ⓜ sa-*mo*-lot
airport *lotnisko* ⓝ lot-*nees*-ko
alcohol *alkohol* ⓜ al-*ko*-khol
all *wszystko* fshist-ko
allergy *alergia* ⓕ a-*ler*-gya
ambulance *karetka pogotowia* ⓕ
   ka-*ret*-ka po-go-*to*-vya
and *i* ee
ankle *kostka* ⓕ *kost*-ka
arm *ręka* ⓕ *ren*-ka
ashtray *popielniczka* ⓕ po-pyel-*neech*-ka
ATM *bankomat* ⓜ ban-*ko*-mat

B

baby *niemowlę* ⓝ nye-*mov*-le
back (body) *plecy* pl *ple*-tsi
backpack *plecak* ⓜ *ple*-tsak
bad *zły* zwi
bag *torba* ⓕ *tor*-ba
baggage claim *odbiór bagażu* ⓝ od-byoor ba-*ga*-zhoo
bank *bank* ⓜ bank
bar *bar* ⓜ bar
bathroom *łazienka* ⓕ wa-*zhyen*-ka
battery *bateria* ⓕ ba-*te*-rya
beautiful *piękny* pyen-kni
bed *łóżko* ⓝ *woozh*-ko
beer *piwo* ⓝ *pee*-vo
before *przed* pshet
behind *za* za
bicycle *rower* ⓜ *ro*-ver
big *duży* doo-zhi
bill *rachunek* ⓜ ra-*khoo*-nek
black *czarny* char-ni
blanket *koc* ⓜ kots

blood group *grupa krwi* ⓕ *groo*-pa krfee
blue *niebieski* nye-*byes*-kee
boat *łódź* ⓕ wooj
book (make a reservation) v *rezerwować*
   re-zer-*vo*-vach
bottle *butelka* ⓕ boo-*tel*-ka
bottle opener *otwieracz do butelek* ⓜ
   ot-*fye*-rach do boo-*te*-lek
boy *chłopiec* ⓜ *khwo*-pyets
brakes (car) *hamulce* pl ha-*mool*-tse
breakfast *śniadanie* ⓝ shnya-*da*-nye
broken (faulty) *połamany* po-wa-*ma*-ni
bus *autobus* ⓜ *ow*-to-boos
business *firma* ⓕ *feer*-ma
buy *kupować* koo-*po*-vach

C

café *kawiarnia* ⓕ ka-*vyar*-nya
camera *aparat* ⓜ a-*pa*-rat
camp site *kamping* ⓜ *kam*-peeng
cancel *unieważniać* oo-nye-*vazh*-nyach
can opener *otwieracz do konserw* ⓜ
   ot-*fye*-rach do kon-*serf*
car *samochód* ⓜ sa-*mo*-khoot
cash *gotówka* ⓕ go-*toof*-ka
cash (a cheque) v *zrealizować czek*
   zre-a-lee-*zo*-vach chek
cell phone *telefon komórkowy* ⓜ
   te-*le*-fon ko-moor-*ko*-vi
centre *środek* ⓜ *shro*-dek
change (money) v *rozmieniać* roz-*mye*-nyach
cheap *tani* ta-nee
check (bill) *sprawdzenie* ⓝ sprav-*dze*-nye
check-in *zameldowanie* ⓝ za-mel-do-*va*-nye
chest *klatka piersiowa* ⓕ *klat*-ka pyer-*shyo*-va
child *dziecko* ⓝ *jye*-tsko
cigarette *papieros* ⓜ pa-*pye*-ros
city *miasto* ⓝ *myas*-to
clean a *czysty* chi-sti
closed *zamknięty* zam-*knyen*-ti
coffee *kawa* ⓕ *ka*-va
coins *monety* pl mo-*ne*-ti
cold a *zimny* zheem-ni

collect call *rozmowa opłacona przez odbierającego* ⓘ
roz-mo-va ɔ-pwa-tso-na pshes od-bye-ra-yon-tse-go

come (by vehicle) *przyjść* pshiyshch

come (on foot) *przychodzić* pshi-kho-jeech

computer *komputer* ⓜ kom-poo-ter

condom *kondom* ⓜ kon-dom

contact lenses *soczewki kontaktowe* ⓘ pl
so-*chef*-kee kon-tak-to-ve

cook v *gotować* go-to-vach

cost *koszt* ⓜ kosht

credit card *karta kredytowa* ⓘ *kar*-ta kre-di-*to*-va

cup *filiżanka* ⓘ fee-lee-*zhan*-ka

currency exchange *kantor* ⓜ *kan*-tor

customs (immigration) *urząd celny* ⓜ
oo-zhont *tsel*-ni

D

dangerous *niebezpieczny* nye-bes-*pyech*-ni

date (time) *data* ⓘ *da*-ta

day *dzień* jyen

delay *opóźnienie* ⓘ o-poozh-*nye*-nye

dentist *dentysta* ⓜ den-*tis*-ta

depart *odjeżdżać* od-*yezh*-jach

diaper *pieluszka* ⓘ pye-*loosh*-ka

dictionary *słownik* ⓜ *swov*-neek

dinner *kolacja* ⓘ ko-*la*-tsya

direct *bezpośredni* bes-po-*shred*-nee

dirty *brudny* *brood*-ni

disabled *niepełnosprawny* nye-pew-no-*sprav*-ni

discount *zniżka* ⓘ *zneesh*-ka

doctor *lekarz* ⓜ *le*-kash

double bed *łóżko małżeńskie* ⓜ
woozh-ko mow-*zhen′*-skye

double room *pokój dwuosobowy* ⓜ
po-kooy dvoo-ɔ-so-*bo*-vi

drink *napój* ⓜ *na*-pooy

drive v *kierować* kye-ro-*vach*

drivers licence *prawo jazdy* ⓜ *pra*-vo *yaz*-di

drugs (illicit) *narkotyki* ⓜ pl nar-ko-*ti*-kee

dummy (pacifier) *smoczek* ⓜ *smo*-chek

E

ear *ucho* ⓜ *oo*-kho

east *wschód* ⓜ vskhood

eat *jeść* yeshch

economy class *klasa oszczędnościowa* ⓘ
kla-sa osh-chend-nosh-*ćiyo*-va

electricity *elektryczność* ⓘ e-lek-*trich*-noshch

elevator *winda* ⓘ *veen*-da

email *email* ⓜ e-mail

embassy *ambasada* ⓘ am-ba-*sa*-da

emergency *nagły przypadek* ⓜ *nag*-wi pshi-*pa*-dek

English (language) *angielski* an-*gyel*-skee

entrance *wejście* ⓜ *veysh*-chye

evening *wieczór* ⓜ *vye*-choor

exchange rate *kurs wymiany* ⓜ koors vi-*mya*-ni

exit *wyjście* ⓜ *viysh*-chye

expensive *drogi* *dro*-gee

express mail *list ekspresowy* ⓜ leest eks-pre-*so*-vi

eye *oko* ⓜ *o*-ko

F

far *daleki* da-*le*-kee

fast *szybki* *shib*-kee

father *ojciec* ⓜ *oy*-chyets

film (camera) *film* ⓜ feelm

finger *palec* ⓜ *pa*-lets

first-aid kit *apteczka pierwszej pomocy* ⓘ
ap-*tech*-ka pyerf-shey po-*mo*-tsi

first class *pierwsza klasa* ⓘ *pyerf*-sha *kla*-sa

fish *ryba* ⓘ *ri*-ba

food *żywność* ⓘ *zhiv*-noshch

foot *stopa* ⓘ *sto*-pa

fork *widelec* ⓜ vee-*de*-lets

free (of charge) *bezpłatny* bes-*pwat*-ni

friend *przyjaciel/przyjaciółka* ⓜ/ⓘ
pshi-ya-*chyel*/pshi-ya-*choow*-ka

fruit *owoc* ⓜ *o*-vots

full *pełny* *pew*-ni

funny *zabawny* za-*bav*-ni

G

gift *prezent* ⓜ *pre*-zent

girl *dziewczyna* ⓘ jyev-*chi*-na

glass (drinking) *szklanka* ⓘ *shklan*-ka

glasses *okulary* pl o-koo-*la*-ri

go (by vehicle) *jechać* *ye*-khach

go (on foot) *iść* eeshch

good *dobry* *do*-bri

green *zielony* zhye-*lo*-ni

guide *przewodnik* ⓜ pshe-*vod*-neek

H

half *połówka* ⓘ po-*woof*-ka

hand *ręka* ⓘ *ren*-ka

handbag *torebka* ⓘ to-*rep*-ka

happy *szczęśliwy* shchen-*shlee*-vi

have *mieć* myech

he *on* on

head *głowa* ① *gwo*-va
heart *serce* ⓝ *ser*-tse
heat *upał* ⓜ *oo*-pow
heavy *ciężki* *chyensh*-kee
help ∨ *pomagać* po-*ma*-gach
here *tutaj* *too*-tai
high *wysoki* vi-*so*-kee
highway *szosa* ① *sho*-sa
hike ∨ *wędrować* ven-*dro*-vach
holiday *święto* ⓝ *shyen*-to
homosexual n *homoseksualista* ⓜ
ho-mo-sek-soo-a-*lees*-ta
hospital *szpital* ⓜ *shpee*-tal
hot *gorący* go-*ron*-tsi
hotel *hotel* ⓜ *ho*-tel
hungry *głodny* *gwo*-dni
husband *mąż* ⓜ monzh

I

I *ja* ya
identification (card) *dowód tożsamości* ⓜ
do-vood tozh-sa-*mosh*-chee
ill *chory* *kho*-ri
important *ważny* *vazh*-ni
included *wliczony* vlee-*cho*-ni
injury *rana* ① *ra*-na
insurance *ubezpieczenie* ⓝ oo-bes-pye-*che*-nye
Internet *internet* ⓜ een-*ter*-net
interpreter *tłumacz/tłumaczka* ⓜ / ①
twoo-mach/twoo-*mach*-ka

J

jewellery *biżuteria* ① bee-zhoo-*ter*-ya
job *praca* ① *pra*-tsa

K

key *klucz* ⓜ klooch
kilogram *kilogram* ⓜ kee-*lo*-gram
kitchen *kuchnia* ① *kookh*-nya
knife *nóż* ⓜ noosh

L

laundry (place) *pralnia* ① *pral*-nya
lawyer *prawnik* ⓜ *prav*-neek
left (direction) *lewy* ① *le*-vi
left-luggage office *przechowalnia bagażu* ①
pshe-kho-*val*-nya ba-*ga*-zhoo

leg *noga* ① *no*-ga
lesbian n *lesbijka* ① les-*beey*-ka
less *mniej* mnyey
letter (mail) *list* ⓜ leest
lift (elevator) *winda* ① *veen*-da
light *światło* ⓝ *shvyat*-wo
like ∨ *lubić* *loo*-beech
lock *zamek* ⓜ *za*-mek
long *długi* *dwoo*-gee
lost *zgubiony* zgoo-*byo*-ni
lost-property office *biuro rzeczy znalezionych* ⓝ
byoo-ro zhe-chi zna-le-*zhyo*-nikh
love ∨ *kochać* *ko*-khach
luggage *bagaż* ⓜ *ba*-gash
lunch *lunch* ⓜ lanch

M

mail (letters) *list* ⓜ leest
mail (postal system) *poczta* ① *poch*-ta
man *mężczyzna* ⓜ menzh-*chiz*-na
map (of country) *mapa* ① *ma*-pa
map (of town) *plan* ⓜ plan
market *rynek* ⓜ *ri*-nek
matches *zapałki* ① pl za-*pow*-kee
meat *mięso* ⓝ *myen*-so
medicine *lekarstwo* ⓝ le-*karst*-fo
menu *jadłospis* ⓜ ya-*dwo*-spees
message *wiadomość* ① vya-*do*-moshch
milk *mleko* ⓝ *mle*-ko
minute *minuta* ① mee-*noo*-ta
mobile phone *telefon komórkowy* ⓜ
te-le-fon ko-moor-*ko*-vi
money *pieniądze* ① pl pye-*nyon*-dze
month *miesiąc* ⓜ *mye*-shonts
morning *rano* ⓝ *ra*-no
mother *matka* ① *mat*-ka
motorcycle *motor* ⓜ *mo*-tor
motorway *autostrada* ① ow-to-*stra*-da
mouth *usta* pl *oos*-ta
music *muzyka* ① *moo*-zi-ka

N

name *imię* ⓝ *ee*-mye
napkin *serwetka* ① ser-*vet*-ka
nappy *pieluszka* ① pye-*loosh*-ka
near *bliski* *blees*-kee
neck *szyja* ① *shi*-ya
new *nowy* *no*-vi
news *wiadomości* ① pl vya-do-*mosh*-chee
newspaper *gazeta* ① ga-*ze*-ta
night *noc* ① nots

o *nie* nye
noisy *hałaśliwy* ha-wa-*shlee*-vi
nonsmoking *niepalący* nye-pa-*lon*-tsi
north *północ* @ *poow*-nots
nose *nos* @ nos
now *teraz* *te*-ras
number *numer* @ *noo*-mer

O

oil (engine) *olej* @ *o*-ley
old *stary* *sta*-ri
one-way ticket *bilet w jedną stronę* @
   bee-let v yed-nom *stro*-ne
open a *otwarty* ot-*far*-ti
outside *na zewnątrz* na zev-*nontsh*

P

package *paczka* ① *pach*-ka
paper *papier* @ *pa*-pyer
park (car) v *parkować* par-*ko*-vach
passport *paszport* @ *pash*-port
pay *płacić* *pwa*-cheech
pen *długopis* @ dwoo-*go*-pees
petrol *benzyna* ① ben-*zi*-na
pharmacy *apteka* ① ap-*te*-ka
phonecard *karta telefoniczna* ① *kar*-ta te-le-fo-*neech*-na
photo *zdjęcie* @ *zdyen*-chye
plate *talerz* @ *ta*-lesh
Poland *Polska* ① *pol*-ska
police *policja* ① po-*lee*-tsya
Polish (language) *polski* @ *pol*-skee
postcard *pocztówka* ① poch-*toof*-ka
post office *urząd pocztowy* ① *oo*-zhond poch-*to*-vi
pregnant *w ciąży* v chyon-zhi
price *cena* ① *tse*-na

Q

quiet *cichy* chee-khi

R

rain *deszcz* @ deshch
razor *brzytwa* ① *bzhit*-fa
receipt *rachunek* ① ra-*khoo*-nek
red *czerwony* cher-*vo*-ni
refund *zwrot pieniędzy* @ zvrot pye-*nyen*-dzi
registered mail *list polecony* @ leest po-le-*tso*-ni
rent v *wynająć* vi-*na*-yonch

repair v *naprawić* na-*pra*-veech
reservation *rezerwacja* ① re-zer-*va*-tsya
restaurant *restauracja* ① res-tow-*ra*-tsya
return v *wracać* vra-*tsach*
return ticket *bilet powrotny* @ *bee*-let po-*vro*-tni
right (direction) *prawoskrętny* pra-vo-*skrent*-ni
road *droga* ① *dro*-ga
room *pokój* @ *po*-kooy

S

safe a *bezpieczny* bes-*pyech*-ni
sanitary napkin *podpaski higieniczne* ① pl
   pod-*pas*-kee hee-gye-*neech*-ne
seat *miejsce* @ *myeys*-tse
send *wysyłać* vi-*si*-wach
service station *stacja obsługi* ① *sta*-tsya ob-*swoo*-gee
sex *seks* @ seks
shampoo *szampon* @ *sham*-pon
share (a dorm) v *mieszkać z kimś* *myesh*-kach z keemsh
shaving cream *krem do golenia* @ krem do go-*le*-nya
she *ona* *o*-na
sheet (bed) *prześcieradło* ① pshesh-chye-*ra*-dwo
shirt *koszula* ① ko-*shoo*-la
shoes *buty* @ pl *boo*-ti
shop *sklep* @ sklep
short *krótki* *kroot*-kee
shower *prysznic* @ *prish*-neets
single room *pokój jednoosobowy* @
   po-kooy ye-dno-o-so-*bo*-vi
skin *skóra* ① *skoo*-ra
skirt *spódnica* ① spood-*nee*-tsa
sleep v *spać* spach
slowly *powoli* po-*vo*-lee
small *mały* *ma*-wi
smoke (cigarettes) v *palić* *pa*-leech
soap *mydło* ① *mid*-wo
some *kilka* *keel*-ka
soon *wkrótce* *fkroot*-tse
south *południe* ① po-*wood*-nye
souvenir shop *sklep z pamiątkami* @
   sklep z pa-*myont*-ka-mi
speak *mówić* *moo*-veech
spoon *łyżka* ① *wish*-ka
stamp *znaczek* @ *zna*-chek
stand-by ticket *bilet z listy rezerwowej* @
   bee-let z *lees*-ti re-zer-*vo*-vey
station (train) *stacja* ① *sta*-tsya
stomach *żołądek* @ zho-*won*-dek
stop v *przestać* pshes-*tach*
stop (bus) *przystanek* @ pshis-*ta*-nek
street *ulica* ① oo-*lee*-tsa
student *student* @ *stoo*-dent

sun *słońce* ⓝ swon'-tse
sunscreen *krem przeciwsłoneczny* ⓜ
  krem pshe-cheef-swo-*nech*-ni
swim v *pływać* pwi-vach

T

tampon *tampon* ⓜ tam-pon
taxi *taksówka* ⓕ tak-*soof*-ka
teaspoon *łyżeczka* ⓕ wi-*zhech*-ka
teeth *zęby* ⓜ pl zem-bi
telephone *telefon* ⓜ te-le-fon
television *telewizja* ⓕ te-le-*veez*-ya
temperature (weather) *temperatura* ⓕ
  tem-pe-ra-*too*-ra
tent *namiot* ⓜ *na*-myot
that (one) *który* ktoo-ri
they *oni* o-nee
thirsty *spragniony* sprag-*nyo*-ni
this (one) *ten* ⓜ ten
throat *gardło* gard-wo
ticket *bilet* ⓜ bee-let
time *czas* ⓜ chas
tired *zmęczony* zmen-cho-ni
tissues *chusteczki* ⓕ pl khoos-*tech*-kee
today *dzisiaj* jee-shyai
toilet *toaleta* ⓕ to-a-*le*-ta
tomorrow *jutro* yoo-tro
tonight *dzisiaj wieczorem* jee-shyai vye-*cho*-rem
toothbrush *szczotka do zębów* ⓕ *shchot*-ka do *zem*-boof
toothpaste *pasta do zębów* ⓕ *pas*-ta do zem-boof
torch (flashlight) *latarka* ⓕ la-*tar*-ka
tour *wycieczka* ⓕ vi-*chyech*-ka
tourist office *biuro turystyczne* ⓜ byoo-ro too-ris-*tich*-ne
towel *ręcznik* ⓜ rench-neek
train *pociąg* ⓜ po-chyonk
translate *przetłumaczyć* pshe-twoo-*ma*-chich
travel agency *biuro podróży* ⓜ byoo-ro po-*droo*-zhi
travellers cheques *czeki podróżne* ⓜ pl
  che-kee po-*droozh*-ne
trousers *spodnie* pl *spo*-dnye
twin beds *dwa łóżka* ⓝ pl dva *woosh*-ka
tyre *opona* ⓕ o-*po*-na

U

underwear *bielizna* ⓕ bye-*leez*-na
urgent *pilny* peel-ni

V

vacant *wolny* vol-ni
vacation *wakacje* pl va-*ka*-tsye
vegetable *warzywo* ⓝ va-zhi-vo
vegetarian a *wegetariański* ve-ge-tar-*yan'*-skee
visa *wiza* ⓕ vee-za

W

waiter *kelner* ⓜ kel-ner
walk v *spacerować* spa-tse-*ro*-vach
wallet *portfel* ⓜ port-fel
warm a *ciepły* chyep-wi
Warsaw *Warszawa* ⓕ var-sha-va
wash (something) *prać* prach
watch *zegarek* ⓜ ze-*ga*-rek
water *woda* ⓕ vo-da
we *my* mi
weekend *weekend* ⓜ wee-kend
west *zachód* ⓜ za-khood
wheelchair *wózek inwalidzki* ⓜ
  voo-zek een-va-*leets*-kee
when *kiedy* kye-di
where *gdzie* gjye
white *biały* bya-wi
who *kto* kto
why *dlaczego* dla-*che*-go
wife *żona* ⓕ zho-na
window *okno* ⓝ *ok*-no
wine *wino* ⓝ vee-no
with *z* z
without *bez* bes
woman *kobieta* ⓕ ko-*bye*-ta
write *pisać* pee-sach

Y

yellow *żółty* zhoow-ti
yes *tak* tak
yesterday *wczoraj* fcho-rai
you sg inf *ty* ti
you sg pol *pan/pani* ⓜ/ⓕ pan/*pa*-nee
you pl inf *wy* vi
you pl pol *panowie/panie* ⓜ/ⓕ pa-*no*-vye/*pa*-nye
you pl pol *państwo* ⓜ & ⓕ *pan'*-stfo

Slovak

slovak alphabet

A a uh	Á á dl-hair a	Ä ä shi-ro-kair e	B b bair	C c tsair	Č č ch
D d dair	Ď ď dy	Dz dz dz	Dž dž j	E e e	É é dl-hair air
F f ef	G g gair	H h ha	Ch ch kh	I i i	Í í dl-hair ee
J j yair	K k ka	L l el	Ĺ ĺ dl-hair el	Ľ ľ ly	M m em
N n en	Ň ň ny	O o o	Ó ó dl-hair aw	Ô ô wo	P p pair
Q q quair	R r er	Ŕ ŕ dl-hair er	S s es	Š š sh	T t tair
Ť ť ty	U u u	Ú ú dl-hair oo	V v vair	W w dvo-yi-tair vair	X x iks
Y y ip-si-lon	Ý ý ee	Z z zet	Ž ž zh		

SLOVENČINA

■ slovak

Poland

Czech
Republic

• Žilina

SLOVAKIA

• Prešov
• Košice

• Banská Bystrica

Ukraine

Trnava
• Nitra

⊗ *Bratislava*

Austria

Hungary

Danube

Romania

0 ———— 100 km
0 ———— 50 mi

introduction

The cosy position of the Slovak language (slovenčina slo·ven·chi·na) in Central Europe makes it a perfect base for learning or understanding the languages of other Slavic nations. It shares certain features with its close relatives in the West Slavic group – Czech and Polish. To a lesser extent, Slovak is similar to the South Slavic languages (particularly Slovene, from which it was distanced by the arrival of the Hungarians to their present day homeland in the 9th century). There are even similarities between Slovak and Ukranian, which represents the East Slavic branch.

Not surprisingly, however, the language that bears the closest resemblance to Slovak is Czech, since ties between the two now independent countries date back to the 9th century and the Great Moravian Empire. More recently, the 20th-century Czechoslovakian affair established even closer relations between Czech and Slovak, to the extent that the two languages are mutually intelligible (although less so in the colloquial form or among the younger generation). Hungarian influence on Slovak (mainly in the vocabulary) is a result of the centuries during which Slovaks formed first part of the Kingdom of Hungary, and later the Austro-Hungarian Empire.

The literary standard of Slovak emerged in the mid-19th century, during a national revival movement marked on the linguistic front by the work of L'udovít Štúr. In earlier times, it was mostly a spoken language, subordinated in writing to Latin and Czech, although texts with elements of Slovak or written entirely in Slovak can be traced back to the 15th century. The Great Moravian Empire was originally the place of St Cyril and Methodius' mission, which used the Glagolitic script, the precursor of the Cyrillic alphabet, for Old Church Slavonic literature. However, the West Slavic languages, including Slovak, soon adopted the Roman alphabet due to the influence of the Catholic Church.

Since 1993, Slovak has stepped out of the shadow of its larger neighbour, Czech, with which it shared official status during the Czechoslovakian days. It is now the official language of about 5 million speakers in Slovakia and there are Slovak speaking minorities in Poland, Hungary, Romania, Ukraine, the northern Serbian province of Vojvodina, and of course, the Czech Republic.

Even if you don't speak Slovak, be sure to look up your name in the official Slovak calendar – in which each day corresponds to a personal name and entitles people to celebrate their 'name day' (sviatok svyuh·tok or meniny me·nyi·ni) with equal pomp as their birthday!

pronunciation

vowel sounds

Slovak is rich in vowels, including a number of vowel combinations (or 'diphthongs').

symbol	english equivalent	slovak example	transliteration
a	father	*pán*	pan
ai	aisle	*raňajky*	*ruh*·nyai·ki
air	hair	*volné*	*vol*·**nair**
aw	law	*pól*	pawl
e	bet	*sestra, mäso*	*ses*·truh, *me*·so
ee	see	*prosím, bývať*	*pro*·seem, *bee*·vuht'
ey	hey	*olej*	*o*·ley
i	bit	*izba, byt*	*iz*·buh, bit
o	pot	*meno*	*me*·no
oh	oh	*zmesou*	*zme*·**soh**
oo	zoo	*pavúk*	*puh*·**vook**
ow	how	*auto*	*ow*·to
oy	toy	*ahoj*	*a*·hoy
uh	run	*matka*	*muht*·kuh
wo	quote	*môžem*	*mwo*·zhem

word stress

In Slovak, stress always falls on the first syllable, but it's quite light.

consonant sounds

Slovak consonants are shown opposite. Most have equivalents in English.

symbol	english equivalent	slovak example	transliteration
b	bed	*obed*	o·**bed**
ch	cheat	*večer*	ve·**cher**
d	dog	*adresa*	uh·**dre**·suh
dy	during	*ďaleko, džem*	**dyuh**·le·ko, **dyem**
dz	adds	*prichádza*	pri·kha·**dzuh**
f	fat	*fotka*	**fot**·kuh
g	go	*margarin*	muhr·**guh**·reen
h	hat	*hlava*	**hluh**·vuh
k	kit	*oko*	**o**·ko
kh	loch	*chorý*	**kho**·ree
l	lot	*lampa*	**luhm**·puh
ly	million	*doľava*	do·**lyuh**·vuh
m	man	*matka*	**muht**·kuh
n	not	*noviny*	**no**·vi·ni
ny	canyon	*kuchyňa*	ku·khi·**nyuh**
p	pet	*pero*	**pe**·ro
r	run	*ráno*	**ra**·no
s	sun	*sukňa*	**suk**·nyuh
sh	shot	*štyri*	**shti**·ri
t	top	*tri*	**tri**
ts	hats	*anglicky*	uhng·**lits**·ki
ty	tutor	*ťava*	**tyuh**·vuh
v	very	*vízum, watt*	**vee**·zum, **vuht**
y	yes	*ja*	**yuh**
z	zero	*zub*	**zub**
zh	pleasure	*manžel*	muhn·**zhel**
'	a slight y sound	*meď*	med'

tools

language difficulties

Do you speak English?
Hovoríte po anglicky?   ho·vo·ree·tye po *uhng*·lits·ki

Do you understand?
Rozumiete?   ro·zu·mye·tye

I understand.
Rozumiem.   ro·zu·myem

I don't understand.
Nerozumiem.   nye·ro·zu·myem

What does (*jablko*) mean?
Čo znamená (jablko)?   cho znuh·me·na (*yuh*·bl·ko)

How do you ...?	*Ako sa ...?*	*uh*·ko suh ...
pronounce this	*toto vyslovuje*	*to*·to *vi*·slo·vu·ye
write (*cesta*)	*píše (cesta)*	pee·she (*tses*·tuh)

Could you please ...?	*Môžete prosím ...?*	mwo·zhe·tye pro·seem ...
repeat that	*to zopakovať*	to zo·puh·ko·vuht'
speak more slowly	*hovoriť pomalšie*	ho·vo·riť *po*·muhl·shye
write it down	*to napísať*	to nuh·pee·suht'

essentials

Yes.	*Áno.*	*a*·no
No.	*Nie.*	*ni*·ye
Please.	*Prosím.*	pro·seem
Thank you	*Ďakujem*	dyuh·ku·yem
(very much).	*(veľmi pekne).*	(*veľ*·mi *pek*·nye)
You're welcome.	*Prosím.*	pro·seem
Excuse me.	*Prepáčte.*	pre·pach·tye
Sorry.	*Prepáčte.*	pre·pach·tye

numbers

0	*nula*	*nu·luh*	15	*pätnásť*	*pet·nast'*	
1	*jeden* m	*ye·den*	16	*šestnásť*	*shes·nast'*	
	jedna f	*yed·na*	17	*sedemnásť*	*se·dyem·nast'*	
	jedno n	*yed·no*	18	*osemnásť*	*o·sem·nast'*	
2	*dva* m	*dvuh*	19	*devätnásť*	*dye·vet·nast'*	
	dve n/f	*dve*	20	*dvadsať*	*dvuh·tsuht'*	
3	*tri*	*tri*	21	*dvadsať-*	*dvuh·tsuht'·*	
4	*štyri*	*shti·ri*		*jeden*	*ye·den*	
5	*päť*	*pet'*	22	*dvadsaťdva*	*dvuh·tsuht'·dvuh*	
6	*šesť*	*shest'*	30	*tridsať*	*tri·tsuht'*	
7	*sedem*	*se·dyem*	40	*štyridsať*	*shti·ri·tsuht'*	
8	*osem*	*o·sem*	50	*päťdesiat*	*pe·dye·syuht*	
9	*deväť*	*dye·vet'*	60	*šesťdesiat*	*shes·dye·syuht*	
10	*desať*	*dye·suht'*	70	*sedemdesiat*	*se·dyem·dye·syuht*	
11	*jedenásť*	*ye·de·nast'*	80	*osemdesiat*	*o·sem·dye·syuht*	
12	*dvanásť*	*dvuh·nast'*	90	*deväťdesiat*	*dye·ve·dye·syuht*	
13	*trinásť*	*tri·nast'*	100	*sto*	*sto*	
14	*štrnásť*	*shtr·nast'*	1000	*tisíc*	*tyi·seets*	

time & dates

What time is it?	*Koľko je hodín?*	*koľ·ko ye ho·dyeen*
It's one o'clock.	*Je jedna hodina.*	*ye yed·nuh ho·dyi·nuh*
It's (two) o'clock.	*Sú (dve) hodiny.*	*soo (dve) ho·dyi·ni*
Quarter past (one).	*Štvrť na (dve).*	*shtvrt' nuh (dve)*
Half past (one).	*Pól (druhej).*	*pol (dru·hey)*
	(lit: half two)	
Quarter to (eight).	*Tri štvrte na (osem).*	*tri·shtvr·tye nuh (o·sem)*
At what time ...?	*O koľkej ...?*	*o koľ·key ...*
At ...	*O ...*	*o ...*
am (before 10)	*ráno*	*ra·no*
pm (10 to 12)	*dobedu*	*do·be·du*
pm	*pobede*	*po·be·dye*

Monday	pondelok	pon·dye·lok
Tuesday	utorok	u·to·rok
Wednesday	streda	stre·duh
Thursday	štvrtok	shtvr·tok
Friday	piatok	pyuh·tok
Saturday	sobota	so·bo·tuh
Sunday	nedeľa	nye·dye·lyuh
January	január	yuh·nu·ar
February	február	feb·ru·ar
March	marec	muh·rets
April	apríl	uhp·reel
May	máj	mai
June	jún	yoon
July	júl	yool
August	august	ow·gust
September	september	sep·tem·ber
October	október	ok·taw·ber
November	november	no·vem·ber
December	december	de·tsem·ber

What date is it today?
Koľkého je dnes?   kol·kair·ho ye dnyes

It's (15 December).
Je (pätnásteho decembra).   ye (pet·nas·te·ho de·tsem·bruh)

since (May)	od (mája)	od (ma·yuh)
until (June)	do (júna)	do (yoo·nuh)
last night	minulú noc	mi·nu·loo nots
last/next ...	minulý/budúci ...	mi·nu·lee/bu·doo·tsi ...
week	týždeň	teezh·dyen'
month	mesiac	me·syuhts
year	rok	rok
yesterday/tomorrow ...	včera/zajtra ...	vche·ruh/zai·truh ...
morning	ráno	ra·no
afternoon	popoludnie	po·po·lud·ni·ye
evening	večer	ve·cher

weather

What's the weather like?	*Aké je počasie?*	*uh*·kair ye *po*·chuh·si·ye

It's ...

cloudy	*Je zamračené.*	ye *zuh*·mruh·che·nair
cold	*Je zima.*	ye *zi*·muh
hot	*Je horúco.*	ye *ho*·roo·tso
raining	*Prší.*	*pr*·shee
snowing	*Sneží.*	*sne*·zhee
sunny	*Je slnečno.*	ye *sl*·nyech·no
warm	*Je teplo.*	ye *tyep*·lo
windy	*Je veterno.*	ye *ve*·tyer·no

spring	*jar* f	yuhr
summer	*leto* n	*le*·to
autumn	*jeseň* f	ye·sen'
winter	*zima* f	*zi*·muh

border crossing

I'm here ...	*Som* ...	som tu ...
on business	*v obchodnej*	v *ob*·khod·ney
	záležitosti	za·le·zhi·tos·tyi
on holiday	*na dovolenke*	nuh *do*·vo·len·ke

I'm here for ...	*Som tu na* ...	som tu nuh ...
(10) days	*(desať) dni*	*(dye*·suht') dnyee
(two) months	*(dva) mesiace*	(dvuh) *me*·syuh·tse
(three) weeks	*(tri) týždne*	(tri) *teezhd*·nye

I'm going to (Bratislava).
Idem do (Bratislavy). — *i*·dyem do (*bruh*·tyi·sluh·vi)

I'm staying at the (Hotel Grand).
Zostávam v (hoteli Grand). — zo·sta·vuhm v (*ho*·te·li gruhnd)

I have nothing to declare.
Nemám nič na preclenie. — *nye*·mam nyich nuh *prets*·le·ni·ye

I have something to declare.
Mám niečo na preclenie. — mam ni·*ye*·cho nuh *prets*·le·ni·ye

That's (not) mine.
To (nie) je moje. — to (*ni*·ye) ye *mo*·ye

transport

tickets & luggage

Where can I buy a ticket?
Kde si môžem kúpiť
cestovný lístok?
kdye si *mwo*·zhem *koo*·pit'
tses·tov·nee *lees*·tok

Do I need to book a seat?
Potrebujem si rezervovať
miestenku?
po·tre·bu·yem si *re*·zer·vo·vuht'
myes·tyen·ku

One ... ticket	*Jeden ... lístok*	ye·den ... *lees*·tok
(to Poprad), please.	*(do Popradu), prosím.*	(do *pop*·ruh·du) *pro*·seem
one-way	*jednosmerný*	yed·no·smer·nee
return	*spiatočný*	spyuh·toch·nee

I'd like to ... my	*Chcel/Chcela by som ...*	khtsel/*khtse*·luh bi som ...
ticket, please.	*môj lístok, prosím.* m/f	mwoy *lees*·tok *pro*·seem
cancel	*zrušiť*	zru·shit'
change	*zmeniť*	zme·nyit'
collect	*vyzdvihnúť*	vizd·vih·noot'
confirm	*potvrdiť*	po·tvr·dyit'

I'd like a ... seat, please.	*Prosím si ... miesto.*	*pro*·seem si ... *mye*·sto
nonsmoking	*nefajčiarske*	nye·fai·chyuhr·ske
smoking	*fajčiarske*	fai·chyuhr·ske

How much is it?
Koľko to stojí?
kol'·ko to *sto*·yee

Is there air conditioning?
Je tam klimatizácia?
ye tuhm *kli*·muh·ti·za·tsi·yuh

Is there a toilet?
Je tam toaleta?
ye tuhm *to*·uh·le·tuh

How long does the trip take?
Koľko trvá cesta?
kol'·ko tr·va tses·tuh

Is it a direct route?
Je to priamy smer?
ye to *pryuh*·mi smer

I'd like a luggage locker.
Chcel/Chcela by som skrinku
na batožinu. m/f
khtsel/*khtse*·luh bi som *skrin*·ku
nuh *buh*·to·zhi·nu

My luggage has been ...   *Moja batožina ...*   *mo·yuh buh·to·zhi·nuh ...*
- **damaged**   *bola poškodená*   *bo·luh posh·ko·dye·na*
- **lost**   *sa stratila*   suh *struh·tyi·luh*
- **stolen**   *bola ukradnutá*   *bo·luh u·kruhd·nu·ta*

getting around

Where does flight (number 333) arrive?
    Kam prilieta let   kuhm *pri·li·ye·tuh* let
    (číslo 333)?   (*chees·*lo *tri·*sto·*tri·tsat'·*tri)

Where does flight (number 333) depart?
    Odkiaľ odlieta let   *od·*kyuhl *od·*li·ye·tuh let
    (číslo 333)?   (*chees·*lo *tri·*sto·*tri·tsat'·*tri)

Where's (the) ...?   *Kde je ...?*   kdye ye ...
- **arrivals hall**   *príletová hala*   *pree·*le·to·va *huh·*luh
- **departures hall**   *odletová hala*   *od·*le·to·va *huh·*luh
- **duty-free shop**   *duty-free obchod*   *uyu·*ti-free *ob·*khod
- **gate (12)**   *vchod (dvanásť)*   vkhod (*dvuh·*nast')

Is this the ...   *Je toto ...*   ye *to·*to ...
to (Komárno)?   *do (Komárna)?*   do (*ko·*mar·nuh)
- **boat**   *loď*   lod'
- **bus**   *autobus*   *ow·*to·bus
- **plane**   *lietadlo*   li·*ye·*tuhd·lo
- **train**   *vlak*   vluhk

What time's the ... bus?   *Kedy príde ... autobus?*   ke·di *pree·*dye ... *ow·*to·bus
- **first**   *prvý*   *pr·*vee
- **last**   *posledný*   po·sled·nee
- **next**   *nasledujúci*   *nuh·*sle·du·yoo·tsi

At what time does it arrive/leave?
    O koľkej prichádza/odchádza?   o *kol'·*key *pri·*khu·dzuh/*od·*kha·dzuh

How long will it be delayed?
    Koľko je spozdenie?   *kol'·*ko ye *spoz·*dye·ni·ye

What station/stop is this?
    Ktorá stanica/zastávka je toto?   *kto·*ra *stuh·*nyi·tsuh/*zuhs·*tav·kuh ye *to·*to

What's the next station/stop?
    Ktorá je nasledujúca   *kto·*ra ye *nuh·*sle·du·yoo·tsuh
    stanica/zastávka?   *stuh·*nyi·tsuh/*zuhs·*tav·kuh

Does it stop at (Štúrovo námestie)?
Stojí to na (Štúrovom námestí)? sto·yee to nuh (shtoo·ro·vom na·mes·tyee)

Please tell me when we get to (Hlavné námestie).
Môžete ma prosím upozorniť mwo·zhe·tye muh pro·seem u·po·zor·nyit'
keď budeme na ... ked' bu·dye·me nuh ...

How long do we stop here?
Ako dlho tu budeme stáť? uh·ko dl·ho tu bu·dye·me stat'

Is this seat available?
Je toto miesto voľné? ye to·to mye·sto vol·nair

That's my seat.
Toto je moje miesto. to·to ye mo·ye mye·sto

I'd like a taxi ...	*Chcel/Chcela by*	khtsel/khtse·luh bi
	som taxík na ... m/f	som tuhk·seek nuh ...
at (9am)	*(deviatu ráno)*	*(dye·vyuh·tu ra·no)*
now	*teraz*	*te·ruhz*
tomorrow	*zajtra*	*zai·truh*

Is this taxi available?
Je tento taxík voľný? ye ten·to tuhk·seek vol'·nee

How much is it to ...?
Koľko to bude stáť do ...? kol'·ko to bu·dye stat' do ...

Please put the meter on.
Zapnite taxameter, prosím. zuhp·nyi·tye tuhk·suh·me·ter pro·seem

Please take me to (this address).
Zavezte ma (na túto adresu), zuh·vez·tye muh (nuh too·to uh·dre·su)
prosím. pro·seem

Please ...	*..., prosím.*	... pro·seem
slow down	*Spomaľte*	spo·muhl'·tye
stop here	*Zastavte tu*	zuhs·tuhv·tye tu
wait here	*Počkajte tu*	poch·kai·tye tu

car, motorbike & bicycle hire

I'd like to hire a ...	*Chcel/Chcela by som si*	khtsel/khtse·luh bi som si
	prenajať ... m/f	pre·nuh·yuht' ...
bicycle	*bicykel*	bi·tsi·kel
car	*auto*	ow·to
motorbike	*motorku*	mo·tor·ku

with ...	s ...	s ...
a driver	šoférom	sho·fair·rom
air conditioning	klimatizáciou	kli·muh·ti·za·tsi·oh
antifreeze	protimrazovou	pro·tyi·mruh·zo·voh
	zmesou	zme·soh
snow chains	snehovými	snye·ho·vee·mi
	reťazami	re·tyuh·zuh·mi
How much for	Koľko stojí	koľ·ko sto·yee
... hire?	prenájom na ...?	pre·na·yom nuh ...
hourly	hodinu	ho·dyi·nu
daily	deň	dyen'
weekly	týždeň	teezh·dyen'
air	stlačený vzduch m	stluh·che·nee vzdukh
oil	olej m	o·ley
petrol	benzín m	ben·zeen
tyres	pneumatiky f pl	pne·u·muh·ti·ki

I need a mechanic.
Potrebujem automechanika. — po·tre·bu·yem ow·to·me·khuh·ni·kuh

I've run out of petrol.
Minul sa mi benzín. — mi·nul suh mi ben·zeen

I have a flat tyre.
Dostal/Dostala som defekt. m/f — dos·tuhl/dos·tuh·luh som de·fekt

directions

Where's the ...?	Kde je ...?	kdye ye ...
bank	banka	buhn·kuh
city centre	mestské centrum	mes·kair tsen·trum
hotel	hotel	ho·tel
market	trh	trh
police station	policajná stanica	po·li·tsai·na stuh·nyi·tsuh
post office	pošta	posh·tuh
public toilet	verejný záchod	ve·rey·nee za·khod
tourist office	turistická	tu·ris·tits·ka
	kancelária	kuhn·tse·la·ri·yuh

Is this the road to ...? *Je toto cesta na ...?* — ye to·to tses·tuh nuh ...

Can you show me (on the map)?
Môžete mi ukázať (na mape)?
mwo·zhe·tye mi u·ka·zuht' (nuh muh·pe)

What's the address?
Aká je adresa?
uh·ka ye uh·dre·suh

How far is it?
Ako je to ďaleko?
uh·ko ye to dyuh·le·ko

How do I get there?
Ako sa tam dostanem?
uh·ko suh tuhm dos·tuh·nyem

Turn ...	*Zabočte ...*	zuh·boch·tye ...
at the corner	*na rohu*	nuh ro·hu
at the traffic lights	*na svetelnej križovatke*	nuh sve·tyel·ney kri·zho·vuht·ke
left	*doľava*	do·lyuh·vuh
right	*doprava*	do·pruh·vuh

It's ...	*Je to ...*	ye to ...
behind ...	*za ...*	zuh ...
far away	*ďaleko*	dyuh·le·ko
here	*tu*	tu
in front of ...	*pred ...*	pred ...
left	*vľavo*	vlyuh·vo
near (to ...)	*blízko (k ...)*	bleez·ko (k ...)
next to ...	*vedľa ...*	ved·lyuh ...
on the corner	*na rohu*	nuh ro·hu
opposite ...	*oproti ...*	o·pro·tyi ...
right	*vpravo*	vpruh·vo
straight ahead	*rovno*	rov·no
there	*tam*	tuhm

by bus	*autobusom*	ow·to·bu·som
by taxi	*taxíkom*	tuhk·see·kom
by train	*vlakom*	vluh·kom
on foot	*peši*	pe·shi

north	*sever*	se·ver
south	*juh*	yooh
east	*východ*	vee·khod
west	*západ*	za·puhd

Vchod/Východ	vkhod/vee-khod	Entrance/Exit
Otvorené/Zatvorené	ot-vo-re-nair/zuht-vo-re-nair	Open/Closed
Ubytovanie	u-bi-to-vuh-ni-ye	Rooms Available
Plne obsadené	pl-nye ob-suh-dye-nair	No Vacancies
Informácie	in-for-ma-tsi-ye	Information
Policajná stanica	po-li-tsai-na stuh-nyi-tsuh	Police Station
Zakázané	zuh-ka-zuh-nair	Prohibited
Záchody/WC/Toalety	za-kho-di/vair-tsair/to-uh-le-ti	Toilets
Páni	pa-nyi	Men
Dámy	da-mi	Women
Horúca/Studená	ho-roo-tsuh/stu-dye-na	Hot/Cold

accommodation

finding accommodation

Where's a ...?	Kde je ...?	kdye ye ...
camping ground	táborisko	ta-bo-ris-ko
guesthouse	penzión	pen-zi-awn
hotel	hotel	ho-tel
youth hostel	nocľaháreň	nots-lyuh-ha-ren'
	pre mládež	pre mla-dyezh
Can you recommend somewhere ...?	Môžete odporučiť niečo ...?	mwo-zhe-tye od-po-ru-chit' ni-ye-cho ...
cheap	lacné	luhts-nair
good	dobré	dob-rair
nearby	nablízku	nuh-bleez-ku
I have a reservation.	Mám rezerváciu.	mam re-zer-va-tsi-yu
My name's ...	Volám sa ...	vo-lam suh ...
Do you have a twin room?	Máte dve oddelené postele?	ma-tye dve od-dye-le-nair pos-tye-le
Do you have a single room?	Máte jednoposteľovú izbu?	ma-tye yed-no-pos-tye-lyo-voo iz-bu
Do you have a double room?	Máte izbu s manželskou posteľou?	ma-tye iz-bu s muhn-zhels-koh pos-tye-lyoh

How much is it per ...?	Koľko to stojí na ...?	kol'·ko to sto·yee nuh ...
night	noc	nots
person	osobu	o·so·bu

Can I pay by ...?	Môžem platiť ...?	mwo·zhem pluh·tyit' ...
credit card	kreditnou kartou	kre·dit·noh kuhr·toh
travellers cheque	cestovnými šekmi	tses·tov·nee·mi shek·mi

I'd like to stay for (two) nights.
Chcel/Chcela by som   khtsel/khtse·luh bi som
zostať (dve) noci. m/f   zos·tuht' (dve) no·tsi

From (2 July) to (6 July).
Od (druhého júla)   od (dru·hair·ho yoo·luh)
do (šiesteho júla).   do (shyes·te·ho yoo·luh)

Can I see it?
Môžem to vidieť?   mwo·zhem to vi·di·yet'

Am I allowed to camp here?
Môžem tu stanovať?   mwo·zhem tu stuh·no·vuht'

Is there a camp site nearby?
Je tu nablízku táborisko?   ye tu nuh·blees·ku ta·bo·ris·ko

requests & queries

When/Where is breakfast served?
Kedy/Kde sa podávajú   ke·di/kdye suh po·da·vuh·yoo
raňajky?   ruh·nyai·ki

Please wake me at (seven).
Zobuďte ma o (siedmej), prosím.   zo·buď·tye muh o (syed·mey) pro·seem

Could I have my key, please?
Prosím si môj kľúč.   pro·seem si mwoy klyooch

Can I get another (blanket)?
Môžem dostať inú (prikrývku)?   mwo·zhem dos·tuht' i·noo (pri·kreev·ku)

Is there a/an ...?	Je tam ...?	ye tuhm ...
elevator	výťah	vee·tyah
safe	bezpečnostný trezor	bez·pech·nos·nee tre·zor

The room is too ...	Izba je príliš ...	iz·buh ye pree·lish ...
expensive	drahá	druh·ha
noisy	hlučná	hluch·na
small	malá	muh·la

The ... doesn't work.   *... nefunguje.*   *... nye·fun·gu·ye*
- air conditioning   *Klimatizácia*   *kli·muh·ti·za·tsi·yuh*
- fan   *Ventilátor*   *ven·ti·la·tor*
- toilet   *Toaleta*   *to·uh·le·tuh*

This ... isn't clean.   *Tento ... nie je čistý.*   *ten·to ... ni·ye ye chis·tee*
- pillow   *vankúš*   *vuhn·koosh*
- towel   *uterák*   *u·tye·rak*

This sheet isn't clean.
Táto plachta nie je chistaa.   *ta·to pluhkh·tuh ni·ye ye chis·ta*

checking out

What time is checkout?
O koľkej sa odhlasuje?   *o kol'·key suh od·hluh·su·ye*

Can I leave my luggage here?
Môžem si tu nechať batožinu?   *mwo·zhem si tu nye·khuht' buh·to·zhi·nu*

Could I have my ...?   *Poprosím vás o ...*   *po·pro·seem vas o ...*
- deposit   *moju zálohu*   *mo·yu za·lo·hu*
- passport   *môj cestovný pas*   *mwoy tses·tov·nee puhs*
- valuables   *moje cennosti*   *mo·ye tsen·nos·tyi*

communications & banking

the internet

Where's the local Internet café?
Kde je miestne internet café?   *kdye ye myes·ne in·ter·net kuh·fair*

How much is it per hour?
Koľko stojí na hodinu?   *kol'·ko sto·yee nuh ho·dyi·nu*

I'd like to ...   *Chcel/Chcela*   *khtsel/khtse·luh*
   by som ... m/f   *bi som ...*
- check my email   *si skontrolovať email*   *si skon·tro·lo·vuht' ee·meyl*
- get Internet access   *sa pripojiť na*   *suh pri·po·yit' nuh*
   internet   *in·ter·net*
- use a printer   *použiť tlačiareň*   *po·u·zhit' tluh·chyuh·ren'*
- use a scanner   *použiť scanner*   *po·u·zhit' ske·ner*

mobile/cell phone

I'd like a ...	Chcel/Chcela	khtsel/khtse·luh
	by som ... m/f	bi som ...
mobile/cell phone for hire	si prenajať mobilný telefón	si pre·nuh·yuhť mo·bil·nee te·le·fawn
SIM card for your network	SIM kartu pre vašu sieť	sim kuhr·tu pre vuh·shu syeť

What are the rates?	Aké sú poplatky?	uh·kair soo pop·luht·ki

telephone

What's your phone number?
Aké je vaše telefónne číslo?   uh·kair ye vuh·she te·le·faw·ne chees·lo

The number is ...
Číslo je ...   chees·lo ye ...

Where's the nearest public phone?
Kde je najbližší verejný telefón?   kdye ye nai·blizh·shee ve·rey·nee te·le·fawn

I'd like to buy a phonecard.
Chcel/Chcela by som si kúpiť   khtsel/khtse·luh bi som si koo·piť
telefónnu kartu. m/f   te·le·faw·nu kuhr·tu

I want to ...	Chcem ...	khtsem ...
call (Singapore)	volať (do Singapúru)	vo·luhť (do sin·guh·poo·ru)
make a local call	volať miestne číslo	vo·luhť myes·ne chees·lo
reverse the charges	hovor na účet volaného	ho·vor nuh oo·chet vo·luh·nair·ho

How much does ... cost?	Koľko ...?	koľ·ko ...
a (three)-minute call	stoja (tri) minúty volania	sto·yuh (tri) mi·noo·ti vo·luh·ni·yuh
each extra minute	stojí každá ďalšia minúta	sto·yee kuhzh·da dyuhl·shyuh mi·noo·tuh

(One) euro per minute.
(Jedno) euro za minútu.   (yed·no) e·u·ro zuh mi·noo·tu

(Forty) Slovak crowns per minute.
(Štyridsať) korún za minútu.   (shti·ri·tsať) ko·roon zuh mi·noo·tu

post office

I want to send a …	Chcel/Chcela by som poslať … m/f	khtsel/khtse·luh bi som pos·luht' …
fax	fax	fuhks
letter	list	list
parcel	balík	buh·leek
postcard	pohľadnicu	po·hlyuhd·nyi·tsu

I want to buy a/an …	Chcel/Chcela by som si kúpiť … m/f	khtsel/ khtse·luh bi som si koo·pit' …
envelope	obálku	o·bal·ku
stamp	známku	znam·ku

Please send it (to Australia) by …	Prosím pošlite to (do Austrálie) …	pro·seem posh·li·tye to (do ows·tra·li·ye) …
airmail	leteckou poštou	le·tyets·koň posh·toh
express mail	expresne	eks·pres·nye
registered mail	doporučene	do·po·ru·che·nye
surface mail	obyčajnou poštou	o·bi·chai·noh posh·toh

Is there any mail for me?
Je tam nejaká pošta pre mňa?　　ye tuhm nye·yuh·ka posh·tuh pre mnyuh

bank

Where's a/an …?	Kde je …?	kdye ye …
ATM	nejaký bankomat	nye·yuh·kee buhn·ko·muht
foreign exchange office	nejaká zmenáreň	nye·yuh·ka zme·na·ren'

I'd like to …	Chcel/Chcela by som … m/f	khtsel/khtse·luh bi som …
Where can I …?	Kde môžem …?	kdye mo·zhem …
arrange a transfer	zariadiť prevod	zuh·ryuh·dyit' pre·vod
cash a cheque	preplatiť šek	pre·pluh·tyit' shek
change a travellers cheque	zameniť cestovný šek	zuh·me·nyit' tses·tov·nee shek
change money	zmeniť peniaze	zuh·me·nyit' pe·ni·yuh·ze
get a cash advance	dostať vopred hotovosť	dos·tuht' vo·pred ho·to·vost'
withdraw money	vybrať peniaze	vib·ruht' pe·ni·yuh·ze

What's the ...?	Aký je ...?	uh·kee ye ...
charge for that	za to poplatok	zuh to pop·luh·tok
exchange rate	výmenný kurz	vee·men·nee kurz

It's ...	Je to ...	ye to ...
(12) euros	(dvanásť) euro	(dvuh·nast') e·u·ro
(100) Slovak crowns	(sto) korún	(sto) ko·roon
free	zadarmo	zuh·duhr·mo

What's the commission?
Aká je provízia? — uh·ka ye pro·vee·zi·yuh

What time does the bank open?
O koľkej otvára banka? — o koľ·key ot·va·ruh buhn·kuh

Has my money arrived yet?
Prišli už moje peniaze? — prish·li uzh mo·ye pe·ni·yuh·ze

sightseeing

getting in

What time does it open/close?
O koľkej otvárajú/ — o koľ·key ot·va·ruh·yoo/
zatvárajú? — zuht·va·ruh·yoo

What's the admission charge?
Koľko je vstupné? — koľ·ko ye vstup·nair

Is there a discount for students/children?
Je nejaká zľava pre — ye nye·yuh·ka zlyuh·vuh pre
študentov/deti? — shtu·den·tov/dye·tyi

I'd like a ...	Chcel/Chcela	khtsel/khtse·luh
	by som ... m/f	bi som ...
catalogue	katalóg	kuh·tuh·lawg
guide	sprievodcu	sprye·vod·tsu
local map	miestnu mapu	myest·nu muh·pu

I'd like to see ...
Rád/Rada by som — rad/ruh·duh bi som
videl/videla ... m/f — vi·dyel/vi·dye·luh ...

What's that?	Čo je to?	cho ye to
Can I take a photo?	Môžem	mwo·zhem
	fotografovať?	fo·to·gruh·fo·vuht'

tours

When's the next ...?	Kedy je ďalší ...?	ke·di ye dyuhl·shee ...
day trip	celodenný výlet	tse·lo·den·nee vee·let
tour	zájazd	za·yuhzd

Is ... included?	Je zahrnuté ...?	ye zuh·hr·nu·tair ...
accommodation	ubytovanie	u·bi·to·vuh·ni·ye
the admission charge	vstupné	vstup·nair
food	jedlo	yed·lo

Is transport included?
Je zahrnutá doprava?   ye zuh·hr·nu·ta do·pruh·vuh

How long is the tour?
Koľko trvá zájazd?   koľ·ko tr·va za·yuhzd

What time should we be back?
O koľkej by sme mali byť späť?   o koľ·key bi sme muh·li bit' spet'

sightseeing

castle	zámok m	za·mok
cathedral	katedrála f	kuh·ted·ra·luh
church	kostol m	kos·tol
main square	hlavné námestie n	hluhv·nair na·mes·ti·ye
monastery	kláštor m	klash·tor
monument	pamätník m	puh·met·nyeek
museum	múzeum n	moo·ze·um
old city	staré mesto n	stuh·rair mes·to
palace	palác m	puh·lats
ruins	zrúcaniny pl	zroo·tsuh·nyi·ni
stadium	štadión m	shtuh·di·awn
statue	socha f	so·khuh

shopping

enquiries

Where's a ...?	Kde je ...?	kdye ye ...
bank	banka	buhn·kuh
bookshop	kníhkupectvo	knyeeh·ku·pets·tvo
camera shop	fotografický obchod	fo·to·gruh·fits·kee ob·khod
department store	obchodný dom	ob·khod·nee dom
grocery store	potraviny	po·truh·vi·ni
market	trh	trh
newsagency	predajňa novín	pre·dai·nyuh no·veen
supermarket	samoobsluha	suh·mo·ob·slu·huh

Where can I buy (a padlock)?
*Kde si môžem kúpiť
(visiaci zámok)?*
kdye si mwo·zhem koo·pit'
(vi·syuh·tsi za·mok)

I'm looking for ...
Hľadám ...
hlyuh·dam ...

Can I look at it?
Môžem sa na to pozrieť?
mwo·zhem suh nuh to poz·ryet'

Do you have any others?
Máte nejaké iné?
ma·tye nye·yuh·kair i·nair

Does it have a guarantee?
Je na to záruka?
ye nuh to za·ru·kuh

Can I have it sent abroad?
*Môžem si to dať poslať do
zahraničia?*
mwo·zhem si to duht' pos·luht' do
zuh·hruh·nyi·chyuh

Can I have my ... repaired?
Môžem si dať opraviť môj ...?
mwo·zhem si duht' o·pruh·vit' mwoy ...

It's faulty.
Je to pokazené.
ye to po·kuh·ze·nair

I'd like ..., please.	Poprosil/Poprosila by som ... m/f	po·pro·sil/po·pro·si·luh bi som ...
a bag	tašku	tuhsh·ku
a refund	vrátenie peňazi	vra·tye·ni·ye pe·nyuh·zee
to return this	toto vrátiť	to·to vra·tyit'

paying

How much is it?
Koľko to stojí? — kol'·ko to sto·yee

Can you write down the price?
Môžete napísať cenu? — mwo·zhe·tye nuh·pee·suhť tse·nu

That's too expensive.
To je príliš drahé. — to ye pree·lish druh·hair

What's your lowest price?
Aká je vaša najnižšia cena? — uh·ka ye vuh·shuh nai·nizh·shyuh tse·nuh

I'll give you (five) euros.
Dám vám (päť) euro. — dam vam (peť) e·u·ro

I'll give you (100) Slovak crowns.
Dám vám (sto) korún. — dam vam (sto) ko·roon

There's a mistake in the bill.
V účte je chyba. — v ooch·tye ye khi·buh

Do you accept ...? *Prijímate ...?* — pree·muh·tye ...
  credit cards   *kreditné karty* — kre·dit·nair kuhr·ti
  debit cards   *debetné karty* — de·bet·nair kuhr·ti
  travellers cheques   *cestovné šeky* — tses·tov·nair she·ki

I'd like ..., please. *Prosím si ...* — pro·seem si ...
  a receipt   *potvrdenie* — pot·vr·dye·ni·ye
  my change   *môj výdavok* — mwoy vee·duh·vok

clothes & shoes

Can I try it on?
Môžem si to vyskúšať? — mwo·zhem si to vis·koo·shuhť

My size is (42).
Moja veľkosť je (štyridsaťdva). — mo·yuh veľ·kosť ye (shti·rid·suhť·dvuh)

It doesn't fit.
Nesedí mi to. — nye·se·dyee mi to

small   *malý* — muh·lee
medium   *stredný* — stred·nee
large   *veľký* — veľ·kee

books & music

I'd like a ...	Môžem dostať ...	mwo·zhem dos·tuht' ...
newspaper	noviny	no·vi·ni
(in English)	(v angličtine)	(v uhn·glich·tyi·nye)
pen	pero	pe·ro

Is there an English-language bookshop?
Je tu anglické kníhkupectvo?   ye tu uhn·glits·kair kneeh·ku·pets·tvo

I'm looking for something by (Milan Lasica/Boris Filan).
Hľadám niečo od (Milana Lasicu/   hlyuh·dam ni·ye·cho od (mi·luh·nuh luh·si·tsu/
Borisa Filana).   bo·ri·suh fi·luh·nuh)

Can I listen to this?
Môžem si to vypočut'?   mwo·zhem si to vi·po·chut'

photography

Can you ...?	Mohli by ste ...?	mo·hli bi stye ...
burn a CD from	napáliť CD z	nuh·pa·liť tsair·dair z
my memory card	mojej pamäťovej	mo·yey puh·me·tyo·vey
	karty	kuhr·ti
develop this film	vyvolať tento film	vi·vo·luhť ten·to film
load my film	zaviesť môj film	zuh·vyesť mwoy film

I need a/an ... film	Potrebujem ... film	po·tre·bu·yem ... film
for this camera.	do tohto fotoaparátu.	do to·hto fo·to·uh·puh·ra·tu
APS	APS	a pair es
B&W	čiernobiely	chyer·no·bye·li
colour	farebný	fuh·reb·nee
slide	navíjací	nuh·vee·yuh·tsee
(200) speed	(dvestovku) citlivosť	(dve·stov·ku) tsit·li·vosť

When will it be ready?
Kedy to bude hotové?   ke·di to bu·dye ho·to·vair

meeting people

greetings, goodbyes & introductions

Hello/Hi.	Dobrý deň/Ahoj.	do·bree dyen'/uh·hoy
Good night.	Dobrú noc.	do·broo nots
Goodbye/Bye.	Do videnia/Ahoj.	do vi·dye·ni·yuh/uh·ho
Mr/Mrs	pán/pani	pan/puh·nyi
Miss	slečna	slech·nuh
How are you?	Ako sa máte/máš? pol/inf	uh·ko suh ma·tye/mash
Fine, thanks.	Dobre, ďakujem.	do·bre dyuh·ku·yem
And you?	A vy/ty? pol/inf	uh vi/ti
What's your name?	Ako sa voláte/	uh·ko suh vo·la·tye/
	voláš? pol/inf	vo·lash
My name is ...	Volám sa ...	vo·lam suh ...
I'm pleased to meet you.	Teší ma.	tye·shee muh

This is my ...	Toto je môj/moja ... m/f	to·to ye mwoy/mo·yuh ...
boyfriend	priateľ	pryuh·tyel'
brother	brat	bruht
daughter	dcéra	tsair·ruh
father	otec	o·tyets
friend	kamarát m	kuh·muh·rat
	kamarátka f	kuh·muh·rat·kuh
girlfriend	priateľka	pryuh·tyel'·kuh
husband	manžel	muhn·zhel
mother	matka	muht·kuh
partner (intimate)	partner/partnerka m/f	part·ner/part·ner·kuh
sister	sestra	ses·truh
son	syn	sin
wife	manželka	muhn·zhel·kuh

What's your ...?	Aká je vaša ...?	uh·ka ye vuh·shuh ...
address	adresa	uhd·re·suh
email address	emailová adresa	ee·mey·lo·va uhd·re·suh

Here's my ...	Tu je môj ...	tu ye mwoy ...
What's your ...?	Aké je vaše ...?	uh·kair ye vuh·she ...
fax number	faxové číslo	fuhk·so·vair chees·lo
phone number	telefónne číslo	te·le·fuhwn·ne chees·lo

occupations

What's your occupation?
Aké je vaše povolanie? uh·kair ye vuh·she po·vo·luh·ni·ye

I'm a/an ...	*Som ...*	som ...
artist	*umelec/umelkyňa* m/f	*u*·me·lets/*u*·mel·ki·nyuh
businessperson	*podnikateľ* m	pod·nyi·kuh·tyel'
	podnikateľka f	pod·nyi·kuh·tyel'·kuh
farmer	*pestovateľ* m	pes·to·vuh·tyel'
	pestovateľka f	pes·to·vuh·tyel'·ka
manual worker	*robotník* m	ro·bot·nyeek
	robotníčka f	ro·bot·nyeech·kuh
office worker	*úradník* m	oo·ruhd·nyeek
	úradníčka f	oo·ruhd·nyeech·kuh
scientist	*vedecký*	ve·dyets·kee
	pracovník m	pruh·tsov·nyeek
	vedecká	ve·dets·ka
	pracovníčka f	pruh·tsov·nyeech·kuh
student	*študent/študentka* m/f	shtu·dent/shtu·dent·kuh
tradesperson	*živnostník* m	zhiv·nos·nyeek
	živnostníčka f	zhiv·nos·nyeech·kuh

background

Where are you from? *Odkiaľ ste?* od·kyuhl' stye

I'm from ...	*Som z ...*	som z ...
Australia	*Austrálie*	ows·tra·li·ye
Canada	*Kanady*	kuh·nuh·di
England	*Anglicka*	uhng·lits·kuh
New Zealand	*Nového Zélandu*	no·vair·ho zair·luhn·du
the USA	*USA*	oo·es·a

Are you married? *Ste ženatý/vydatá?* m/f stye zhe·nuh·tee/vi·duh·ta

I'm ...	*Som ...*	som ...
married	*ženatý/vydatá* m/f	zhe·nuh·tee/vi·duh·ta
single	*slobodný* m	slo·bod·nee
	slobodná f	slo·bod·na

age

How old ...?	Koľko ... rokov?	koľ·ko ... ro·kov
are you	máte/máš pol/inf	ma·tye/mash
is your daughter	má vaša dcéra	ma vuh·shuh tsair·ruh
is your son	má váš syn	ma vash sin
I'm ... years old.	Ja mám ... rokov.	yuh mam ... ro·kov
He/She is ... years old.	On/Ona má ... rokov.	on/onuh ma ... ro·kov

feelings

I'm (not) ...	(Nie) Je mi ...	(ni·ye) ye mi ...
Are you ...?	Je vám ...?	ye vam ...
cold	zima	zi·muh
hot	teplo	tye·plo
I'm (not) ...	(Nie) Som ...	(ni·ve) som ...
Are you ...?	Ste ...?	stye ...
happy	šťastný/šťastná m/f	shtyuhs·nee/shtyuhs·na
hungry	hladný/hladná m/f	hluhd·nee/hluhd·na
sad	smutný/smutná m/f	smut·nee/smut·na
thirsty	smädný/smädná m/f	smed·nee/smed·na

entertainment

going out

Where can I find ...?	Kde nájdem ...?	kdye nai·dyem ...
clubs	kluby	klu·bi
gay venues	podniky pre	pod·nyi·ki pre
	homosexuálov	ho·mo·sek·su·a·lov
pubs	krčmy	krch·mi
I feel like going to a/the ...	Mám chuť ísť ...	mam khuť eest' ...
concert	na koncert	nuh kon·tsert
movies	do kina	do ki·nuh
restaurant	do reštaurácie	do resh·tow·ra·tsi·ye
theatre	do divadla	do dyi·vuhd·luh

interests

Do you like ...?	Máte radi ...?	ma·tye ruh·di ...
I like ...	Mám rád/rada ... m/f	mam rad/ruh·duh ...
I don't like ...	Nemám rád/ rada ... m/f	nye·mam rad/ ruh·duh ...
art	umenie	u·me·ni·ye
cooking	varenie	vuh·re·ni·ye
movies	filmy	fil·mi
nightclubs	nočné kluby	noch·nair klu·bi
reading	čítanie	chee·tuh·ni·ye
shopping	nakupovanie	nuh·ku·po·vuh·ni·ye
sport	šport	shport
travelling	cestovanie	tses·to·vuh·ni·ye

Do you like to ...?	Radi ...?	ruh·dyi ...
dance	tancujete	tuhn·tsu·ye·tye
go to concerts	chodíte na koncerty	kho·dyee·tye nuh kon·tser·ti
listen to music	počúvate hudbu	po·choo·vuh·tye hud·bu

food & drink

finding a place to eat

Can you recommend a ...?	Môžete mi odporučiť ...?	mwo·zhe·tye mi od·po·ru·chit' ...
bar	bar	buhr
café	kaviareň	kuh·vyuh·ren'
restaurant	reštauráciu	resh·tow·ra·tsi·yu

I'd like ..., please.	Chcel/Chcela by som ..., prosím. m/f	khtsel/khtse·luh bi som ... pro·seem
a table for (four)	stôl pre (štyroch)	stwol pre (shti·rokh)
the nonsmoking section	nefajčiarsku časť	nye·fai·chyuhr·sku chuhst'
the smoking section	fajčiarsku časť	fai·chyuhr·sku chuhst'

ordering food

breakfast	raňajky pl	ruh·nyai·ki
lunch	obed m	o·bed
dinner	večera f	ve·che·ruh
snack	občerstvenie n	ob·cherst·ve·ni·ye
What would you recommend?	Čo by ste mi odporučili?	cho bi stye mi od·po·ru·chi·li
'd like (the) ..., please.	Prosím si ...	pro·seem si ...
bill	účet	oo·chet
drink list	nápojový lístok	na·po·yo·vee lees·tok
menu	jedálny lístok	ye·dal·ni lees·tok
that dish	toto jedlo	to·to yed·lo

drinks

(cup of) coffee/tea ...	(šálka) kávy/čaju ...	(shal·kuh) ka·vi/chuh·yu ...
with milk	s mliekom	s mlye·kom
without sugar	bez cukru	bez tsuk·ru
(orange) juice	(pomarančový) džús m	(po·muh·ruhn·cho·vee) dyoos
soft drink	nealkoholický nápoj m	nye·uhl·ko·ho·lits·kee na·poy
(boiled/mineral) water	(prevarená/minerálna) voda f	(pre·vuh·re·na/mi·ne·ral·nuh) vo·duh

in the bar

'll have ...	Dám si ...	dam si ...
'll buy you a drink.	Kúpim ti/vám drink. inf/pol	koo·pim tyi/vam drink
What would you like?	Čo si dáš/dáte? inf/pol	cho si dash/da·tye
Cheers!	Nazdravie!	nuhz·druh·vi·ye
a shot of (whisky)	štamperlík (whisky)	shtuhm·per·leek (vís·ki)
a bottle/glass of beer	fľaša/pohár piva	flyuh·shuh/po·har pi·vuh
a bottle/glass of ...wine	fľaša/pohár ... vína	flyuh·shuh/po·har ... vee·nuh
red	červeného	cher·ve·nair·ho
sparkling	šumivého	shu·mi·vair·ho
white	bieleho	bye·le·ho

self-catering

What's the local speciality?
Čo je miestna špecialita?   cho ye *myes*·nuh shpe·tsyuh·li·tuh

What's that?
Čo je to?   cho ye to

How much is (a kilo of cheese)?
Koľko stojí (kilo syra)?   koľ·ko *sto*·yee (*ki*·lo *si*·ruh)

I'd like ...	*Môžem dostať ...*	mwo·zhem *dos*·tuhť ...
(100) grams	*(sto) gramov*	(sto) gruh·mov
(two) kilos	*(dve) kilá*	(dve) *ki*·la
(three) pieces	*(tri) kusy*	(tri) *ku*·si
(six) slices	*(šesť) plátkov*	(shesť) *plat*·kov

Less.	*Menej.*	me·nyey
Enough.	*Stačí.*	stuh·chee
More.	*Viac.*	vyuhts

special diets & allergies

Is there a vegetarian restaurant near here?
Je tu nablízku vegetariánska   ye tu *nuh*·bleez·ku ve·ge·tuh·ri·yan·skuh
reštaurácia?   resh·tow·ra·tsi·yuh

Do you have vegetarian food?
Máte vegetariánske jedlá?   ma·tye ve·ge·tuh·ri·yan·ske *yed*·la

Could you prepare	*Mohli by ste pripraviť*	*mo*·hli bi stye *pri*·pruh·viť
a meal without ...?	*jedlo bez ...?*	*yed*·lo bez ...
butter	*masla*	muhs·luh
eggs	*vajec*	vuh·yets
meat stock	*mäsového vývaru*	me·so·vair·ho *vee*·vuh·ru

I'm allergic to ...	*Som alergický/*	som uh·ler·gits·kee/
	alergická na ... m/f	uh·ler·gits·ka nuh ...
dairy produce	*mliečne produkty*	mlyech·ne *pro*·duk·ti
gluten	*lepok*	le·pok
MSG	*zvýrazňovač*	zvee·ruhz·nyo·vuhch
	chute	khu·tye
nuts	*orechy*	o·re·khi
seafood	*dary mora*	duh·ri *mo*·ruh

balkánský šalát m	*buhl*-kan-ski *shuh*-lat	lettuce, tomato, onion & cheese salad
bravčové pečené s rascou n	*bruhv*-cho-vair pe-che-nair s *ruhs*-tsoh	roast pork with caraway seeds
držková polievka f	drzh-ko-va *po*-lyev-kuh	sliced tripe soup
dusené hovädzie na prírodno n	du-se-nair *ho*-ve-dzye nuh *pree*-rod-no	braised beef slices in sauce
guláš m	*gu*-lash	thick, spicy beef & potato soup
hovädzí guláš m	*ho*-ve-dzee *gu*-lash	beef chunks in brown sauce
hovädzí vývar m	*ho*-ve-dzee *vee*-vuhr	beef in broth
hrachová polievka f	*hruh*-kho-va *po*-lyev-kuh	thick pea soup with bacon
jablkový závin m	*yuh*-bl-ko-vee *za*-vin	apple strudel
kapor na víne m	*kuh*-por nuh *vee*-nye	carp braised in wine
koložvárska kapusta f	*ko*-lozh-var-skuh *kuh*-pus-tuh	goulash with beef, pork, lamb & sauerkraut in a cream sauce
krokety m pl	*kro*-ke-ti	deep-fried mashed potato
kuracia polievka f	*ku*-ruh-tsyuh *po*-lyev-kuh	chicken soup
kurací paprikáš m	*ku*-ruh-tsee *puhp*-ri-kash	chicken braised in red (paprika) sauce
kyslá uhorka f	*kis*-la *u*-hor-kuh	dill pickle (gherkin)
opékané zemiaky f pl	*o*-pe-kuh-nair *ze*-myuh-ki	fried potatoes
ovocné knedle f pl	*o*-vots-nair *kned*-le	fruit dumplings
palacinky f pl	*puh*-luh-tsin-ki	pancakes
paradajková polievka s cibuľkou f	*puh*-ruh-dai-ko-va *po*-lyev-kuh s *tsi*-buľ-koh	tomato & onion soup

pečené zemiaky f pl	pe·che·nair ze·myuh·ki	roast potatoes
plnená paprika v paradajkovej omáčke f	pl·nye·na puhp·ri·kuh v puh·ruh·dai·ko·vey o·mach·ke	capsicum stuffed with minced meat & rice, served with tomato sauce
polievka z bažanta f	po·lyev·kuh z buh·zhuhn·tuh	pheasant soup
praženica f	pruh·zhe·nyi·tsuh	scrambled eggs
prírodný rezeň m	pree·rod·nee re·zen'	unbreaded pork or veal schnitzel
rizoto n	ri·zo·to	mixture of pork, onion, peas & rice
ruské vajcia n pl	rus·kair vai·tsyuh	hard-boiled egg, potato & salami, with mayonnaise
rybacia polievka f	ri·buh·tsyuh po·lyev·kuh	fish soup
ryžový nákyp m	ri·zho·vee na·kip	rice soufflé
salámový tanier s oblohou m	suh·la·mo·vee tuh·nyer s ob·lo·hoh	salami platter with fresh or pickled vegetables
sviečková na smotane f	svyech·ko·va nuh smo·tuh·nye	roast beef with sour cream sauce & spices
špenát m	shpe·nat	finely chopped spinach, cooked with onion, garlic & cream
šunka pečená s vajcom f	shun·kuh pe·che·na s vai·tsom	fried ham with egg
tatárska omáčka f	tuh·tar·skuh o·mach·kuh	creamy tartar sauce
tatársky bifték m	tuh·tar·ski bif·tek	raw steak
teľacie pečené n	tye·lyuh·tsye pe·che·nair	roast veal
tlačenka s octom a cibuľou f	tluh·chen·kuh s ots·tom uh tsi·bu·loh	jellied meat loaf with vinegar & onion
vyprážané rybacie filé n	vi·pra·zhuh·nair ri·buh·tsye fi·lair	fillet of fish fried in breadcrumbs

emergencies

basics

Help!	Pomoc!	po·mots
Stop!	Stoj!	stoy
Go away!	Choďte preč!	khoď·tye prech
Thief!	Zlodej!	zlo·dyey
Fire!	Oheň!	o·hen'
Watch out!	Pozor!	po·zor
Call a doctor!	Zavolajte lekára!	zuh·vo·lai·tye le·ka·ruh
Call an ambulance!	Zavolajte záchranku!	zuh·vo·lai·tye zakh·ruhn·ku
Call the police!	Zavolajte políciu!	zuh·vo·lai·tye po·lee·tsi·yu

It's an emergency!
Je to pohotovostný prípad!   ye to po·ho·to·vos·nee pree·puhd

Could you help me, please?
Môžete mi prosím pomôcť?   mwo·zhe·tye mi pro·seem po·mwotsť

I have to use the telephone.
Potrebujem telefón.   po·tre·bu·yem te·le·fawn

I'm lost.
Stratil/Stratila som sa. m/f   struh·tyil/struh·tyi·luh som suh

Where are the toilets?
Kde sú tu záchody?   kdye soo tu za·kho·di

police

Where's the police station?
Kde je policajná stanica?   kdye ye po·li·tsai·na stuh·nyi·tsuh

I want to report an offence. (serious/minor)
Chcem nahlásiť zločin/priestupok.   khtsem nuh·hla·siť zlo·chin/prye·stu·pok

I've been ...	Bol/Bola som ... m/f	bol/bo·luh som ...
assaulted	prepadnutý m	pre·puhd·nu·tee
	prepadnutá f	pre·puhd·nu·ta
raped	znásilnený m	zna·sil·nye·nee
	znásilnená f	zna·sil·nye·na
robbed	okradnutý m	o·kruhd·nu·tee
	okradnutá f	o·kruhd·nu·ta

I've lost my ...	Stratil/Stratila	struh·tyil/struh·tyi·luh
	som ... m/f	som ...
My ... was/were stolen.	Ukradli mi ...	u·kruhd·li mi ...
backpack	plecniak	plets·ni·yuhk
bags	batožinu	buh·to·zhi·nu
credit card	kreditnú kartu	kre·dit·noo kuhr·tu
handbag	kabelku	kuh·bel·ku
jewellery	šperky	shper·ki
money	peniaze	pe·nyuh·ze
passport	cestovný pas	tses·tov·nee puhs
travellers cheques	cestovné šeky	tses·tov·nair she·ki
wallet	peňaženku	pe·nyuh·zhen·ku
I want to contact my ...	Chcem sa spojiť's ...	khtsem suh spo·yit' s ...
consulate	mojím konzulátom	mo·yeem kon·zu·la·tom
embassy	mojou ambasádou	mo·yoh uhm·buh·sa·doh

health

medical needs

Where's the nearest ...?	Kde je najbližší/ najbližšia ...? m/f	kdye ye nai·blizh·shee/ nai·blizh·shyuh ...
dentist	zubár m	zu·bar
doctor	doktor m	dok·tor
hospital	nemocnica f	ne·mots·nyi·tsuh
(night) pharmacist	(pohotovostná) lekáreň f	(po·ho·to·vost·na) le·ka·ren'

I need a doctor (who speaks English).
Potrebujem lekára,
(ktorý hovorí po anglicky).
po·tre·bu·yem le·ka·ruh
(kto·ree ho·vo·ree po uhng·lits·ki)

Could I see a female doctor?
Mohla by som navštíviť
ženského lekára?
mo·hluh bi som nuhv·shtyee·vit'
zhen·skair·ho le·ka·ruh

I've run out of my medication.
Minuli sa mi lieky.
mi·nu·li suh mi li·ye·ki

| I'm sick. | Som chorý/chorá. m/f | som kho·ree/kho·ra |
| It hurts here. | Tu ma to bolí. | tu muh to bo·lee |

I have (a) ...

	Mám ...	mam ...
asthma	Mám astmu.	mam uhst·mu
bronchitis	Mám zápal priedušiek.	mam za·puhl prye·du·shyek
constipation	Mám zápchu.	mam zap·khu
cough	Mám kašeľ.	mam kuh·shel
diarrhoea	Mám hnačku.	mam hnuhch·ku
fever	Mám horúčku.	mam ho·rooch·ku
headache	Bolí ma hlava.	bo·lee muh hluh·vuh
heart condition	Mám srdcovú príhodu.	mam srd·tso·voo pree·ho·du
nausea	Je mi nazvracanie.	ye mi nuhz·vruh·tsuh·ni·ye
pain	Mám bolesti.	mam bo·les·tyi
sore throat	Bolí ma hrdlo.	bo·lee muh hrd·lo
toothache	Bolí ma zub.	bo·lee muh zub

I'm allergic to ...

	Som alergický/ alergická na ... m/f	som uh·ler·gits·kee/ uh·ler·gits·ka nuh ...
antibiotics	antibiotiká	uhn·ti·bi·o·ti·ka
anti-inflammatories	protizápalové lieky	pro·ti·za·puh·lo·vair lye·ki
aspirin	aspirín	uhs·pi·reen
bees	včely	fche·li
codeine	kodeín	ko·de·een
penicillin	penicilín	pe·ni·tsi·leen

antiseptic	antiseptikum n	uhn·ti·sep·ti·kum
bandage	obväz n	ob·vez
condoms	kondómy m pl	kon·daw·mi
contraceptives	antikoncepcia f	uhn·ti·kon·tsep·tsi·yuh
diarrhoea medicine	lieky proti hnačke m	li·ye·ki pro·tyi hnuhch·ke
insect repellent	repelent proti hmyzu m	re·pe·lent pro·tyi hmi·zu
laxatives	preháňadlá n pl	pre·ha·nyuhd·la
painkillers	analgetiká n pl	uh·nuhl·ge·ti·ka
rehydration salts	rehydratujúce soli f pl	re·hid·ruh·tu·yoo·tse so·li
sleeping tablets	tabletky na spanie f pl	tuhb·let·ki nuh spuh·ni·ye

english–slovak dictionary

Slovak nouns in this dictionary have their gender indicated by ⓜ (masculine), ⓕ (feminine) or ⓝ (neuter). If it's a plural noun, you'll also see pl. Adjectives are given in the masculine form only. Wor are also marked as a (adjective), v (verb), sg (singular), pl (plural), inf (informal) or pol (polite) whe necessary.

A

accident *nehoda* ⓕ nye-ho-duh
accommodation *ubytovanie* ⓝ u-bi-to-vuh-ni-ye
adaptor *rozvodka* ⓕ roz-vod-kuh
address *adresa* ⓕ uh-dre-suh
after *po* po
air-conditioned *klimatizovaný* klí-muh-ti-zo-vuh-nee
airplane *lietadlo* ⓝ li-ye-tuhd-lo
airport *letisko* ⓝ le-tis-ko
alcohol *alkohol* ⓜ uhl-ko-hol
all (everything) *všetko* fshet-ko
allergy *alergia* ⓕ uh-ler-gi-yuh
ambulance *ambulancia* ⓕ uhm-bu-luhn-tsi-yuh
and *a* uh
ankle *členok* ⓜ chle-nok
arm *rameno* ⓝ ruh-me-no
ashtray *popolník* ⓜ po-pol-nyeek
ATM *bankomat* ⓜ buhn-ko-muht

B

baby *dieťatko* ⓝ di-ye-tyuht-ko
back (body) *chrbát* ⓜ khr-baat
backpack *ruksak* ⓜ ruk-suhk
bad *zlý* zlee
bag *taška* ⓕ tuhsh-kuh
baggage claim *úložňa batožiny* ⓕ oo-lozh-nyuh buh-to-zhi-ni
bank *banka* ⓕ buhn-kuh
bar *bar* ⓜ buhr
bathroom *kúpeľňa* ⓕ koo-peľ-nyuh
battery *batéria* ⓕ buh-tair-ri-yuh
beautiful *krásny* kras-ni
bed *posteľ* ⓕ pos-tyeľ
beer *pivo* ⓝ pi-vo
before *pred* pred
behind *za* zuh
bicycle *bicykel* ⓜ bi-tsi-kel
big *veľký* veľ-kee
bill *účet* ⓜ oo-chet
black *čierny* chyer-ni
blanket *prikrývka* ⓕ pri-kreev-kuh

blood group *krvná skupina* ⓕ krv-na sku-pi-nuh
blue *modrý* mod-ree
boat *loď* ⓕ loď
book (make a reservation) v *rezervovať* re-zer-vo-vuhť
bottle *fľaša* ⓕ flyuh-shuh
bottle opener *otvárač na fľašu* ⓜ ot-va-ruhch nuh flyuh-shu
boy *chlapec* ⓜ khluh-pets
brakes (car) *brzdy* ⓕ pl brz-di
breakfast *raňajky* ⓕ pl ruh-nyai-ki
broken (faulty) *pokazený* po-kuh-ze-nee
bus *autobus* ⓜ ow-to-bus
business *obchod* ⓜ ob-khod
buy *kúpiť* koo-piť

C

café *kaviareň* ⓕ kuh-vyuh-reň
camera *fotoaparát* ⓜ fo-to-uh-puh-rat
camp site *táborisko* ⓝ ta-bo-ris-ko
cancel *zrušiť* zru-shiť
can opener *otvárač na konzervu* ⓜ ot-va-ruhch nuh kon-zer-vu
car *auto* ⓝ ow-to
cash *hotovosť* ⓕ ho-to-vosť
cash (a cheque) v *preplatiť (šek)* prep-luh-tyiť (shek)
cell phone *mobil* ⓜ mo-bil
centre *centrum* ⓝ tsen-trum
change (money) v *zameniť (peniaze)* zuh-me-nyiť (pe-ni-yuh-ze)
cheap *lacný* luhts-nee
check (bill) *účet* ⓜ oo-chet
check-in *registrácia* ⓕ re-gis-tra-tsi-yuh
chest *hruď* ⓜ hruď
child *dieťa* ⓝ di-ye-tyuh
cigarette *cigareta* ⓕ tsi-guh-re-tuh
city *mesto* ⓝ mes-to
clean a *čistý* chis-tee
closed *zatvorený* zuht-vo-re-nee
coffee *káva* ⓕ ka-vuh
coins *mince* ⓕ pl min-tse
cold a *studený* stu-dye-nee

llect call *hovor na účet volaného* ⓜ
ho-vor nuh oo-chet vo-luh-nair-ho
me *prísť* preesť
mputer *počítač* ⓜ po-chee-tuhch
ndom *kondóm* ⓜ kon-duhwm
ntact lenses *kontaktné šošovky* ⓕ pl
kon-tuhkt-nair sho-shov-ki
ook v *variť* vuh-riť
ost *cena* ⓕ tse-nuh
redit card *kreditná karta* ⓕ kre-dit-na kuhr-tuh
up *šálka* ⓕ shaal-ka
urrency exchange *výmena peňazí* ⓕ
vee-me-nuh pe-nyuh-zee
ustoms (immigration) *colnica* ⓕ tsol-nyi-tsuh

D

angerous *nebezpečný* ne-bez-pech-nee
late (time) *dátum* ⓜ da-tum
lay deň ⓜ dyen'
lelay *meškanie* ⓝ mesh-kuh-ni-ye
lentist *zubár* ⓜ zu-bar
lepart *odchádzať* od-kha-dzať
liaper *plienka* ⓕ pli-yen-kuh
lictionary *slovník* ⓜ slov-nyeek
linner *večera* ⓕ ve-che-ruh
lirect a *priamy* pryuh-mi
lirty *špinavý* shpi-nuh-vee
lisabled *postihnutý* pos-tyih-nu-tee
liscount *zľava* ⓕ zlyuh-vuh
loctor *lekár* ⓜ le-kar
louble bed *dvojitá posteľ* ⓕ dvo-yi-ta pos-tyeľ
louble room *dvojposteľová izba* ⓕ
dvoy-pos-tye-lyo-va iz-buh
lrink *nápoj* ⓜ na-poy
lrive v *riadiť* ryuh-dyiť
lrivers licence *vodičský preukaz* ⓜ
vo-dyich-skee pre-u-kuhz
lrug (illicit) *droga* ⓕ dro-guh
lummy (pacifier) *cumeľ* ⓜ tsu-meľ

E

ear *ucho* ⓝ u-kho
east *východ* vee-khod
eat *jesť* yesť
economy class *ekonomická trieda* ⓕ
e-ko-no-mits-ka trye-duh
electricity *elektrika* ⓕ e-lek-tri-kuh
elevator *výťah* ⓜ vee-ťah
email *email* ⓜ ee-meyl
embassy *veľvyslanectvo* ⓝ veľ'-vis-luh-nyets-tvo
emergency *pohotovosť* ⓕ po-ho-to-vosť

English (language) *angličtina* ⓕ uhng-lich-tyi-nuh
entrance *vchod* ⓜ vkhod
evening *večer* ⓜ ve-cher
exchange rate *výmenný kurz* ⓜ vee-men-nee kurz
exit *východ* ⓜ vee-khod
expensive *drahý* druh-hee
express mail *expresná pošta* ⓕ eks-pres-na posh-tuh
eye *oko* ⓝ o-ko

F

far *ďaleko* dyuh-le-ko
fast *rýchly* reekh-li
father *otec* ⓜ o-tyets
film (camera) *film* ⓜ film
finger *prst* ⓜ prst
first-aid kit *lekárnička* ⓕ le-kar-nyich-kuh
first class *prvá trieda* ⓕ pr-va trye-duh
fish *ryba* ⓕ ri-buh
food *jedlo* ⓝ yed-lo
foot *noha* ⓕ no-huh
fork *vidlička* ⓕ vid-lich-kuh
free (of charge) *zadarmo* zuh-duhr-mo
friend *priateľ/priateľka* ⓜ/ⓕ pryuh-teľ/prya-tyeľ-ka
fruit *ovocie* ⓝ o-vo-tsye
full *plný* pl-nee
funny *smiešny* smyesh-ni

G

gift *dar* ⓜ duhr
girl *dievča* ⓝ di-yev-chuh
glass (drinking) *pohár* ⓜ po-har
glasses *okuliare* pl o-ku-lyuh-re
go *ísť* eesť
good *dobrý* dob-ree
green *zelený* ze-le-nee
guide *sprievodca* ⓜ sprye-vod-tsuh

H

half *polovica* ⓕ po-lo-vi-tsuh
hand *ruka* ⓕ ru-kuh
handbag *kabelka* ⓕ kuh-bel-kuh
happy *šťastný* shtyuhs-nee
have *mať* muhť
he *on* on
head *hlava* ⓕ hluh-vuh
heart *srdce* ⓝ srd-tse
heat *teplo* ⓝ tyep-lo
heavy *ťažký* tyuhzh-kee
help v *pomôcť* pom-wotsť

here *tu* tu
high *vysoký* vi-so-kee
highway *diaľnica* ① di-yuhl-nyi-tsuh
hike v *ísť na turistiku* eesť nuh *tu*-ris-ti-ku
holiday *dovolenka* ① do-vo-len-kuh
homosexual *homosexuál* ⓜ ho-mo-sek-su-al
hospital *nemocnica* ① ne-mots-nyi-tsuh
hot *horúci* ho-roo-tsi
hotel *hotel* ⓜ ho-tel
hungry *hladný* hluhd-nee
husband *manžel* ⓜ muhn-zhel

I

I *ja* yuh
identification (card) *občiansky preukaz* ⓜ ob-chyuhns-ki *pre*-u-kuhz
ill *chorý* kho-ree
important *dôležitý* dwo-le-zhi-tee
included *zahrnutý* zuh-hr-nu-tee
injury *poranenie* ① po-ruh-nye-ni-ye
insurance *poistenie* ① po-is-tye-ni-ye
Internet *internet* ⓜ in-ter-net
interpreter *tlmočník* ⓜ tl-moch-nyeek

J

jewellery *šperky* ⓜ pl shper-ki
job *zamestnanie* ⓝ zuh-mest-nuh-ni-ye

K

key *kľúč* ⓜ kľooch
kilogram *kilogram* ⓜ ki-log-ruhm
kitchen *kuchyňa* ① ku-khi-nyuh
knife *nôž* ⓜ nwozh

L

laundry (place) *práčovňa* ① pra-chov-nyuh
lawyer *právnik* ⓜ prav-nyik
left (direction) *vľavo* vluh-vo
left-luggage office *úschovňa batožiny* ①
  oos-khov-nyuh buh-to-zhi-ni
leg *noha* ① no-huh
lesbian *lesbia* ① les-bi-yuh
less *menej* me-nyey
letter (mail) *list* ⓜ list
lift (elevator) *výťah* ⓜ vee-ťah
light *svetlo* ⓝ svet-lo
like v *mať rád* muhť rad

lock *zámok* ⓜ za-mok
long *dlhý* dl-hee
lost *stratený* struh-tye-nee
lost-property office *straty a nálezy* ①
  struh-ti uh na-le-zi
love v *ľúbiť/ľ1yoo-biť*
luggage *batožina* ① buh-to-zhi-nuh
lunch *obed* ⓜ o-bed

M

mail *pošta* ① posh-tuh
man *muž* ⓜ muzh
map *mapa* ① muh-puh
market *trh* ⓜ trh
matches *zápalky* ① pl za-puhl-ki
meat *mäso* ⓝ me-so
medicine *liek* ⓜ li-yek
menu *jedálny lístok* ⓜ ye-dal-ni lees-tok
message *správa* ① spra-vuh
milk *mlieko* ⓝ mli-ye-ko
minute *minúta* ① mi-noo-tuh
mobile phone *mobil* ⓜ mo-bil
money *peniaze* ⓜ pl pe-ni-yuh-ze
month *mesiac* ⓜ me-syuhts
morning *ráno* ⓝ ra-no
mother *matka* ① muht-kuh
motorcycle *motorka* ① mo-tor-kuh
motorway *hlavná cesta* ① hluhv-na tses-tuh
mouth *ústa* pl oos-tuh
music *hudba* ① hud-buh

N

name *meno* ⓝ me-no
napkin *obrúsok* ⓜ ob-roo-sok
nappy *plienka* ① plyen-kuh
near *blízko* bleez-ko
neck *krk* ⓜ krk
new *nový* no-vee
news *správy* ① pl spra-vi
newspaper *noviny* pl no-vi-ni
night *noc* ① nots
no *nie* ni-ye
noisy *hlučný* hluch-nee
nonsmoking *nefajčiarsky* ne-fai-chyuhr-ski
north *sever* se-ver
nose *nos* ⓜ nos
now *teraz* te-ruhz
number *číslo* ⓝ chees-lo

oil (engine) *olej* ⓜ *o-ley*
old *starý* *stuh-ree*
one-way ticket *jednosmerný lístok* ⓜ
  yed-no-smer-nee lees-tok
open a *vlečený* *ot-vo-re-nee*
outside *vonku* *von-ku*

P

package *balík* ⓜ *buh-leek*
paper *papier* ⓜ *puh-pyer*
park (car) v *zaparkovať* *zuh-puhr-ko-vuhť*
passport *cestovný pas* ⓜ *tses-tov-nee puhs*
pay *platiť* *pluh-tyiť*
pen *pero* ⓝ *pe-ro*
petrol *benzín* ⓜ *ben-zeen*
pharmacy *lekáreň* ⓕ *le-ka-reň*
phonecard *telefónna karta* ⓕ
  te-le-fuhwn-nuh kuhr-tuh
photo *fotografia* ⓕ *fo-to-gruh-fi-yuh*
plate *tanier* ⓜ *tuh-ni-yer*
police *polícia* ⓕ *po-lee-tsi-yuh*
postcard *pohľadnica* ⓕ *poh-ľuhd-nyi-tsuh*
post office *pošta* ⓕ *posh-tuh*
pregnant *tehotná* *tye-hot-na*
price *cena* ⓕ *tse-nuh*

Q

quiet *tichý* *tyi-khee*

R

rain *dážď* ⓜ *dazhď*
razor *žiletka* ⓕ *zhi-let-kuh*
receipt *potvrdenie* ⓝ *pot-vr-dye-ni-ye*
red *červený* *cher-ve-nee*
refund *vrátenie peňazí* ⓝ
  vra-tye-ni-ye pe-nyuh-zee
registered mail *doporučená pošta* ⓕ
  do-po-ru-che-na posh-tuh
rent v *prenajať* *pre-nuh-yuhť*
repair v *opraviť* *o-pruh-viť*
reservation *rezervácia* ⓕ *re-zer-va-tsi-yuh*
restaurant *reštaurácia* ⓕ *resh-tow-ra-tsi-yuh*
return v *vrátiť* *vra-tyiť*
return ticket *spiatočný lístok* ⓜ
  spyuh-toch-nee lees-tok
right (direction) *vpravo* *vpruh-vo*

road *cesta* ⓕ *tses-tuh*
room *izba* ⓕ *iz-buh*

S

safe a *bezpečný* *bez-pech-nee*
sanitary napkin *dámska vložka* ⓕ *dams-kuh*
  vlozh-kuh
seat *sedadlo* ⓝ *se-duhd-lo*
send *poslať* *pos-luhť*
service station *benzínová stanica* ⓕ
  ben-zee-no-va stuh-nyi-tsuh
sex *sex* ⓜ *seks*
shampoo *šampón* ⓜ *shuhm-puhwn*
share (a dorm) *deliť sa (o izbu)*
  dye-liť suh (o iz-bu)
shaving cream *krém na holenie* ⓜ
  kraimr nuh ho-le-ni-ye
she *ona* *o-nuh*
sheet (bed) *plachta* ⓕ *pluhkh-tuh*
shirt *košeľa* ⓕ *ko-she-ľuh*
shoes *topánky* ⓕ pl *to-pan-ki*
shop *obchod* ⓜ *ob-khod*
short *krátky* *krat-ki*
shower *sprcha* ⓕ *spr-khuh*
single room *jednoposteľová izba* ⓕ
  yed-no-pos-tye-ľyo-va iz-buh
skin *koža* ⓕ *ko-zhuh*
skirt *sukňa* ⓕ *suk-nyuh*
sleep v *spať* *spuhť*
Slovakia *Slovensko* ⓝ *slo-vens-ko*
Slovak (language) *slovenčina* ⓕ *slo-ven-chi-na*
Slovak a *slovenský* *slo-vens-kee*
slowly *pomaly* *po-muh-li*
small *malý* *muh-lee*
smoke (cigarettes) v *fajčiť* *fai-chiť*
soap *mydlo* ⓝ *mid-lo*
some *nejaký* *nye-yuh-kee*
soon *skoro* *sko-ro*
south *juh* *yooh*
souvenir shop *obchod so suvenírmi* ⓜ
  ob-khod zo su-ve-neer-mi
speak *hovoriť* *ho-vo-riť*
spoon *lyžica* ⓕ *li-zhi-tsuh*
stamp *známka* ⓕ *znam-kuh*
stand-by ticket *lístok na čakacom zozname* ⓜ
  lees-tok nuh chuh-kuh-tsom zoz-nuh-me
station (train) *železničná stanica* ⓕ
  zhe-lez-nich-na stuh-ni-tsuh
stomach *žalúdok* ⓜ *zhuh-loo-dok*
stop v *stáť* *stať*

stop (bus) *autobusová zastávka* ⓕ
ow-to-bu-so-va zuhs-tav-kuh
street *ulica* ⓕ u-li-tsuh
student *študent/študentka* ⓜ/ⓕ
shtu-dent/shtu-dent-ka
sun *slnko* ⓝ sln-ko
sunscreen *ochranný faktor* ⓜ o-khruhn-nee fuhk-tor
swim v *plávať* pla-vuht'

T

tampons *tampóny* ⓜ pl tuhm-puhw-ni
taxi *taxik* ⓜ tuhk-seek
teaspoon *lyžička* ⓕ li-zhich-ku
teeth *zuby* ⓜ pl zu-bi
telephone *telefón* ⓜ te-le-fuhwn
television *televízia* ⓕ te-le-vee-zi-yuh
temperature (weather) *teplota* ⓕ tep-lo-tuh
tent *stan* ⓜ stuhn
that (one) *to* to
they *oni* o-nyi
thirsty *smädný* smed-nee
this (one) *toto* to-to
throat *hrdlo* ⓝ hrd-lo
ticket *lístok* ⓜ lees-tok
time *čas* ⓜ chuhs
tired *unavený* u-nuh-ve-nee
tissues *servítky* ⓕ pl ser-veet-ki
today *dnes* dnyes
toilet *záchod* ⓜ za-khod
tomorrow *zajtra* zai-truh
tonight *dnes večer* dnyes ve-cher
toothbrush *zubná kefka* ⓕ zub-na kef-kuh
toothpaste *zubná pasta* ⓕ zub-na puhs-tuh
torch (flashlight) *baterka* ⓕ buh-ter-kuh
tour *zájazd* ⓜ za-yuhzd
tourist office *turistická kancelária* ⓕ
tu-ris-tits-ka kuhn-tse-la-ri-yuh
towel *uterák* ⓜ u-tye-rak
train *vlak* ⓜ vluhk
translate *prekladať* pre-kluh-duht'
travel agency *cestovná kancelária* ⓕ
tses-tov-na kuhn-tse-la-ri-yuh
travellers cheque *cestovný šek* ⓜ tses-tov-nee shek
trousers *nohavice* pl no-huh-vi-tse
twin beds *dve oddelené postele* ⓕ pl
dve od-dye-le-nair pos-tye-le
tyre *pneumatika* ⓕ pne-u-muh-ti-kuh

U

underwear *spodné prádlo* ⓝ spod-nair prad-lo
urgent *súrny* soor-ni

V

vacant *voľný* voly-nee
vacation *dovolenka* ⓕ do-vo-len-kuh
vegetable *zelenina* ⓕ ze-le-nyi-nuh
vegetarian a *vegetariánsky* ve-ge-tuh-ri-yans-ki
visa *vízum* ⓝ vee-zum

W

waiter *čašník* ⓜ chuhsh-nyeek
walk v *kráčať* kra-chuht'
wallet *peňaženka* ⓕ pe-nyuh-zhen-kuh
warm a *teplý* tep-lee
wash (something) *umývať* u-mee-vuht'
watch *hodinky* pl ho-dyin-ki
water *voda* ⓕ vo-duh
we *my* mi
weekend *víkend* ⓜ vee-kend
west *západ* za-puhd
wheelchair *invalidný vozík* ⓜ in-vuh-lid-nee vo-zeek
when *kedy* ke-di
where *kde* kdye
white *biely* bye-li
who *kto* kto
why *prečo* pre-cho
wife *manželka* ⓕ muhn-zhel-kuh
window *okno* ⓝ ok-no
wine *víno* ⓝ vee-no
with *s* s
without *bez* bez
woman *žena* ⓕ zhe-nuh
write *písať* pee-suht'

Y

yellow *žltý* zhl-tee
yes *áno* a-no
yesterday *včera* vche-ruh
you sg inf *ty* ti
you sg pol & pl *vy* vi

Slovene

slovene alphabet

A a a	*B b* buh	*C c* tsuh	*Č č* chuh	*D d* duh
E e e	*F f* fuh	*G g* guh	*H h* huh	*I i* ee
J j yuh	*K k* kuh	*L l* luh	*M m* muh	*N n* nuh
O o o	*P p* puh	*R r* ruh	*S s* suh	*Š š* shuh
T t tuh	*U u* oo	*V v* vuh	*Z z* zuh	*Ž ž* zhuh

SLOVENŠČINA

SLOVENE

slovenščina

introduction

The language spoken by about 2 million people 'on the sunny side of the Alps', Slovene (*slovenščina* slo·*vensh*·chee·na) is sandwiched between German, Italian and Hungarian, against the backdrop of its wider South Slavic family. Its distinctive geographical position parallels its unique evolution, beginning with Slav settlement in this corner of Europe back in the 6th century, then becoming the official language of Slovenia – first as a part of Yugoslavia and since 1991 an independent republic.

Although Croatian and Serbian are its closest relatives within the South Slavic group, Slovene is nevertheless much closer to Croatia's northwestern and coastal dialects. It also shares some features with the more distant West Slavic languages (through contact with a dialect of Slovak, from which it was later separated by the arrival of the Hungarians to Central Europe in the 9th century). Unlike any other modern Slavic language, it has preserved the archaic Indo-European dual grammatical form, which means, for example, that instead of *pivo pee*·vo (a beer) or *piva pee*·va (beers), you and a friend could simply order *pivi pee*·vee (two beers).

German, Italian and Hungarian words entered Slovene during the centuries of foreign rule (in the Austro-Hungarian Empire or under the control of Venice), as these were the languages of the elite when all three countries coexisted, while the common people spoke one of the Slovene dialects. Croatian and Serbian influence on Slovene was particularly significant during the 20th century within the Yugoslav state.

For a language with a relatively small number of speakers, Slovene abounds in regional variations – eight major dialect groups have been identified, which are further divided into fifty or so regional dialects. Some of these cover the neighbouring areas of Austria, Italy and Hungary. The modern literary language is based largely on the central dialects and was shaped through a gradual process that lasted from the 16th to the 19th century.

Slovenia has been called 'a nation of poets', and what better way to get immersed in that spirit than to plunge into this beautiful language first? While you're soaking up the atmosphere of the capital, Ljubljana (whose central square is graced with a monument in honour of the nation's greatest poet, France Prešeren), remember that its name almost equals 'beloved' (*ljubljena lyoob*·lye·na) in Slovene!

introduction – SLOVENE

pronunciation

vowel sounds

The vowels in Slovene can be pronounced differently, depending on whether they're stressed or unstressed, long or short. Don't worry about these distinctions though, as you shouldn't have too much trouble being understood if you follow our coloured pronunciation guide. Note that we've used the symbols oh and ow to help you pronounce vowels followed by the letters l and v in written Slovene – when they appear at the end of a syllable, these combinations sometimes produce a sound similar to the 'w' in English.

symbol	english equivalent	slovene example	transliteration
a	father	*dan*	dan
ai	aisle	*srajca*	*srai*-tsa
e	bet	*center*	*tsen*-ter
ee	see	*riba*	*ree*-ba
o	pot	*oče*	*o*-che
oh	oh	*pol, nov*	poh, noh
oo	zoo	*jug*	yoog
ow	how	*ostal, prav*	os-*tow*, prow
uh	ago	*pes*	puhs

word stress

Slovene has free stress, which means there's no general rule regarding which syllable the stress falls on – it simply has to be learned. You'll be fine if you just follow our coloured pronunciation guides, in which the stressed syllable is always in italics.

consonant sounds

Most Slovene consonant sounds are pronounced more or less as they are in English. Don't be intimidated by the vowel-less words such as *trg* tuhrg (square) or *vrt* vuhrt (garden) – we've put a slight 'uh' sound before the *r*, which serves as a semi-vowel between the two other consonants.

symbol	english equivalent	slovene example	transliteration
b	bed	*brat*	brat
ch	cheat	*hči*	hchee
d	dog	*datum*	*da*·toom
f	fat	*telefon*	te·le·*fon*
g	go	*grad*	grad
h	hat	*hvala*	*hva*·la
k	kit	*karta*	*kar*·ta
l	lot	*ulica*	*oo*·lee·tsa
m	man	*mož*	mozh
n	not	*naslov*	nas·*loh*
p	pet	*pošta*	*po*·shta
r	run (rolled)	*brez*	brez
s	sun	*sin*	seen
sh	shot	*tuš*	toosh
t	top	*sto*	sto
ts	hats	*cesta*	*tse*·sta
v	very	*vlak*	vlak
y	yes	*jesen*	ye·*sen*
z	zero	*zima*	*zee*·ma
zh	pleasure	*žena*	*zhe*·na
'	a slight y sound	*kašelj, manj*	*ka*·shel', man'

tools

language difficulties

Do you speak English?
Ali govorite angleško?
a·lee go·vo·*ree*·te ang·*lesh*·ko

Do you understand?
Ali razumete?
a·lee ra·*zoo*·me·te

I (don't) understand.
(Ne) Razumem.
(ne) ra·*zoo*·mem

What does (*danes*) mean?
Kaj pomeni (danes)?
kai po·*me*·nee (*da*·nes)

Could you repeat that?
Lahko ponovite?
lah·*ko* po·no·*vee*·te

How do you ...?
Kako se ...?
ka·*ko* se ...

   pronounce this word
izgovori to besedo
eez·go·vo·*ree* to be·*se*·do

   write (*hvala*)
napiše (hvala)
na·*pee*·she (*hva*·la)

Could you please ...?
Prosim ...
pro·seem ...

   speak more slowly
govorite počasneje
go·vo·*ree*·te po·cha·*sne*·ye

   write it down
napišite
na·*pee*·shee·te

essentials

Yes.	*Da.*	da
No.	*Ne.*	ne
Please.	*Prosim.*	*pro*·seem
Thank you (very much).	*Hvala (lepa).*	*hva*·la (*le*·pa)
You're welcome.	*Ni za kaj.*	nee za kai
Excuse me.	*Dovolite.*	do·vo·lee·te
Sorry.	*Oprostite.*	op·ros·*tee*·te

numbers

0	*nula*	*noo·*la	16	*šestnajst*	*shest·*naist
1	*en/ena* m/f	*en/e·*na	17	*sedemnajst*	*se·*dem·naist
2	*dva/dve* m/f	*dva/dve*	18	*osemnajst*	*o·*sem·naist
3	*trije/tri* m/f	*tree·*ye/tree	19	*devetnajst*	*de·*vet·naist
4	*štirje* m	*shtee·*rye	20	*dvajset*	*dvai·*set
	štiri f	*shtee·*ree	21	*enaindvajset*	*e·*na·een·dvai·set
5	*pet*	*pet*	22	*dvaindvajset*	*dva·*een·dvai·set
6	*šest*	*shest*			
7	*sedem*	*se·*dem	30	*trideset*	*tree·*de·set
8	*osem*	*o·*sem	40	*štirideset*	*shtee·*ree·de·set
9	*devet*	*de·*vet	50	*petdeset*	*pet·*de·set
10	*deset*	*de·*set	60	*šestdeset*	*shest·*de·set
11	*enajst*	*e·*naist	70	*sedemdeset*	*se·*dem·de·set
12	*dvanajst*	*dva·*naist	80	*osemdeset*	*o·*sem·de·set
13	*trinajst*	*tree·*naist	90	*devetdeset*	*de·*vet·de·set
14	*štirinajst*	*shtee·*ree·naist	100	*sto*	*sto*
15	*petnajst*	*pet·*naist	1000	*tisoč*	*tee·*soch

time & dates

What time is it?	*Koliko je ura?*	*ko·*lee·ko ye *oo·*ra
It's one o'clock.	*Ura je ena.*	*oo·*ra ye *e·*na
It's (10) o'clock.	*Ura je (deset).*	*oo·*ra ye (de·*set*)
Quarter past (one).	*Četrt čez (ena).*	*che·tuhrt* chez (*e·*na)
Half past (one).	*Pol (dveh).* (lit: half two)	pol (dveh)
Quarter to (one).	*Petnajst do (enih).*	*pet·*naist do (*e·*neeh)
At what time ...?	*Ob kateri uri ...?*	ob ka·*te·*ree *oo·*ree ...
At ...	*Ob ...*	ob ...
am	*dopoldne*	do·*poh·*dne
pm	*popoldne*	po·*poh·*dne
Monday	*ponedeljek*	po·ne·*del·*yek
Tuesday	*torek*	*to·*rek
Wednesday	*sreda*	*sre·*da
Thursday	*četrtek*	che·*tuhr·*tek
Friday	*petek*	*pe·*tek
Saturday	*sobota*	so·*bo·*ta
Sunday	*nedelja*	ne·*del·*ya

January	januar	ya·noo·ar
February	februar	feb·roo·ar
March	marec	ma·rets
April	april	ap·reel
May	maj	mai
June	junij	yoo·neey
July	julij	yoo·leey
August	avgust	av·goost
September	september	sep·tem·ber
October	oktober	ok·to·ber
November	november	no·vem·ber
December	december	de·tsem·ber

What date is it today?
Katerega smo danes? ka·te·re·ga smo da·nes

It's (18 October).
Smo (osemnajstega oktobra). smo (o·sem·nai·ste·ga) ok·tob·ra

| since (May) | od (maja) | od (ma·ya) |
| until (June) | do (junija) | do (yoo·nee·ya) |

last ...
night	prejšnji večer	preysh·nyee ve·cher
week	prejšnji teden	preysh·nyee te·den
month	prejšnji mesec	preysh·nyee me·sets
year	prejšnje leto	preysh·nye le·to

next ...
week	naslednji teden	nas·led·nyee te·den
month	naslednji mesec	nas·led·nyee me·sets
year	naslednje leto	nas·led·nye le·to

yesterday/tomorrow ...
	včeraj/jutri ...	vche·rai/yoot·ree ...
morning	zjutraj	zyoot·rai
afternoon	popoldne	po·poh·dne
evening	zvečer	zve·cher

weather

What's the weather like?	Kakšno je vreme?	kak·shno ye vre·me
It's raining/snowing.	Dežuje/Sneži.	de·zhoo·ye/sne·zhee

It's	... je.	... ye
cloudy	Oblačno	ob·lach·no
cold	Mrzlo	muhr·zlo
hot	Vroče	vro·che
sunny	Sončno	sonch·no
warm	Toplo	top·lo
windy	Vetrovno	vet·roh·no

spring	pomlad f	pom·lad
summer	poletje n	po·let·ye
autumn	jesen f	ye·sen
winter	zima f	zee·ma

border crossing

I'm here ...	Tu sem ...	too sem ...
on business	poslovno	pos·lov·no
on holiday	na počitnicah	na po·cheet·nee·tsah

I'm here for ...	Ostanem ...	os·ta·nem ...
(10) days	(deset) dni	(de·set) dnee
(two) months	(dva) meseca	(dva) me·se·tsa
(three) weeks	(tri) tedne	(tree) ted·ne

I'm going to ...
Namenjen/Namenjena sem v ... m/f   na·*men*·yen/na·*men*·ye·na sem v ...

I'm staying at the (Slon).
Stanujem v (Slonu).   sta·*noo*·yem v (*slo*·noo)

I have nothing to declare.
Ničesar nimam za prijaviti.   nee·*che*·sar *nee*·mam za pree·*ya*·vee·tee

I have something to declare.
Nekaj imam za prijaviti.   ne·kai ee·*mam* za pree·*ya*·vee·tee

That's mine.
To je moje.   to ye *mo*·ye

That's not mine.
To ni moje.   to nee *mo*·ye

transport

tickets & luggage

Where can I buy a ticket?
Kje lahko kupim vozovnico?   kye lah·*ko* koo·peem vo·*zov*·nee·tso

Do I need to book a seat?
Ali moram rezervirati sedež?   a·lee *mo*·ram re·zer·*vee*·ra·tee se·dezh

One ... ticket to (Koper), please.	... vozovnico do (Kopra), prosim.	... vo·*zov*·nee·tso do (*ko*·pra) pro·seem
one-way	Enosmerno	e·no·*smer*·no
return	Povratno	pov·*rat*·no

I'd like to ... my ticket, please.	Želim ... vozovnico, prosim.	zhe·*leem* ... vo·*zov*·nee·tso pro·seem
cancel	preklicati	prek·*lee*·tsa·tee
change	zamenjati	za·*men*·ya·tee
collect	dvigniti	dveeg·nee·tee
confirm	potrditi	po·tuhr·*dee*·tee

I'd like a ... seat, please.	Želim ... sedež, prosim.	zhe·*leem* ... se·dezh pro·seem
nonsmoking	nekadilski	ne·ka·*deel*·skee
smoking	kadilski	ka·*deel*·skee

How much is it?
Koliko stane?   ko·lee·ko *sta*·ne

Is there air conditioning?
Ali ima klimo?   a·lee ee·*ma klee*·mo

Is there a toilet?
Ali ima stranišče?   a·lee ee·*ma* stra·*neesh*·che

How long does the trip take?
Kako dolgo traja potovanje?   ka·*ko dol*·go *tra*·ya po·to·*van*·ye

Is it a direct route?
Je to direktna proga?   ye to dee·*rekt*·na *pro*·ga

I'd like a luggage locker.
Želim garderobno omarico.   zhe·*leem* gar·de·*rob*·no o·*ma*·ree·tso

My luggage has been ...	Moja prtljaga je ...	mo·ya puhrt·lya·ga ye ...
damaged	poškodovana	posh·ko·do·va·na
lost	izgubljena	eez·goob·lye·na
stolen	ukradena	oo·kra·de·na

getting around

Where does flight (AF 46) arrive/depart?
Kje pristane/odleti let — kye pree·sta·ne/od·le·tee let
številka (AF 46)? — shte·veel·ka (a fuh shtee·ree shest)

Where's (the) ...?	Kje je/so ...? sg/pl	kye ye/so ...
arrivals hall	prihodi pl	pree·ho·dee
departures hall	odhodi pl	od·ho·dee
duty-free shop	brezcarinska	brez·tsa·reen·ska
	trgovina sg	tuhr·go·vee·na
gate (12)	izhod (dvanajst) sg	eez·hod (dva·naist)

Is this the ... to (Venice)?	Je to ... za (Benetke)?	ye to ... za (be·net·ke)
boat	ladja	lad·ya
bus	avtobus	av·to·boos
plane	letalo	le·ta·lo
train	vlak	vlak

What time's the ... bus?	Kdaj odpelje ... avtobus?	kdai od·pel·ye ... av·to·boos
first	prvi	puhr·vee
last	zadnji	zad·nyee
next	naslednji	nas·led·nyee

At what time does it arrive/leave?
Kdaj prispe/odpelje? — kdai prees·pe/od·pel·ye

How long will it be delayed?
Koliko ze zamujen? — ko·lee·ko ye za·moo·yen

What station is this?
Katera postaja je to? — ka·te·ra pos·ta·ya ye to

What stop is this?
Katero postajališče je to? — ka·te·ro pos·ta·ya·leesh·che ye to

What's the next station?
Katera je naslednja postaja? — ka·te·ra ye nas·led·nya pos·ta·ya

What's the next stop?
Katero je naslednje postajališče? — ka·te·ro ye nas·led·nye pos·ta·ya·leesh·che

Does it stop at (Postojna)?
Ali ustavi v (Postojni)? — a·lee oos·ta·vee v (pos·toy·nee)

Please tell me when we get to (Kranj).
Prosim povejte mi, — pro·seem po·vey·te mee
ko prispemo v (Kranj). — ko prees·pe·mo v (kran)

How long do we stop here?
Kako dolgo stojimo tu? — ka·ko dol·go sto·yee·mo too

Is this seat available?
Je ta sedež prost? — ye ta se·dezh prost

That's my seat.
To je moj sedež. — to ye moy se·dezh

I'd like a taxi ...	*Želim taksi ...*	zhe·leem tak·see ...
at (9am)	*ob (devetih*	ob (de·ve·teeh
	dopoldne)	do·poh·dne)
now	*zdaj*	zdai
tomorrow	*jutri*	yoot·ree

Is this taxi available?
Je ta taksi prost? — ye ta tak·see prost

How much is it to ...?
Koliko stane do ...? — ko·lee·ko sta·ne do ...

Please put the meter on.
Prosim, vključite taksimeter. — pro·seem vklyoo·chee·te tak·see·me·ter

Please take me to (this address).
Prosim, peljite me na (ta naslov). — pro·seem pel·yee·te me na (ta nas·loh)

Please ...	*Prosim ...*	pro·seem ...
slow down	*vozite počasneje*	vo·zee·te po·chas·ne·ye
stop here	*ustavite tukaj*	oos·ta·vee·te too·kai
wait here	*počakajte tukaj*	po·cha·kai·te too·kai

car, motorbike & bicycle hire

I'd like to hire a ...	*Želim najeti ...*	zhe·leem na·ye·tee ...
bicycle	*kolo*	ko·lo
car	*avto*	av·to
motorbike	*motor*	mo·tor

with ...	s ...	s ...
a driver	šoferjem	sho·*fer*·yem
air conditioning	klimo	klee·mo
antifreeze	sredstvom proti	sreds·tvom pro·tee
	zmrzovanju	zmuhr·zo·van·yoo
snow chains	snežnimi	snezh·nee·mee
	verigami	ve·ree·ga·mee

How much for	Koliko stane najem	ko·lee·ko sta·ne na·yem
... hire?	na ...?	na ...
hourly	uro	oo·ro
daily	dan	dan
weekly	teden	te·den

air	zrak m	zrak
oil	olje n	ol·ye
petrol	bencin m	ben·tseen
tyres	gume f	goo·me

I need a mechanic.
  Potrebujem mehanika.   pot·re·boo·yem me·ha·nee·ka

I've run out of petrol.
  Zmanjkalo mi je bencina.   zman'·ka·lo mee ye ben·tsee·na

I have a flat tyre.
  Počila mi je guma.   po·chee·la mee ye goo·ma

directions

Where's the ...?	Kje je ...?	kye ye ...
bank	banka	ban·ka
city centre	center mesta	tsen·ter mes·ta
hotel	hotel	ho·tel
market	tržnica	tuhrzh·nee·tsa
police station	policijska	po·lee·tseey·ska
	postaja	pos·ta·ya
post office	pošta	posh·ta
public toilet	javno stranišče	yav·no stra·neesh·che
tourist office	turistični	too·rees·teech·nee
	urad	oo·rad

Is this the road to (Ptuj)?
Pelje ta cesta do (Ptuja)? — pel·ye ta tses·ta do (ptoo·ya)

Can you show me (on the map)?
Mi lahko pokažete (na zemljevidu)? — mee lah·ko po·ka·zhe·te (na zem·lye·vee·doo)

What's the address?
Na katerem naslovu je? — na ka·te·rem nas·lo·voo ye

How far is it?
Kako daleč je? — ka·ko da·lech ye

How do I get there?
Kako pridem tja? — ka·ko pree·dem tya

Turn ...	*Zavijte ...*	za·veey·te ...
at the corner	*na vogalu*	na vo·ga·loo
at the traffic lights	*pri semaforju*	pree se·ma·for·yoo
left/right	*levo/desno*	le·vo/des·no

It's ...		
behind ...	*Za ...*	za ...
far away	*Daleč.*	da·lech
here	*Tukaj.*	too·kai
in front of ...	*Pred ...*	pred ...
left	*Levo.*	le·vo
near (to ...)	*Blizu ...*	blee·zoo ...
next to ...	*Poleg ...*	po·leg ...
on the corner	*Na vogalu.*	na vo·ga·loo
opposite ...	*Nasproti ...*	nas·pro·tee ...
right	*Desno.*	des·no
straight ahead	*Naravnost naprej.*	na·rav·nost na·prey
there	*Tam.*	tam

by bus	*z avtobusom*	z av·to·boo·som
by taxi	*s taksijem*	s tak·see·yem
by train	*z vlakom*	z vla·kom
on foot	*peš*	pesh

north	*sever*	se·ver
south	*jug*	yoog
east	*vzhod*	vzhod
west	*zahod*	za·hod

Vhod/Izhod	vhod/eez-*hod*	**Entrance/Exit**
Odprto/Zaprto	od-*puhr*-to/za-*puhr*-to	**Open/Closed**
Proste sobe	*pros*-te so-be	**Rooms Available**
Ni prostih mest	nee *pros*-teeh mest	**No Vacancies**
Informacije	een-for-*ma*-tsee-ye	**Information**
Policijska postaja	po-lee-*tseey*-ska pos-*ta*-ya	**Police Station**
Prepovedano	pre-po-*ve*-da-no	**Prohibited**
Stranišče	stra-*neesh*-che	**Toilets**
Moški	*mosh*-kee	**Men**
Ženske	*zhen*-ske	**Women**
Vroče/Mrzlo	*vro*-che/*muhr*-zlo	**Hot/Cold**

accommodation

finding accommodation

Where's a ...?	*Kje je ... ?*	kye ye ...
camping ground	*kamp*	kamp
guesthouse	*gostišče*	gos-*teesh*-che
hotel	*hotel*	ho-*tel*
youth hostel	*mladinski hotel*	mla-*deen*-skee ho-*tel*

Can you recommend	*Mi lahko priporočite*	mee lah-*ko* pree-po-ro-*chee*-te
a ... hotel?	*... hotel?*	... ho-*tel*
cheap	*poceni*	po-*tse*-nee
good	*dober*	*do*-ber

Can you recommend a hotel nearby?
Mi lahko priporočite hotel v   mee lah-*ko* pree-po-ro-*chee*-te ho-*tel* oo
bližini?   blee-*zhee*-nee

I'd like to book a room, please.
Želim rezervirati sobo, prosim.   zhe-*leem* re-zer-*vee*-ra-tee *so*-bo *pro*-seem

I have a reservation.
Imam rezervacijo.   ee-*mam* re-zer-*va*-tsee-yo

My name's ...
Ime mi je ...   ee-*me* mee ye ...

Do you have a twin room?
Imate sobo z ločenima posteljama?   ee·*ma*·te *so*·bo z *lo*·che·nee·ma *pos*·tel·ya·ma

Do you have a ... room?	*Ali imate ... sobo?*	a·lee ee·*ma*·te ... *so*·bo
single	*enoposteljno*	e·no·*pos*·tel'·no
double	*dvoposteljno*	dvo·*pos*·tel'·no

How much is it per ...?	*Koliko stane na ...?*	ko·lee·ko *sta*·ne na ...
night	*noč*	noch
person	*osebo*	o·*se*·bo

Can I pay by ...?	*Lahko plačam s ...?*	lah·*ko* pla·cham s ...
credit card	*kreditno kartico*	kre·*deet*·no *kar*·tee·tso
travellers cheque	*potovalnim čekom*	po·to·*val*·neem *che*·kom

I'd like to stay for (three) nights.
Rad bi ostal (tri) noči. m   rada bee os·*tow* (tree) no·*chee*
Rada bi ostala (tri) noči. f   ra·da bee os·*ta*·la (tree) no·*chee*

From (2 July) to (6 July).
Od (drugega julija)   od (*droo*·ge·ga *yoo*·lee·ya)
do (šestega julija).   do (*shes*·te·ga *yoo*·lee·ya)

Can I see the room?
Lahko vidim sobo?   lah·*ko vee*·deem *so*·bo

Am I allowed to camp here?
Smem tu kampirati?   smem too kam·*pee*·ra·tee

Is there a camp site nearby?
Je v bližini kakšen kamp?   ye v blee·*zhee*·nee *kak*·shen kamp

requests & queries

When/Where is breakfast served?
Kdaj/Kje strežete zajtrk?   kdai/kye *stre*·zhe·te *zai*·tuhrk

Please wake me at (seven).
Prosim, zbudite me ob (sedmih).   *pro*·seem zboo·*dee*·te me ob (*sed*·meeh)

Could I have my key, please?
Lahko prosim dobim ključ?   lah·*ko pro*·sim do·*beem* klyooch

Can I get another (blanket)?
Lahko dobim drugo (odejo)?   lah·*ko* do·*beem droo*·go (o·*de*·yo)

Is there an elevator/a safe?
Imate dvigalo/sef?   ee·*ma*·te dvee·*ga*·lo/sef

The room is too...   *Soba je ...*   so·ba ye ...
- expensive   *predraga*   pre·*dra*·ga
- noisy   *prehrupna*   pre·*hroop*·na
- small   *premajhna*   pre·*mai*·hna

This ... isn't clean.   *Ta ... ni čista.*   ta ... nee *chees*·ta
- pillow   *blazina*   bla·*zee*·na
- sheet   *rjuha*   *ryoo*·ha
- towel   *brisača*   bree·*sa*·cha

The fan doesn't work.
Ventilator je pokvarjen.   ven·tee·*la*·tor ye pok·*var*·yen
The air conditioning doesn't work.
Klima je pokvarjena.   *klee*·ma ye pok·*var*·ye·na
The toilet doesn't work.
Stranišče je pokvarjeno.   stra·*neesh*·che ye pok·*var*·ye·no

checking out

What time is checkout?
Kdaj se moram odjaviti?   kdai se *mo*·ram od·*ya*·vee·tee

Can I leave my luggage here?
Lahko pustim prtljago tu?   lah·*ko* poos·*teem* puhrt·*lya*·go too

Could I have my ...,   *Lahko prosim*   lah·*ko* pro·seem
please?   *dobim ...?*   do·*beem* ...
- deposit   *moj polog*   moy *po*·log
- passport   *moj potni list*   moy *pot*·nee leest
- valuables   *moje dragocenosti*   *mo*·ye dra·go·*tse*·nos·tee

communications & banking

the internet

Where's the local Internet café?
Kje je najbližja internetna   kye ye nai·*bleezh*·ya een·ter·*net*·na
kavarna?   ka·*var*·na

How much is it per hour?
Koliko stane ena ura?   ko·lee·ko *sta*·ne e·na *oo*·ra

I'd like to ...	Želim ...	zhe-leem ...
check my email	preveriti elektronsko pošto	pre-ve-ree-tee e-lek-tron-sko posh-to
get Internet access	dostop do interneta	dos-top do een-ter-ne-ta
use a printer	uporabiti tiskalnik	oo-po-ra-bee-tee tees-kal-neek
use a scanner	uporabiti optični čitalnik	oo-po-ra-bee-tee op-teech-nee chee-tal-neek

mobile/cell phone

I'd like a ...	Želim ...	zhe-leem ...
mobile/cell phone for hire	najeti mobilni telefon	na-ye-tee mo-beel-nee te-le-fon
SIM card for your network	SIM kartico za vaše omrežje	seem kar-tee-tso za va-she om-rezh-ye
What are the rates?	Kakšne so cene?	kak-shne so tse-ne

telephone

What's your phone number?
Lahko izvem vašo telefonsko številko?
lah-ko eez-vem va-sho te-le-fon-sko shte-veel-ko

The number is ...
Številka je ...
shte-veel-ka ye ...

Where's the nearest public phone?
Kje je najbližja govorilnica?
kye ye nai-bleezh-ya go-vo-reel-nee-tsa

I'd like to buy a phonecard.
Želim kupiti telefonsko kartico.
zhe-leem koo-pee-tee te-le-fon-sko kar-tee-tso

I want to ...	Želim ...	zhe-leem ...
call (Singapore)	poklicati (Singapur)	pok-lee-tsa-tee (seen-ga-poor)
make a local call	klicati lokalno	klee-tsa-tee lo-kal-no
reverse the charges	klicati na stroške klicanega	klee-tsa-tee na strosh-ke klee-tsa-ne-ga

How much does ... cost?	Koliko stane ...?	ko-lee-ko sta-ne ...
a (three)-minute call	(tri)minutni klic	(tree-)mee-noot-nee kleets
each extra minute	vsaka dodatna minuta	vsa-ka do-dat-na mee-noo-ta

post office

I want to send a ...	Želim poslati ...	zhe-*leem* pos-*la*-tee ...
letter	pismo	*pees*-mo
parcel	paket	pa-*ket*
postcard	razglednico	raz-*gled*-nee-tso
I want to buy a/an ...	Želim kupiti ...	zhe-*leem* koo-*pee*-tee ...
envelope	kuverto	koo-*ver*-to
stamp	znamko	*znam*-ko
Please send it by ...	Prosim, pošljite ...	pro-seem posh-*lyee*-te ...
airmail	z letalsko pošto	z le-*tal*-sko *posh*-to
express mail	s hitro pošto	s *heet*-ro *posh*-to
registered mail	s priporočeno pošto	s pree-po-ro-*che*-no *posh*-to
surface mail	z navadno pošto	z na-*vad*-no *posh*-to

bank

Where's a/an ...?	Kje je ...?	kye ye ...
ATM	bankomat	ban-ko-*mat*
foreign exchange office	menjalnica	men-*yal*-nee-tsa
I'd like to ...	Želim ...	zhe-*leem* ...
Where can I ...?	Kje je mogoče ...?	kye ye mo-*go*-che ...
cash a cheque	unovčiti ček	oo-*nov*-chee-tee chek
change a travellers cheque	zamenjati potovalni ček	za-*men*-ya-tee po-to-*val*-nee chek
change money	zamenjati denar	za-*men*-ya-tee de-*nar*
withdraw money	dvigniti denar	dveeg-nee-tee de-*nar*
What's the ...?	Kakšen/Kakšna je ...? m/f	kak-*shen*/kak-*shna* ye ...
commission	provizija f	pro-*vee*-zee-ya
exchange rate	menjalni tečaj m	men-*yal*-nee te-*chai*

Can I arrange a transfer of money?
Lahko uredim prenos denarja?   lah-*ko* oo-re-*deem* pre-*nos* de-*nar*-ya

What time does the bank open?
Kdaj se banka odpre?   kdai se *ban*-ka od-*pre*

Has my money arrived yet?
Je moj denar že prispel?   ye moy de-*nar* zhe prees-*pe*-oo

sightseeing

getting in

What time does it open/close?
Kdaj se odpre/zapre?
kdai se od·*pre*/za·*pre*

What's the admission charge?
Koliko stane vstopnica?
ko·lee·ko *sta*·ne *vstop*·nee·tsa

Is there a discount for students/children?
Imate popust za
ee·*ma*·te po·*poost* za
študente/otroke?
shtoo·*den*·te/ot·*ro*·ke

I'd like a ...	*Želim ...*	zhe·*leem* ...
catalogue	*katalog*	ka·ta·*log*
guide	*vodnik*	vod·*neek*
local map	*zemljevid kraja*	zem·lye·*veed kra*·ya

I'd like to see ... *Želim videti ...* zhe·*leem vee*·de·tee ...
What's that? *Kaj je to?* kai ye to
Can I take a photo? *Ali lahko fotografiram?* a·lee lah·*ko* fo·to·gra·*fee*·ram

tours

When's the next ...?	*Kdaj je naslednji ...?*	kdai ye nas·*led*·nyee ...
boat trip	*izlet s čolnom*	eez·*let* s *choh*·nom
day trip	*dnevni izlet*	*dnev*·nee eez·*let*
tour	*izlet*	eez·*let*

Is ... included?	*Je ... vključena?*	ye ... *vklyoo*·che·na
accommodation	*nastanitev*	nas·ta·*nee*·tev
the admission charge	*vstopnina*	vstop·*nee*·na
food	*hrana*	*hra*·na

Is transport included?
Je prevoz vključen?
ye pre·*voz* vklyoo·chen

How long is the tour?
Koliko časa traja izlet?
ko·lee·ko *cha*·sa *tra*·ya eez·*let*

What time should we be back?
Kdaj naj se vrnemo?
kdai nai se *vuhr*·ne·mo

castle	grad m	grad
cathedral	stolnica f	stol·nee·tsa
church	cerkev f	tser·kev
main square	glavni trg m	glav·nee tuhrg
monastery	samostan m	sa·mos·tan
monument	spomenik m	spo·me·neek
museum	muzej m	moo·zey
old city	staro mesto n	sta·ro mes·to
palace	palača f	pa·la·cha
ruins	ruševine f	roo·she·vee·ne
stadium	stadion m	sta·dee·on
statue	kip m	keep

shopping

enquiries

Where's a …?	Kje je …?	kye ye …
bank	banka	ban·ka
bookshop	knjigarna	knyee·gar·na
camera shop	trgovina s	tuhr·go·vee·na s
	fotografsko opremo	fo·to·graf·sko op·re·mo
department store	blagovnica	bla·gov·nee·tsa
grocery store	trgovina s	tuhr·go·vee·na s
	špecerijo	shpe·tse·ree·yo
market	tržnica	tuhrzh·nee·tsa
newsagency	kiosk	kee·osk
supermarket	trgovina	tuhr·go·vee·na

Where can I buy (a padlock)?
   Kje lahko kupim (ključavnico)?   kye lah·ko koo·peem (klyoo·chav·nee·tso)

I'm looking for …
   Iščem …   eesh·chem …

Can I look at it?
   Lahko pogledam?   lah·ko pog·le·dam

Do you have any others?
Imate še kakšnega/kakšno? m/f — ee·*ma*·te she kak·shne·ga/kak·shno

Does it have a guarantee?
Ali ima garancijo? — *a*·lee ee·*ma* ga·ran·*tsee*·yo

Can I have it sent abroad?
Mi lahko pošljete v tujino? — mee lah·*ko* posh·lye·te v too·*yee*·no

Can I have my ... repaired?
Mi lahko popravite ...? — mee lah·ko po·*pra*·vee·te ...

It's faulty.
Ne deluje. — ne de·*loo*·ye

I'd like ..., please. — *Želim ..., prosim.* — zhe·*leem* ... *pro*·seem
  a bag — *vrečko* — *vrech*·ko
  a refund — *vračilo denarja* — vra·*chee*·lo de·*nar*·ya
  to return this — *vrniti tole* — vr·*nee*·tee *to*·le

paying

How much is this?
Koliko stane? — ko·lee·ko *sta*·ne

Can you write down the price?
Lahko napišete ceno? — lah·*ko* na·*pee*·she·te *tse*·no

That's too expensive.
To je predrago. — to ye pre·dra·*go*

What's your lowest price?
Povejte vašo najnižjo ceno. — po·*vey*·te *va*·sho nai·*neezh*·yo *tse*·no

I'll give you (five) euros.
Dam vam (pet) evrov. — dam vam (pet) *ev*·roh

There's a mistake in the bill.
Na računu je napaka. — na ra·*choo*·noo ye na·*pa*·ka

Do you accept ...? — *Ali sprejemate ...?* — *a*·lee spre·*ye*·ma·te ...
  credit cards — *kreditne kartice* — kre·*deet*·ne *kar*·tee·tse
  debit cards — *debetne kartice* — de·*bet*·ne *kar*·tee·tse
  travellers cheques — *potovalne čeke* — po·to·*val*·ne *che*·ke

I'd like ..., please. — *Želim ..., prosim.* — zhe·*leem* ... *pro*·seem
  a receipt — *račun* — ra·*choon*
  my change — *drobiž* — dro·*beezh*

clothes & shoes

Can I try it on?	Lahko pomerim?	lah·ko po·me·reem
My size is (42).	Nosim številko	no·seem shte·veel·ko
	(dvainštirideset).	(dva·een·shtee·ree·de·set)
It doesn't fit.	Ni mi prav.	nee mee prow
... size	... številka	... shte·veel·ka
small	majhna	mai·hna
medium	srednja	sred·nya
large	velika	ve·lee·ka

books & music

I'd like a ...	Želim ...	zhe·leem ...
newspaper	časopis	cha·so·pees
(in English)	(v angleščini)	(v ang·lesh·chee·nee)
pen	pisalo	pee·sa·lo

I'm looking for an English-language bookshop.
Iščem angleško knjigarno.   eesh·chem ang·lesh·ko knyee·gar·no

I'm looking for a book/music by (Miha Mazzini/Zoran Predin).
Iščem knjigo/glasbo   eesh·chem knyee·go/glaz·bo
(Mihe Mazzinija/Zorana Prediña).   (mee·he ma·tsee·nee·ya/zo·ra·na pre·dee·na)

Can I listen to this?
Lahko tole poslušam?   lah·ko to·le pos·loo·sham

photography

Can you ...?	Lahko ...?	lah·ko ...
burn a CD from	zapečete CD z moje	za·pe·che·te tse·de z mo·ye
my memory card	spominske kartice	spo·meen·ske kar·tee·tse
develop this film	razvijete ta film	raz·vee·ye·te ta feelm
load this film	vstavite ta film	vsta·vee·te ta feelm

I need a/an ... film	Potrebujem ... film	pot·re·boo·yem ... feelm
for this camera.	za ta fotoaparat.	za ta fo·to·a·pa·rat
APS	APS	a pe es
B&W	črno-bel	chuhr·no·be·oo
colour	barvni	barv·nee
(200) speed	(dvesto) ASA	(dve·sto) a·sa

I need a slide film for this camera.

Potrebujem film za diapozitive pot·re·*boo*·yem feelm za dee·a·po·zee·*tee*·ve
za ta fotoaparat. za ta fo·to·a·pa·*rat*

When will it be ready?

Kdaj bo gotovo? kdai bo go·*to*·vo

meeting people

greetings, goodbyes & introductions

Hello/Hi.	*Zdravo.*	*zdra*·vo
Good night.	*Lahko noč.*	*lah*·ko noch
Goodbye./Bye.	*Na svidenje/Adijo.*	na *svee*·den·ye/a·*dee*·yo
See you later.	*Se vidiva.*	se *vee*·dee·va
Mr/Mrs	*gospod/gospa*	gos·*pod*/gos·*pa*
Miss	*gospodična*	gos·po·*deech*·na
How are you?	*Kako ste/si?* pol/inf	ka·*ko* ste/see
Fine, thanks.	*Dobro, hvala.*	*dob*·ro *hva*·la
And you?	*Pa vi/ti?* pol/inf	pa vee/tee
What's your name?	*Kako vam/ti je ime?* pol/inf	ka·*ko* vam/tee ye ee·*me*
My name is ...	*Ime mi je ...*	ee·*me* mee ye ...
I'm pleased to	*Veseli me, da sem vas*	ve·se·*lee* me da sem vas
meet you.	*spoznal/spoznala.* m/f	spoz·*now*/spoz·*na*·la
This is my ...	*To je moj/moja ...* m/f	to ye moy/*mo*·ya ...
boyfriend	*fant*	fant
brother	*brat*	brat
daughter	*hči*	hchee
father	*oče*	*o*·che
friend	*prijatelj* m	pree·*ya*·tel'
	prijateljica f	pree·*ya*·tel·yee·tsa
girlfriend	*punca*	*poon*·tsa
husband	*mož*	mozh
mother	*mama*	*ma*·ma
partner (intimate)	*partner/partnerka* m/f	*part*·ner/*part*·ner·ka
sister	*sestra*	*ses*·tra
son	*sin*	seen
wife	*žena*	*zhe*·na

Here's my phone number.
Tu je moja telefonska številka.   too ye *mo*·ya te·le·*fon*·ska shte·*veel*·ka

What's your phone number?
Mi poveste vašo telefonsko številko?   mee po·*ves*·te *va*·sho te·le·*fon*·sko shte·*veel*·ko

Here's my ...   *Tu je moj/moja ...* m/f   too ye moy/*mo*·ya ...
What's your ...?   *Kakšen je vaš ...?* m   *kak*·shen ye vash ...
   Kakšna je vaša ...? f   *kak*·shna ye *va*·sha ...
   (email) address   *(elektronski) naslov* m   (e·lek·*tron*·skee) nas·*loh*
   fax number   *številka faksa* f   shte·*veel*·ka *fak*·sa

occupations

What's your occupation?   *Kaj ste po poklicu?*   kai ste po pok·*lee*·tsoo

I'm a/an ...   *... sem.*   ... sem
   artist   *Umetnik* m   oo·*met*·neek
      Umetnica f   oo·*met*·nee·tsa
   farmer   *Kmet/Kmetica* m/f   kmet/kme·*tee*·tsa
   office worker   *Uradnik* m   oo·*rad*·neek
      Uradnica f   oo·*rad*·nee·tsa
   scientist   *Znanstvenik* m   znans·tve·neek
      Znanstvenica f   znans·tve·nee·tsa
   student   *Študent/Študentka* m/f   shtoo·*dent*/shtoo·*dent*·ka
   tradesperson   *Trgovec/Trgovka* m/f   tuhr·*go*·vets/ tuhr·*gov*·ka

background

Where are you from?   *Od kod ste?*   od kod ste

I'm from ...   *Iz ... sem.*   eez ... sem
   Australia   *Avstralije*   av·*stra*·lee·ye
   Canada   *Kanade*   *ka*·na·de
   England   *Anglije*   an·*glee*·ye
   New Zealand   *Nove Zelandije*   *no*·ve ze·*lan*·dee·ye
   the USA   *Združenih držav*   zdroo·zhe·neeh dr·zhav

Are you married?   *Ste poročeni?*   ste po·ro·*che*·nee
I'm married.   *Poročen/Poročena*   po·ro·chen/po·ro·*che*·na
   sem. m/f   sem
I'm single.   *Samski/Samska sem.* m/f   *sam*·skee/*sam*·ska sem

age

How old ...?	*Koliko ...?*	ko·lee·ko ...
are you	*si star/stara* m/f inf	see star/*sta*·ra
are you	*ste stari* m&f pol	ste *sta*·ree
is your daughter	*je stara vaša hči*	ye *sta*·ra *va*·sha hchee
is your son	*je star vaš sin*	ye star vash seen

| I'm ... years old. | *Imam ... let.* | ee·*mam* ... let |
| He/She is ... years old. | *... let ima.* | ... let ee·*ma* |

feelings

I'm ...	*... sem.*	... sem
hungry	*Lačen/Lačna* m/f	la·chen/*lach*·na
thirsty	*Žejen/Žejna* m/f	zhe·yen/*zhey*·na
tired	*Utrujen* m	oot·*roo*·yen
	Utrujena f	oot·*roo*·ye·na

I'm not ...	*Nisem ...*	nee·sem ...
hungry	*lačen/lačna* m/f	la·chen/*lach*·na
thirsty	*žejen/žejna* m/f	zhe·yen/*zhey*·na
tired	*utrujen/utrujena* m/f	oot·*roo*·yen/oot·*roo*·ye·na

Are you ... ?	*Ste ... ?*	ste ...
hungry	*lačni*	*lach*·nee
thirsty	*žejni*	*zhey*·nee
tired	*utrujeni*	oot·*roo*·ye·nee

I'm ...	*... mi je.*	... mee ye
hot	*Vroče*	*vro*·che
well	*Dobro*	*dob*·ro

I'm not ...	*Ni mi ...*	nee mee ...
Are you ...?	*Vam je ...?*	vam ye ...
hot	*vroče*	*vro*·che
well	*dobro*	*dob*·ro

| I'm (not) cold. | *(Ne) Zebe me.* | ne *ze*·be me |
| Are you cold? | *Vas zebe?* | vas *ze*·be |

entertainment

going out

Where can I find ...?	*Kje je kakšen ...?*	kye ye *kak*·shen ...
clubs	*klub*	kloob
gay venues	*homoseksualski bar*	ho·mo·sek·soo·*al*·skee bar
pubs	*bar*	bar
I feel like going to a/the ...	*Želim iti ....*	zhe·*leem* ee·tee ...
concert	*na koncert*	na kon·*tsert*
movies	*v kino*	oo *kee*·no
party	*na zabavo*	na za·*ba*·vo
restaurant	*v restavracijo*	oo res·tav·*ra*·tsee·yo
theatre	*v gledališče*	oo gle·da·*leesh*·che

interests

Do you like ...?	*Vam je všeč ...?*	vam ye vshech ...
I like ...	*Všeč mi je ...*	vshech mee ye ...
I don't like ...	*Ni mi všeč ...*	nee mee vshech ...
art	*umetnost*	oo·*met*·nost
cooking	*kuhanje*	koo·*han*·ye
reading	*branje*	*bran*·ye
shopping	*nakupovanje*	na·koo·po·*van*·ye
sport	*šport*	shport
Do you like ...?	*So vam všeč ...?*	so vam vshech ...
I like ...	*Všeč so mi ...*	vshech so mee ...
I don't like ...	*Niso mi všeč ...*	*nee*·so mee vshech ...
movies	*filmi*	*feel*·mee
nightclubs	*nočni bari*	*noch*·nee ba·ree
travelling	*potovanja*	po·to·*van*·ya
Do you like to ...?	*Ali radi ...?*	*a*·lee *ra*·dee ...
dance	*plešete*	*ple*·she·te
go to concerts	*hodite na koncerte*	ho·dee·te na kon·*tser*·te
listen to music	*poslušate glasbo*	pos·*loo*·sha·te *glas*·bo

food & drink

finding a place to eat

Can you recommend a ...?	Mi lahko priporočite ...?	mee lah-ko pree-po-ro-chee-te ...
bar	bar	bar
café	kavarno	ka-var-no
restaurant	restavracijo	res-tav-ra-tsee-yo
I'd like ..., please.	Želim ..., prosim.	zhe-leem ... pro-seem
a table for (five)	mizo za (pet)	mee-zo za (pet)
the (non)smoking section	prostor za (ne)kadilce	pros-tor za (ne-)ka-deel-tse

ordering food

breakfast	zajtrk m	zai-tuhrk
lunch	kosilo n	ko-see-lo
dinner	večerja f	ve-cher-ya
snack	malica f	ma-lee-tsa
today's special	danes nudimo	da-nes noo-dee-mo
What would you recommend?	Kaj priporočate?	kai pree-po-ro-cha-te
I'd like (the) ..., please.	Želim ..., prosim.	zhe-leem ... pro-seem
bill	račun	ra-choon
drink list	meni pijač	me-nee pee-yach
menu	jedilni list	ye-deel-nee leest
that dish	to jed	to yed

drinks

cup of coffee ...	skodelica kave ...	sko-de-lee-tsa ka-ve ...
cup of tea ...	skodelica čaja ...	sko-de-lee-tsa cha-ya ...
with milk	z mlekom	z mle-kom
without sugar	brez sladkorja	brez slad-kor-ya

(orange) juice	(pomarančni) sok m	(po·ma·ranch·nee) sok
soft drink	brezalkoholna pijača f	brez·al·ko·hol·na pee·ya·cha
... water	... voda	... vo·da
boiled	prekuhana	pre·koo·ha·na
(sparkling)	mineralna	mee·ne·ral·na
mineral	(gazirana)	(ga·zee·ra·na)

in the bar

I'll have ...
Jaz bom ...   yaz bom ...

I'll buy you a drink.
Povabim te na pijačo. inf   po·va·beem te na pee·ya·cho

What would you like?
Kaj boš? inf   kai bosh

Cheers!
Na zdravje!   na zdrav·ye

brandy	vinjak m	veen·yak
champagne	šampanjec m	sham·pan·yets
cocktail	koktajl m	kok·tail
cognac	konjak m	kon·yak
a shot of (whisky)	kozarček (viskija)	ko·zar·chek (vees·kee·ya)
a ... of beer	... piva	... pee·va
glass	kozarec	ko·za·rets
jug	vrč	vuhrch
pint	vrček	vuhr·chek
a bottle/glass of ... wine	steklenica/kozarec ... vina	stek·le·nee·tsa/ko·za·rets ... vee·na
red	rdečega	rde·che·ga
sparkling	penečega	pe·ne·che·ga
white	belega	be·le·ga

self-catering

What's the local speciality?
Kaj je lokalna specialiteta?   kai ye lo·*kal*·na spe·tsee·a·lee·*te*·ta

What's that?
Kaj je to?   kai ye to

How much is (a kilo of cheese)?
Koliko stane (kila sira)?   ko·lee·ko *sta*·ne (*kee*·la *see*·ra)

I'd like ...	*Želim ...*	zhe·*leem* ...
(200) grams	*(dvesto) gramov*	(dve·sto) *gra*·mov
(two) kilos	*(dva) kilograma*	(dva) kee·lo·*gra*·ma
(three) pieces	*(tri) kose*	(tree) *ko*·se
(six) slices	*(šest) rezin*	(shest) re·*zeen*

Less.	*Manj.*	man'
Enough.	*Dovolj.*	do·*vol*
More.	*Več.*	vech

special diets & allergies

Is there a vegetarian restaurant near here?
Je tu blizu vegetarijanska   ye too *blee*·zoo ve·ge·ta·ree·*yan*·ska
restavracija?   res·tav·*ra*·tsee·ya

Do you have vegetarian food?
Ali imate vegetarijansko hrano?   a·lee ee·*ma*·te ve·ge·ta·ree·*yan*·sko *hra*·no

Could you prepare	*Lahko pripravite*	lah·ko pree·*pra*·vee·te
a meal without ...?	*obed brez ...?*	o·*bed* brez ...
butter	*masla*	*mas*·la
eggs	*jajc*	yaits
meat stock	*mesne osnove*	*mes*·ne os·*no*·ve

I'm allergic to ...	*Alergičen/Alergična*	a·*ler*·gee·chen/a·*ler*·geech·na
	sem na ... m/f	sem na ...
dairy produce	*mlečne izdelke*	*mlech*·ne eez·*del*·ke
gluten	*gluten*	gloo·*ten*
MSG	*MSG*	em es ge
nuts	*oreške*	o·*resh*·ke
seafood	*morsko hrano*	*mor*·sko *hra*·no

menu reader

bograč m	*bog·rach*	*beef goulash*
brancin na maslu m	*bran·tseen na mas·loo*	*sea bass in butter*
čebulna bržola f	*che·bool·na br·zho·la*	*braised beef with onions*
čevapčiči m	*che·vap·chee·chee*	*spicy beef or pork meatballs*
drobnjakovi štruklji m	*drob·nya·ko·vee shtrook·lyee*	*dumplings of cottage cheese & chives*
dunajski zrezek m	*doo·nai·skee zre·zek*	*breaded veal or pork cutlet*
francoska solata f	*fran·tsos·ka so·la·ta*	*diced potatoes & vegetables with mayonnaise*
gobova kremna juha f	*go·bo·va krem·na yoo·ha*	*creamed mushroom soup*
goveja juha z rezanci f	*go·ve·ya yoo·ha z re·zan·tsee*	*beef broth with little egg noodles*
jota f	*yo·ta*	*beans, sauerkraut & potatoes or barley cooked with pork*
kisle kumarice f	*kees·le koo·ma·ree·tse*	*pickled cucumbers*
kmečka pojedina f	*kmech·ka po·ye·dee·na*	*smoked meats with sauerkraut*
kranjska klobasa z gorčico f	*kran·'ska klo·ba·sa z gor·chee·tso*	*sausage with mustard*
kraški pršut z olivami m	*krash·kee puhr·shoot z o·lee·va·mee*	*air-dried ham with black olives*
krofi m	*kro·fee*	*jam-filled doughnuts*
kuhana govedina s hrenom f	*koo·ha·na go·ve·dee·na s hre·nom*	*boiled beef with horseradish*
kuhana postrv f	*koo·ha·na pos·tuhrv*	*boiled trout*
kumarična solata f	*koo·ma·reech·na so·la·ta*	*cucumber salad*
ljubljanski zrezek m	*lyoob·lyan·skee zre·zek*	*breaded cutlet with cheese*

menu reader – SLOVENE

239

mešano meso na žaru n	*me·sha·no me·so na zha·roo*	*mixed grill*
ocvrt oslič m	*ots·vuhrt os·leech*	*fried cod*
ocvrt piščanec m	*ots·vuhrt peesh·cha·nets*	*fried chicken*
orada na žaru f	*o·ra·da na zha·roo*	*grilled sea bream*
palačinke f	*pa·la·cheen·ke*	*thin pancakes with marmalade, nuts or chocolate*
pečena postrv f	*pe·che·na pos·tuhrv*	*grilled trout*
pečene sardele f	*pe·che·ne sar·de·le*	*grilled sardines*
pleskavica f	*ples·ka·vee·tsa*	*spicy meat patties*
pariški zrezek m	*pa·reesh·kee zre·zek*	*cutlet fried in egg batter*
puranov zrezek s šampinjoni m	*poo·ra·nov zre·zek s sham·peen·yo·nee*	*turkey steak with white mushrooms*
ražnjiči m	*razh·nyee·chee*	*shish kebab*
riba v marinadi f	*ree·ba v ma·ree·na·dee*	*marinated fish*
ričet m	*ree·chet*	*barley stew with smoked pork ribs*
rižota z gobami f	*ree·zho·ta z go·ba·mee*	*risotto with mushrooms*
sadna kupa f	*sad·na koo·pa*	*fruit salad with whipped cream*
srbska solata f	*suhrb·ska so·la·ta*	*salad of tomatoes & green peppers with onions & cheese*
svinjska pečenka f	*sveen'·ska pe·chen·ka*	*roast pork*
škampi na žaru m	*shkam·pee na zha·roo*	*grilled prawns*
školjke f	*shkol'·ke*	*clams*
zelena solata f	*ze·le·na so·la·ta*	*lettuce salad*
zelenjavna juha f	*ze·len·yav·na yoo·ha*	*vegetable soup*

emergencies

basics

Help!	Na pomoč!	na po·*moch*
Stop!	Ustavite (se)!	oos·*ta*·vee·te (se)
Go away!	Pojdite stran!	poy·*dee*·te stran
Thief!	Tat!	tat
Fire!	Požar!	po·*zhar*
Watch out!	Pazite!	pa·*zee*·te
Call ...!	Pokličite ...!	pok·*lee*·chee·te ...
a doctor	zdravnika	zdrav·*nee*·ka
an ambulance	rešilca	re·*sheel*·tsa
the police	policijo	po·lee·*tsee*·yo

It's an emergency.
Nujno je.
nooy·no ye

Could you help me, please?
Pomagajte mi, prosim.
po·*ma*·gai·te mee *pro*·seem

I have to use the telephone.
Poklicati moram.
pok·*lee*·tsa·tee *mo*·ram

I'm lost.
Izgubil/Izgubila sem se. m/f
eez·*goo*·beew/eez·goo·*bee*·la sem se

Where are the toilets?
Kje je stranišče?
kye ye stra·*neesh*·che

police

Where's the police station?
Kje je policijska postaja?
kye ye po·lee·*tseey*·ska pos·*ta*·ya

I want to report an offence.
Želim prijaviti prestopek.
zhe·*leem* pree·*ya*·vee·tee pres·*to*·pek

I have insurance.
Zavarovan/Zavarovana sem. m/f
za·va·ro·*van*/za·va·ro·*va*·na sem

I've been ...	... so me.	... so me
assaulted	Napadli	na·*pad*·lee
raped	Posilili	po·*see*·lee·lee
robbed	Oropali	o·*ro*·pa·lee

I've lost my ...	Izgubil/Izgubila sem ... m/f	eez·goo·beew/eez·goo·bee·la sem ...
My ... was/were stolen.	Ukradli so mi ...	ook·rad·lee so mee ...
backpack	nahrbtnik	na·huhrbt·neek
bags	torbe	tor·be
credit card	kreditno kartico	kre·deet·no kar·tee·tso
handbag	ročno torbico	roch·no tor·bee·tso
jewellery	nakit	na·keet
money	denar	de·nar
passport	potni list	pot·nee leest
travellers cheques	potovalne čeke	po·to·val·ne che·ke
wallet	denarnico	de·nar·nee·tso

I want to contact my ...	Želim poklicati ... svoj/svojo ... m/f	zhe·leem pok·lee·tsa·tee ... svoy/svo·yo ...
consulate	konzulat m	kon·zoo·lat
embassy	ambasado f	am·ba·sa·do

health

medical needs

Where's the nearest ...?	Kje je najbližji/ najbližja ... ? m/f	kye ye nai·bleezh·yee/ nai·bleezh·ya ...
dentist	zobozdravnik m	zo·bo·zdrav·neek
doctor	zdravnik m	zdrav·neek
hospital	bolnišnica f	bol·neesh·nee·tsa
(night) pharmacist	(nočna) lekarna f	(noch·na) le·kar·na

I need a doctor (who speaks English).

Potrebujem zdravnika   pot·re·boo·yem zdrav·nee·ka
(ki govori angleško).   (kee go·vo·ree ang·lesh·ko)

Could I see a female doctor?

Bi me lahko pregledala   bee me lah·ko preg·le·da·la
zdravnica?   zdrav·nee·tsa

I've run out of my medication.

Zmanjkalo mi je zdravil.   zman'·ka·lo mee ye zdra·veel

symptoms, conditions & allergies

I'm sick.	Bolan/Bolna sem. m/f	bo-*lan*/boh-na sem
It hurts here.	Tu me boli.	too me bo-*lee*

I have (a) ...	Imam ...	ee-*mam* ...
asthma	astmo	*ast*-mo
bronchitis	bronhitis	bron-*hee*-tees
constipation	zapeko	za-*pe*-ko
diarrhoea	drisko	*drees*-ko
fever	vročino	vro-*chee*-no
headache	glavobol	gla-vo-*bol*
heart condition	srčno bolezen	*suhr*-chno bo-*le*-zen
toothache	zobobol	zo-bo-*bol*
pain	bolečine	bo-le-*chee*-ne

I'm nauseous.	Slabo mi je.	sla-*bo* mee ye
I'm coughing.	Kašljam.	*kash*-lyam
I have a sore throat.	Boli me grlo.	bo-*lee* me *guhr*-lo

I'm allergic to ...	Alergičen/Alergična sem na ... m/f	a-*ler*-gee-chen/a-*ler*-geech-na sem na ...
antibiotics	antibiotike	an-tee-bee-*o*-tee-ke
anti-inflammatories	protivnetna zdravila	pro-teev-*net*-na zdra-*vee*-la
aspirin	aspirin	as-pee-*reen*
bees	čebelji pik	che-*bel*-yee peek
codeine	kodein	ko-de-*een*
penicillin	penicilin	pe-nee-tsee-*leen*

antiseptic	razkužilo n	raz-koo-*zhee*-lo
bandage	obveza f	ob-*ve*-za
condoms	kondomi m pl	kon-*do*-mee
contraceptives	kontracepcija f	kon-tra-*tsep*-tsee-ya
diarrhoea medicine	zdravilo za drisko n	zdra-*vee*-lo za *drees*-ko
insect repellent	sredstvo proti mrčesu n	*sreds*-tvo *pro*-tee muhr-*che*-soo
laxatives	odvajala n pl	od-va-*ya*-la
painkillers	analgetiki m pl	a-nal-*ge*-tee-kee
rehydration salts	sol za rehidracijo f	sol za re-heed-*ra*-tsee-yo
sleeping tablets	uspavalne tablete f pl	oos-pa-*val*-ne tab-*le*-te

english–slovene dictionary

Slovene nouns in this dictionary have their gender indicated by ⓜ (masculine), ⓕ (feminine) or ⓝ (neuter)
If it's a plural noun, you'll also see pl. Adjectives are given in the masculine form only. Words are also marked
as a (adjective), v (verb), sg (singular), pl (plural), inf (informal) or pol (polite) where necessary.

A

accident *nesreča* ⓕ nes-re-cha
accommodation *nastanitev* ⓕ na-sta-nee-tev
adaptor *adapter* ⓜ a-dap-ter
address *naslov* ⓜ nas-loh
after *po* po
air-conditioned *klimatiziran* klee-ma-tee-zee-ran
airplane *letalo* ⓝ le-ta-lo
airport *letališče* ⓝ le-ta-leesh-che
alcohol *alkohol* ⓜ al-ko-hol
all *vse* vse
allergy *alergija* ⓕ a-ler-gee-ya
ambulance *rešilni avto* ⓜ re-sheel-nee av-to
and *in* een
ankle *gleženj* ⓜ gle-zhen'
arm *roka* ⓕ ro-ka
ashtray *pepelnik* ⓜ pe-pel-neek
ATM *bankomat* ⓜ ban-ko-mat

B

baby *dojenček* ⓜ do-yen-chek
back (body) *hrbet* ⓜ huhr-bet
backpack *nahrbtnik* ⓜ na-huhrbt-neek
bad *slab* slab
bag *torba* ⓕ tor-ba
baggage *prtljaga* ⓕ puhrt-lya-ga
baggage claim *prevzem prtljage* ⓕ
    prev-zem puhrt-lya-ge
bank *banka* ⓕ ban-ka
bar *bar* ⓜ bar
bathroom *kopalnica* ⓕ ko-pal-nee-tsa
battery *baterija* ⓕ ba-te-ree-ya
beautiful *lep* lep
bed *postelja* ⓕ pos-tel-ya
beer *pivo* ⓝ pee-vo
before *prej* prey
behind *zadaj* za-dai
bicycle *bicikel* ⓜ bee-tsee-kel
big *velik* ve-leek
bill *račun* ⓜ ra-choon
black *črn* chuhrn

blanket *odeja* ⓕ o-de-ya
blood group *krvna skupina* ⓕ kuhrv-na skoo-pee-na
blue *moder* mo-der
boat (ship) *ladja* ⓕ lad-ya
boat (small) *čoln* ⓜ chohn
book (make a reservation) v *rezervirati*
    re-zer-vee-ra-tee
bottle *steklenica* ⓕ stek-le-nee-tsa
bottle opener *odpirač* ⓜ od-pee-rach
boy *fant* ⓜ fant
brakes (car) *zavore* ⓕ pl za-vo-re
breakfast *zajtrk* ⓜ zai-tuhrk
broken (faulty) *pokvarjen* pok-var-yen
bus *avtobus* ⓜ av-to-boos
business *posel* ⓜ po-se-oo
buy *kupiti* koo-pee-tee

C

café *kavarna* ⓕ ka-var-na
camera *fotoaparat* ⓜ fo-to-a-pa-rat
camera shop *trgovina s fotografsko opremo* ⓕ
    tr-go-vee-na s fo-to-graf-sko o-pre-mo
campsite *kamp* ⓜ kamp
cancel *preklicati* prek-lee-tsa-tee
can opener *odpirač za pločevinke* ⓜ
    od-pee-rach za plo-che-veen-ke
car *avtomobil* ⓜ av-to-mo-beel
cash *gotovina* ⓕ go-to-vee-na
cash (a cheque) v *unovčiti (ček)* oo-nov-chee-tee (chek)
cell phone *mobilni telefon* ⓜ mo-beel-nee te-le-fon
centre *center* ⓜ tsen-ter
change (money) v *menjati (denar)* men-ya-tee (de-nar)
cheap *poceni* po-tse-nee
check (bill) *račun* ⓜ ra-choon
check-in *prijava za let* pree-ya-va za let
chest *prsni koš* ⓜ puhr-snee kosh
child *otrok* ⓜ ot-rok
cigarette *cigareta* ⓕ tsee-ga-re-ta
city *mesto* ⓝ mes-to
clean a *čist* cheest
closed *zaprt* za-puhrt
coffee *kava* ⓕ ka-va
coins *kovanci* ⓜ pl ko-van-tsee

cold a *hladen* hla-den
collect call *klic na stroške klicanega* ⓜ
  kleets na strosh-ke klee-tsa-ne-ga
come *priti* pree-tee
computer *računalnik* ⓜ ra-choo-nal-neek
condom *kondom* ⓜ kon-dom
contact lenses *kontaktne leče* ⓕ pl kon-takt-ne le-che
cook v *kuhati* koo-ha-tee
cost *strošek* ⓜ stro-shek
credit card *kreditna kartica* ⓕ kre-deet-na kar-tee-tsa
cup *skodelica* ⓕ sko-de-lee-tsa
currency exchange *menjava* ⓕ men-ya-va
customs (immigration) *carina* ⓕ tsa-ree-na

D

dangerous *nevaren* ne-va-ren
date (time) *datum* ⓜ da-toom
day *dan* ⓜ dan
delay *zamuda* ⓕ za-moo-da
dentist *zobozdravnik* ⓜ zo-boz-drav-neek
depart *oditi* o-dee-tee
diaper *plenica* ⓕ ple-nee-tsa
dictionary *slovar* ⓜ slo-var
dinner *večerja* ⓕ ve-cher-ya
direct *direkten* dee-rek-ten
dirty *umazan* oo-ma-zan
disabled (person) *invaliden* een-va-lee-den
discount *popust* ⓜ po-poost
doctor *zdravnik* ⓜ zdrav-neek
double bed *dvojna postelja* ⓕ dvoy-na pos-tel-ya
double room *dvoposteljna soba* ⓕ
  dvo-pos-tel'-na so-ba
drink *pijača* ⓕ pee-ya-cha
drive v *voziti* vo-zee-tee
drivers licence *vozniško dovoljenje* ⓜ
  voz-neesh-ko do-vol-yen-ye
drug (illicit) *mamilo* ⓜ ma-mee-lo
dummy (pacifier) *duda* ⓕ doo-da

E

ear *uho* ⓝ oo-ho
east *vzhod* ⓜ vzhod
eat *jesti* yes-tee
economy class *turistični razred* ⓜ
  too-rees-teech-nee raz-red
electricity *elektrika* ⓕ e-lek-tree-ka
elevator *dvigalo* ⓝ dvee-ga-lo
email *elektronska pošta* ⓕ e-lek-tron-ska posh-ta
embassy *ambasada* ⓕ am-ba-sa-da
emergency *nujen primer* ⓜ noo-yen pree-mer
English (language) *angleščina* ⓕ ang-lesh-chee-na

entrance *vhod* ⓜ vhod
evening *večer* ⓜ ve-cher
exchange rate *menjalni tečaj* ⓜ men-yal-nee te-chai
exit *izhod* ⓜ eez-hod
expensive *drag* drag
express mail *hitra pošta* ⓕ heet-ra posh-ta
eye *oko* ⓝ o-ko

F

far *daleč* da-lech
fast *hitro* heet-ro
father *oče* o-che
film (camera) *film* ⓜ feelm
finger *prst* ⓜ puhrst
first-aid kit *komplet za prvo pomoč* ⓜ
  kom-plet za puhr-vo po-moch
first class *prvi razred* ⓜ puhr-vee raz-red
fish *riba* ⓕ ree-ba
food *hrana* ⓕ hra-na
foot *stopalo* ⓝ sto-pa-lo
fork *vilice* ⓕ pl vee-lee-tse
free (of charge) *brezplačen* brez-pla-chen
friend *prijatelj/prijateljica* ⓜ/ⓕ
  pree-ya-tel/pree-ya-tel-yee-tsa
fruit *sadje* ⓝ pl sad-ye
full *poln* poln
funny *smešen* sme-shen

G

gift *darilo* ⓝ da-ree-lo
girl *dekle* ⓝ dek-le
glass (drinking) *kozarec* ⓜ ko-za-rets
glasses *očala* ⓝ pl o-cha-la
go *iti* ee-tee
good *dober* do-ber
green *zelen* ze-len
guide *vodnik* ⓜ vod-neek

H

half *pol* poh
hand *roka* ⓕ ro-ka
handbag *ročna torbica* ⓕ roch-na tor-bee-tsa
happy *srečen* sre-chen
have *imeti* ee-me-tee
he *on* ⓜ on
head *glava* ⓕ gla-va
heart *srce* ⓝ suhr-tse
heat *vročina* ⓕ vro-chee-na
heavy *težek* te-zhek

help v *pomagati* po-*ma*-ga-tee
here *tukaj* too-kai
high *visok* vee-*sok*
highway *hitra cesta* ① *heet*-ra tses-ta
(go on a) hike v *iti na pohod* ee-tee na po-*hod*
holidays *počitnice* ① pl po-*cheet*-nee-tse
homosexual *homoseksualec* ⓜ ho-mo-sek-soo-*a*-lets
hospital *bolnišnica* ① bol-*neesh*-nee-tsa
hot *vroč* vroch
hungry *lačen* la-*chen*
husband *mož* ⓜ mozh

I

I *jaz* yaz
identification (card) *osebna izkaznica* ①
  o-*seb*-na eez-*kaz*-nee-tsa
ill *bolan* bo-*lan*
important *pomemben* po-*mem*-ben
included *vključen* vklyoo-chen
injury *poškodba* ① posh-*kod*-ba
insurance *zavarovanje* ⓝ za-va-ro-*van*-ye
Internet *internet* ⓜ een-ter-net
interpreter *tolmač* ① tol-*mach*

J

jewellery *nakit* ⓜ na-*keet*
job *služba* ① *sloozh*-ba

K

key *ključ* ⓜ klyooch
kilogram *kilogram* ⓜ kee-lo-*gram*
kitchen *kuhinja* ① *koo*-heen-ya
knife *nož* ⓜ nozh

L

laundry (place) *pralnica* ① *pral*-nee-tsa
lawyer *odvetnik* ⓜ od-*vet*-neek
left (direction) *levo* le-vo
left-luggage office *garderoba* ① gar-de-ro-ba
leg *noga* ① *no*-ga
lesbian *lezbijka* ① *lez*-beey-ka
less *manj* man'
letter (mail) *pismo* ⓝ *pees*-mo
lift (elevator) *dvigalo* ⓝ dvee-*ga*-lo
light *svetloba* ① svet-*lo*-ba
like v *všeč biti* vshech bee-tee

lock *ključavnica* ① klyoo-*chav*-nee-tsa
long *dolg* dohg
lost *izgubljen* eez-goob-*lyen*
lost-property office *urad za izgubljene predmete* ⓜ
  oo-*rad* za eez-goob-*lye*-ne pred-*me*-te
love v *ljubiti* lyoo-bee-tee
luggage *prtljaga* ① puhrt-*lya*-ga
lunch *kosilo* ⓝ ko-*see*-lo

M

mail *pošta* ① *posh*-ta
man *moški* ⓜ *mosh*-kee
map *zemljevid* ⓜ zem-lye-*veed*
market *tržnica* ① *tuhrzh*-nee-tsa
matches *vžigalice* ① pl vzhee-*ga*-lee-tse
meat *meso* ⓝ me-*so*
medicine *zdravilo* ⓝ zdra-*vee*-lo
menu *jedilni list* ⓜ ye-*deel*-nee leest
message *sporočilo* ⓝ spo-ro-*chee*-lo
milk *mleko* ⓝ *mle*-ko
minute *minuta* ① mee-*noo*-ta
mobile phone *mobilni telefon* ⓜ mo-*beel*-nee te-le-*fon*
money *denar* ⓜ de-*nar*
month *mesec* ⓜ *me*-sets
morning *dopoldne* ⓝ do-*pol*-dne
mother *mama* ① *ma*-ma
motorcycle *motorno kolo* ⓝ mo-*tor*-no ko-*lo*
motorway *motorna cesta* ① mo-*tor*-na tses-ta
mouth *usta* ① *oos*-ta
music *glasba* ① *glaz*-ba

N

name *ime* ⓝ ee-*me*
napkin *prtiček* ⓜ puhr-*tee*-chek
nappy *plenica* ① ple-*nee*-tsa
near *blizu* blee-zoo
neck *vrat* ⓜ vrat
new *nov* noh
news *novice* ① pl no-*vee*-tse
newspaper *časopis* ⓜ cha-so-*pees*
night *noč* ① noch
no *ne* ne
noisy *hrupen* hroo-pen
nonsmoking *nekadilski* ne-ka-*deel*-skee
north *sever* ⓜ se-ver
nose *nos* ⓜ nos
now *zdaj* zdai
number *število* ⓝ shte-*vee*-lo

O

oil (engine) *olje* ⓝ *ol*-ye
old *star* star
one-way ticket *enosmerna vozovnica* ⓕ
   e-no-*smer*-na vo-zov-*nee*-tsa
open a *odprt* od-*puhrt*
outside *zunaj* zoo-*nai*

P

package *paket* ⓜ pa-*ket*
paper *papir* ⓜ pa-*peer*
park (car) v *parkirati* par-kee-ra-tee
passport *potni list* ⓜ *pot*-nee leest
pay *plačati* pla-cha-tee
pen *pisalo* ⓝ pee-*sa*-lo
petrol *bencin* ⓜ ben-*tseen*
pharmacy *lekarna* ⓕ le-*kar*-na
phonecard *telefonska kartica* ⓕ
   te-le-*fon*-ska *kar*-tee-tsa
photo *fotografija* ⓕ fo-to-gra-*fee*-ya
picnic *piknik* ⓜ *peek*-neek
plate *krožnik* ⓜ *krozh*-neek
police *policija* ⓕ po-lee-*tsee*-ya
postcard *razglednica* ⓕ raz-*gled*-nee-tsa
post office *pošta* ⓕ *posh*-ta
pregnant *noseča* no-se-cha
price *cena* ⓕ *tse*-na

Q

quiet *tih* teeh

R

rain *dež* ⓜ dezh
razor *brivnik* ⓜ *breev*-neek
receipt *račun* ⓜ ra-*choon*
red *rdeč* rdech
refund *vračilo denarja* ⓝ vra-chee-lo de-*nar*-ya
registered mail *priporočena pošta* ⓕ
   pree-po-ro-che-na *posh*-ta
rent v *najeti* na-ye-tee
repair v *popraviti* pop-*ra*-vee-tee
reservation *rezervacija* ⓕ re-zer-*va*-tsee-ya
restaurant *restavracija* ⓕ res-tav-*ra*-tsee-ya
return v *vrniti* vr-*nee*-tee

return ticket *povratna vozovnica* ⓕ
   pov-*rat*-na vo-zov-*nee*-tsa
right (direction) *desno* des-no
road *cesta* ⓕ *tses*-ta
room *soba* ⓕ *so*-ba

S

safe a *varen* va-*ren*
sanitary napkins *damski vložki* ⓜ pl
   dam-skee *vlozh*-kee
seat *sedež* ⓜ *se*-dezh
send *poslati* pos-*la*-tee
service station *servis* ⓜ *ser*-vees
sex *seks* ⓜ seks
shampoo *šampon* ⓜ sham-*pon*
share (a dorm) *deliti (sobo)* de-*lee*-tee (*so*-bo)
shaving cream *krema za britje* ⓕ *kre*-ma za *breet*-ye
she *ona* ⓕ *o*-na
sheet (bed) *rjuha* ⓕ *ryoo*-ha
shirt *srajca* ⓕ *srai*-tsa
shoes *čevlji* ⓜ pl *chev*-lyee
shop *trgovina* ⓕ *tuhr*-go-*vee*-na
short *kratek* *kra*-tek
shower *prha* ⓕ *puhr*-ha
single room *enoposteljna soba* ⓕ
   e-no-pos-*tel'*-na *so*-ba
skin *koža* ⓕ *ko*-zha
skirt *krilo* ⓝ *kree*-lo
sleep v *spati* *spa*-tee
Slovenia *Slovenija* ⓕ slo-ve-*nee*-ya
Slovene (language) *slovenščina* ⓕ slo-*vensh*-chee-na
Slovene a *slovenski* slo-*ven*-skee
slowly *počasi* po-*cha*-see
small *majhen* mai-hen
smoke (cigarettes) v *kaditi* ka-*dee*-tee
soap *milo* ⓝ *mee*-lo
some *nekaj* ne-kai
soon *kmalu* kma-*loo*
south *jug* ⓜ yoog
souvenir shop *trgovina s spominki* ⓕ
   tuhr-go-vee-na s spo-*meen*-kee
speak *govoriti* go-vo-*ree*-tee
spoon *žlica* ⓕ *zhlee*-tsa
stamp *znamka* ⓕ *znam*-ka
stand-by ticket *stand-by vozovnica* ⓕ
   stend-bai vo-zov-*nee*-tsa
station (train) *postaja* ⓕ *pos-ta*-ya
stomach *želodec* ⓜ zhe-*lo*-dets

stop v *ustaviti* oos-*ta*-vee-tee
stop (bus) *postajališče* ⓝ pos-ta-ya-*leesh*-che
street *ulica* ⓕ oo-lee-tsa
student *študent/študentka* ⓜ/ⓕ
    shtoo-*dent*/shtoo-*dent*-ka
sun *sonce* ⓝ son-tse
sunscreen *krema za sončenje* ⓕ *kre*-ma za *son*-chen-ye
swim v *plavati* pla-*va*-tee

T

tampons *tamponi* ⓜ pl tam-*po*-nee
taxi *taksi* ⓜ *tak*-see
teaspoon *čajna žlička* ⓕ *chai*-na *zhleech*-ka
teeth *zobje* ⓝ zob-ye
telephone *telefon* ⓜ te-le-*fon*
television *televizija* ⓕ te-le-vee-zee-ya
temperature (weather) *temperatura* ⓕ
    tem-pe-ra-*too*-ra
tent *šotor* ⓜ *sho*-tor
that (one) *tisti* tees-tee
they *oni/one* ⓜ/ⓕ *o*-nee/*o*-ne
thirsty *žejen* zhe-yen
this (one) *ta* ta
throat *grlo* ⓝ *guhr*-lo
ticket (entrance) *vstopnica* ⓕ vstop-*nee*-tsa
ticket (travel) *vozovnica* ⓕ vo-zov-*nee*-tsa
time *čas* ⓜ chas
tired *utrujen* oo-*troo*-yen
tissues *robčki* ⓜ pl *rob*-chkee
today *danes* *da*-nes
toilet *stranišče* ⓝ stra-*neesh*-che
tomorrow *jutri* *yoot*-ree
tonight *nocoj* no-*tsoy*
toothbrush *zobna ščetka* ⓕ *zob*-na *shchet*-ka
toothpaste *zobna pasta* ⓕ *zob*-na *pas*-ta
torch (flashlight) *baterija* ⓕ ba-te-*ree*-ya
tour *izlet* ⓜ *eez*-let
tourist office *turistični urad* ⓜ too-*rees*-teech-nee oo-*rad*
towel *brisača* ⓕ bree-*sa*-cha
train *vlak* ⓜ vlak
translate *prevesti* pre-*ves*-tee
travel agency *potovalna agencija* ⓕ
    po-to-*val*-na a-gen-*tsee*-ya
travellers cheque *potovalni ček* ⓜ po-to-*val*-nee chek
trousers *hlače* ⓕ pl *hla*-che
twin beds *ločeni postelji* ⓕ pl *lo*-che-nee *pos*-tel-yee
tyre *guma* ⓕ *goo*-ma

U

underwear *spodnje perilo* ⓝ *spod*-nye pe-*ree*-lo
urgent *nujen* *noo*-yen

V

vacant *prost* prost
vacation *počitnice* ⓕ pl po-*cheet*-nee-tse
vegetable *zelenjava* ⓕ ze-len-*ya*-va
vegetarian a *vegetarijanski* ve-ge-ta-ree-*yan*-skee
visa *viza* ⓕ *vee*-za

W

waiter *natakar* ⓜ na-*ta*-kar
walk v *hoditi* ho-*dee*-tee
wallet *denarnica* ⓕ de-nar-*nee*-tsa
warm a *topel* to-*pe*-oo
wash (something) *prati* *pra*-tee
watch *zapestna ura* ⓕ za-*pest*-na oo-ra
water *voda* ⓕ *vo*-da
we *mi* mee
weekend *vikend* ⓜ *vee*-kend
west *zahod* ⓜ za-*hod*
wheelchair *invalidski voziček* ⓜ
    een-va-*leed*-skee vo-zee-chek
when *kdaj* kdai
where *kje* kye
white *bel* be-oo
who *kdo* kdo
why *zakaj* za-*kai*
wife *žena* ⓕ *zhe*-na
window *okno* ⓝ *ok*-no
wine *vino* ⓝ *vee*-no
with *z/s* z/s
without *brez* brez
woman *ženska* ⓕ *zhen*-ska
write *pisati* pee-*sa*-tee

Y

yellow *rumen* roo-men
yes *da* da
yesterday *včeraj* vche-rai
you sg inf/pol *ti/vi* tee/vee
you pl *vi* vee

INDEX

Berlin Love Parade in June is the largest techno party in the world. Hordes of tour-
come to **Germany** for the famous beer festival in Munich, the *Oktoberfest* – one of
ope's biggest and most drunken parties from late September to early October.

Prague Spring in May, one of Europe's biggest festivals of classical music, kicks off the
mer in the **Czech Republic**. The town of Prachatice goes fairly wild during the mid-
e Gold Trail Festival with medieval costumes, fencing tournaments and fireworks.

ple from all over Europe camp and party at the Sziget Festival in **Hungary**, a week-
world music bash in early August on Budapest's Óbuda Island. The Gyula Theatre
ival has spectacular performances in the castle courtyard during July and August.

Dominican Fair in Gdańsk is the oldest shopping fair in **Poland**, held in August and
mpanied by street theatre, concerts, parades and races. The May Juvenalia in Kraków
student carnival with fancy dress, masquerades and dancing in the street.

uly, artists from all over Europe come to Kežmarok for the biggest Craft Fair in **Slova**-
with food, drinks and live music. Rumours that the Bojnice Castle is haunted are kept
e by the International Festival of Spirits and Ghosts, held in early May.

entovanje, a rite of spring celebrated in February, is the most extravagant folklore
nt in **Slovenia**, held in Ptuj. Maribor hosts both the International Puppet Festival in
and August and a renowned theatre festival in the second half of October.

What kind of traveller are you?

A. You're eating chicken for dinner *again* because it's the only word you know.

B. When no one understands what you say, you step closer and shout louder.

C. When the barman doesn't understand your order, you point frantically at the bee

D. You're surrounded by locals, swapping jokes, email addresses and experiences
– other travellers want to borrow your phrasebook or audio guide.

If you answered A, B, or C, you NEED Lonely Planet's language products ..

- **Lonely Planet Phrasebooks** – for every phrase you need in every language
  you want
- **Lonely Planet Language & Culture** – get behind the scenes of English as it's
  spoken around the world – learn and laugh
- **Lonely Planet Fast Talk & Fast Talk Audio** – essential phrases for short trips
  weekends away – read, listen and talk like a local
- **Lonely Planet Small Talk** – 10 essential languages for city breaks
- **Lonely Planet Real Talk** – downloadable language audio guides from
  lonelyplanet.com to your MP3 player

... and this is why

- **Talk to everyone everywhere**
  Over 120 languages, more than any other publisher
- **The right words at the right time**
  Quick-reference colour sections, two-way dictionary, easy pronunciation,
  every possible subject – and audio to support it

Lonely Planet Offices

Australia
90 Maribyrnong St, Footscray,
Victoria 3011
☎ 03 8379 8000
fax 03 8379 8111
✉ talk2us@lonelyplanet.com.au

USA
150 Linden St, Oakland,
CA 94607
☎ 510 893 8555
fax 510 893 8572
✉ info@lonelyplanet.com

UK
72-82 Rosebery Ave,
London EC1R 4RW
☎ 020 7841 9000
fax 020 7841 9001
✉ go@lonelyplanet

lonelyplanet.com

WHAT THE BIBLE SAYS I AM

JAKE & KEITH PROVANCE

I Am What the Bible Says I AM
ISBN: 9781936314072
Copyright © 2017 by Word and Spirit Publishing

Published by Word and Spirit Publishing
P.O. Box 701403
Tulsa, Oklahoma 74170

Contents

Introduction

Who do you see when you look in the mirror? *Are you good looking? Are you smart? Are you kind? Are you strong? Are you valuable?*

Before you answer, take a moment to think about where your response is coming from. Why do you think these things about yourself? Where did they originate? Have they been spoken to you? Have you pondered them in your secret thoughts? Are they rooted in doubt and insecurity or in confidence and truth?

Too often we tend to conform to the opinions of those around us, and use comparison to build our self-worth. This is a sure recipe for disaster, for it leads to a very fickle, unhappy life. Comparison is a double-edged sword—too often leading to destruction. The stress of trying to fit in, wanting to stand out, the pressure to be perfect, etc., are all self-induced afflictions that rob us of our daily joy, peace, and contentment. That's why the Bible warns us, "But when they measure themselves by one another and compare themselves with one another, they are without understanding" (2 Corinthians 10:12 ESV).

But what if you could base your identity and self-worth on something besides the opinions of those around you or even your own opinions? What if your value was based on something that never changes? Something that is fixed and decided for all eternity—never to be undone? Whether you are a new believer or have been a Christian for many years, it is always important to be reminded of who God says you are. This book is a collection of those truths, to remind you and encourage you to stand tall in the reality of the "new you."

God never changes in His thoughts towards you. He does not look at you as a lump sum of your decisions, nor does He judge you based on your worthiness. The moment you surrender to God by believing in Him, and confessing Him as your Lord and Savior, is the moment God places a new identity on you and in you! He sees you as His child, He delights in your happiness, and it is His firm desire to encourage and affirm your true identity—if you will let Him.

The Word of God is a living book full of life, love, and light. When you read God's words and speak them with faith, their power will take root in your heart, and infiltrate and permeate your mind. The full realization of who you are according to God may not happen overnight, but as you meditate and speak His words, the way you see yourself will begin to mesh with the way God sees you, and you'll be able to see those around you the way God sees them. You will never be the same!

I Am New

You became a new creation when you accepted Jesus as your personal Savior. You experienced the greatest miracle of God's Kingdom—a spiritual metamorphosis. One Bible translation says that you became a new species of being. God has forgiven the sins, mistakes, failures, and shortcomings of your past, never to be remembered again. You may have some of the same thoughts, attitudes, and addictions, and you may even want to do some of the same old stuff, but don't get discouraged. Though Christ made your spirit new, *you* are the one who makes your mind new.

The Bible says to "put on the new you." This means it's a conscious choice to behave like and adopt the attitude of a new person in Christ. Choosing to do what is right, reading and listening to the Word of God, and praying are all part of becoming the new you. It doesn't happen completely overnight, but the moment you start to adapt your lifestyle is the moment your life begins to change! As you stick with it, you will begin to prefer God's way instead of your old ways of doing things.

How cool is it that with God you can actually change the way you think?! As you embrace the new you and renew your mind by reading, contemplating, and speaking His Word, you'll grow more and more aware of God's presence in your life. You'll notice with each passing day that your desires and thoughts are becoming more and more like His. You are *new* on the inside—believe and confess this over yourself daily, and watch your thoughts and actions change to reflect what is already yours.

Scriptures

"Therefore if any man be in Christ, he is a new creature: old things are passed away; behold, all things are become new."

—2 Corinthians 5:17 (KJV)

"Remember not the former things, nor consider the things of old. Behold, I am doing a new thing; now it springs forth, do you not perceive it? I will make a way in the wilderness and rivers in the desert."

—Isaiah 43:18-19 (ESV)

"Don't lie to each other, for you have stripped off your old sinful nature and all its wicked deeds. Put on your new nature, and be renewed as you learn to know your Creator and become like him."

—Colossians 3:9-10 (NLT)

"And I will give you a new heart, and I will put a new spirit in you. I will take out your stony, stubborn heart and give you a tender, responsive heart."

—Ezekiel 36:26 (NLT)

Speak these words over your life

I am a new creation in Christ. All of my sins have been forgiven and forgotten. My old life and everything associated with it has passed away. I have new desires pleasing to God, and new goals for a life of peace, prosperity, and joy. I am committed to living a life of honor and integrity. I am committed to let God's love and light shine through me, and His wisdom guide me, change me, and mold me into what He desires I become. The old me is dead, there is a new person living on the inside of me. The Spirit of the Lord now lives in me and my mind will focus on those things that are pure. I am a new creation in Christ and His life within me will be evident for all to see.

I Am Free

Where the Spirit of the Lord is, there is *freedom*! When you accepted Jesus as your Savior, the supernatural-powered, bondage-breaking, addiction-killing Spirit of Freedom was infused into your very being. You are *free*! You no longer have to be chained up by the guilt of your past, for sin has lost its power over you and you have been forgiven.

You no longer have to be paralyzed by fear, for God will never leave you or forsake you. You no longer have to be a slave to your own lusts and desires, for there is a new force at work within you to equip, energize, and empower you. You no longer have to be confined by sickness and disease, for Christ made healing, wellness, and wholeness available for you. You no longer have to be plagued by the nagging thoughts of worry and anxiety, for God's ability to intervene is great, and greater still is His affection for you! You no longer have to be tortured by the need for others' approval, for you are a child of God, and He affirms you through His Word.

Satan's attacks against you are futile; God is with you, for you, and on your side! You are free to live the life you have always dreamed about. Nothing is too big or too far out of reach to an unshackled champion of God the Almighty. Jesus died on the cross to give you complete and total freedom, for nothing can halt the unstoppable life-altering force that is God's fierce love for those whose faith is audacious enough to believe in a loving God! YOU ARE FREE!

Scripture

"With the arrival of Jesus, the Messiah, that fateful dilemma is resolved. Those who enter into Christ's being-here-for-us no longer have to live under a continuous, low-lying black cloud. A new power is in operation. The Spirit of life in Christ, like a strong wind, has magnificently cleared the air, freeing you from a fated lifetime of brutal tyranny at the hands of sin and death."

–Romans 8:1-2 (MSG)

"In [this] freedom Christ has made us free [and completely liberated us]; stand fast then, and do not be hampered and held ensnared and submit again to a yoke of slavery [which you have once put off]."

–Galatians 5:1 (AMPC)

"So if the Son liberates you [makes you free men], then you are really and unquestionably free."

–John 8:36 (AMPC)

Speak these words over your life

I am free. I am free from the guilt and condemnation of my past failures, for I have been forgiven. I am free from worry, anxiety, and stress, for the peace of God reigns in my heart. I am free from depression, discouragement, and despair, for the Lord encourages me and sustains me. I am free from fear, for God has not given me a spirit of fear, but of power, love, and a sound mind. I am free from addictions and the pull of my lusts and desires, for there is a new force at work within me to equip, energize, and empower me to live a life of honor. I am free from sickness and disease, for when Jesus took stripes on His back, He obliterated any power that sickness and disease had over me. I am free to live the life I have always dreamed about. Nothing is too big or too far out of reach to me—an unshackled champion of God the Almighty!

I Am Strong

Sometimes life can just wear you out! Weariness and fatigue always seem to be nipping at our heels. It's not just physical— the mental and emotional demands of life zap our strength and drain our energy. Our fast-paced lives are sometimes not conducive to the stress-free, worry-free, easy life we all seem to be chasing after. But don't lose heart! Look to God, and He will infuse strength into you, enabling you to not only endure the ever-constant pressures of life, but actually overcome them with joy!

The foundation and supplier of strength is the unfaltering Word of God. Reading, spending time thinking about, and speaking God's Word will allow His strength to flow to you. When you need strength to rise above all the negative words that people have spoken to you and about you, then remind yourself who God said you are and what He said you can do with Him. When you need strength to push through in the tough times, God will be your strength and walk through it with you. When you need strength in the mornings to face the grind, God is up with you to fight for you. When you need strength to get through depression, worry, or anxiety, then lean on God and He'll lift you up out of despair.

God is easily touched by what we are going through, and He never misses a chance to show Himself strong on behalf of those who love Him and put their trust in Him. When you need strength to overcome fear and your own insecurities, let God's strength bolster your heart with courage and confidence so you can face any circumstance head-on.

Scriptures

"In conclusion, be strong in the Lord [draw your strength from Him and be empowered through your union with Him] and in the power of His [boundless] might."

–Ephesians 6:10 (AMP)

"I can do all things [which He has called me to do] through Him who strengthens and empowers me [to fulfill His purpose—I am self-sufficient in Christ's sufficiency; I am ready for anything and equal to anything through Him who infuses me with inner strength and confident peace.]"

–Philippians 4:13 (AMP)

"Have I not commanded you? Be strong and courageous. Do not be frightened, and do not be dismayed, for the Lord your God is with you wherever you go."

–Joshua 1:9 (ESV)

Speak these words over your life

I am strong in the Lord and in the power of His might. I am strong in my body. I am strong in my mind. I am strong in my spirit. I draw my strength through my union with Christ. When I am at my weakest, He is at His strongest. I can do all things through Him who strengthens and empowers me to fulfill His purpose. I am self-sufficient in Christ's sufficiency—I am ready for anything and equal to anything through Him who infuses me with inner strength and confident peace. I have strength to overcome any obstacle, to endure any attack, and to boldly fight the good fight of faith. I will not fear, nor will I allow any doubt to enter my mind, for I am a child of the Almighty and I will not be shaken! I am strong in the Lord!

I Am a Light in the Darkness

Darkness is all around us, seeking to dim our passion, hide our hope, and invade our peace. Christ has made you to be an example in this world—He wants His love and life to shine through you into the hearts of those around you. You are a light in the darkness!

Darkness takes many forms in people's lives. When we are depressed, it takes the form of heaviness; when we are angry, it clouds our judgement; when we are hurt, it feels cold and lonely. Darkness seeks to isolate us using depression, hate, confusion, and fear so we will push people away, develop addictions, and focus on our own inadequacies. But God has made us lights to pull people out of the darkness that envelops them. The only way to combat the darkness is to make the conscious choice to let God's light shine through you.

You can truly be a beacon of God's light, life, and love to a lost and dying world. Your life touches a great number of people every day. You can bring His life to the darkness in the lives around you. A smile, a kind word, a thoughtful gesture, a considerate response, a sympathetic ear, or a small act of kindness could have a significant effect on someone's life. His light in you can bring hope to the discouraged and heartbroken, healing to the sick and hurting, peace to a troubled mind, joy to the weary and distressed, and direction to those who have lost their way. Don't settle to live a life blending in; remember that you are a light in this world, a beacon of hope to those around you. Now, go and be that light in the darkness!

Scriptures

"You are the light of the world. You cannot hide a city that is on a mountain. Men do not light a lamp and put it under a basket. They put it on a table so it gives light to all in the house. Let your light shine in front of men. Then they will see the good things you do and will honor your Father Who is in heaven."

–Matthew 5:14-16 (NLV)

"You were once darkness, but now you are light in the Lord, so live your life as children of light."

–Ephesians 5:8 (CEB)

"Then Jesus again spoke to them, saying, "I am the Light of the world; he who follows Me will not walk in the darkness, but will have the Light of life."

–John 8:12 (NASB)

Speak these words over your life

I am light in the darkness, a beacon of hope to all who see me. I will not settle for a life spent cowering in the shadows, afraid to allow the Light inside me to shine. I will make a difference in this world for the glory of God. Though sickness, sin, and suffering are all around me, they shall by no means affect me in any way, shape, or form. I operate on delegated authority from God the Almighty, and I refuse to allow evil in any form to live on in my spheres of influence. Goodness and mercy shall follow me wherever I go, for God is within me. Where there is a need, God will fulfill it through me. Where there is hurt, God will provide comfort through me. I proclaim that your Light, Father, shines through me more brightly every day.

I Am an Overcomer

This world can be a tough place. Jesus said that in the world we will have tribulation *and* distress *and* suffering, but to be courageous, be confident, be undaunted, and be filled with joy, for He has overcome the world. His conquest is accomplished, His victory abiding. You are an overcomer—God has decreed it through His Word, and it is an established fact. All you have to do is believe, receive, and act on it. The same life-giving, reality-shaping Spirit that raised Christ from the dead, overcoming even death, resides in you!

It is not the will of our Father to see you defeated by a problem, discouraged by an obstacle, or stressed by pressure. It's His firm desire that you choose life, that you choose to activate His gifts, that you choose to operate in faith, and that you live the joyfully fulfilled life of an overcomer.

So how do you overcome? By faith in God's Word. Your faith to overcome is not based on how you feel, and it's not conditional on how good you are. It's an unwavering trust that no matter how insurmountable an obstacle looks, your God will see you through to the other side of it. Take the dare to trust God above all things and to trust that with Him there is nothing you can't overcome. In the midst of the most daunting of challenges, dare to overcome. When faced with impossible odds, dare to overcome. When hope seems lost, dare to overcome! Pray to God, ask for help, find what His Word says about your situation, and then let God's Word guide your thoughts, words, and actions. By doing this, you are stepping into the identity of an overcomer.

Scriptures

"For everyone born of God is victorious *and* overcomes the world; and this is the victory that has conquered *and* overcome the world—our [continuing, persistent] faith [in Jesus the Son of God]. Who is the one who is victorious *and* overcomes the world? It is the one who believes *and* recognizes the fact that Jesus is the Son of God."

–1 John 5:4-5 (AMP)

"I have told you these things, so that in Me you may have [perfect] peace. In the world you have tribulation *and* distress *and* suffering, but be courageous [be confident, be undaunted, be filled with joy]; I have overcome the world." [My conquest is accomplished, My victory abiding.]"

–John 16:33 (AMP)

"He who overcomes [the world by adhering faithfully to Christ Jesus as Lord and Savior] will inherit these things, and I will be his God and he will be My son."

–Revelation 21:7 (AMP)

19

Speak these words over your life

I am an overcomer, strong in the Lord and the power of His might. I am confident, courageous, and undaunted in my faith. Even when I experience tribulation, tests, and trials, I shall overcome. I will not succumb to distress, frustration, or defeat. I am born of God and that makes me a world-overcomer. The same Spirit that raised Christ from the dead lives in me. I have been designed by God to succeed in this life. Through Him I can overcome any obstacle or challenge I might face. In spite of adverse circumstances and regardless of the failures of the past, even when faced with what seems to be impossible situations—I will still overcome by the power of the Holy Spirit. I will never give up; I will fight until I win. The battle is the Lord's and the victory is mine. I am an overcomer!

I Am a Child of God

Why does God treat us so lovingly when we sin constantly, spend our days ignoring Him at every turn, and only come to Him when we need something or a crisis happens in our life? Why would He send His only beloved Son, Jesus, to die a brutal death to save mankind after all of the crimes we have committed against Him (and still commit)? It makes no sense why God would do all of this for us unless there was an underlying reason for all of it. We may never be able to grasp the depth of His unconditional love for us, but God makes it clear why we are here—it's because He wanted to have children. He didn't want a servant, an employee, or a subject—He wanted a son or a daughter.

Have you ever wondered why you were born?

He wanted *you*.

You are His child; even when you mess up, you are still His. It brings joy to your Father when you are happy, when you succeed, and especially when you spend time with Him! He wants to be close to you and walk through life with you. All of the "rules" of the Bible are not set up so you can prove your love and devotion; they are there to protect you and help you live the most fulfilling life possible. Everything God has done has been out of His love for you. That's why He sent the dearest thing to His heart, Jesus, to die for you. He did it to show you just how valuable you are to Him and so He can spend eternity with you. You're His child, and heaven wouldn't be the same without you.

Scriptures

"And, I will be a Father to you, and you will be my sons and daughters, says the Lord Almighty."

–2 Corinthians 6:18 (NIV)

"See how very much our Father loves us, for he calls us his children, and that is what we are! But the people who belong to this world don't recognize that we are God's children because they don't know him."

–1 John 3:1 (NLT)

"For you [who are born-again have been reborn from above—spiritually transformed, renewed, sanctified and] are all children of God [set apart for His purpose with full rights and privileges] through faith in Christ Jesus."

–Galatians 3:26 (AMP)

Speak these words over your life

I am a child of the Almighty, with all the rights, privileges, and blessings that go with that position. The Creator of the universe is my Father. He loves me unconditionally. He wants me to succeed. He provides for all my needs. He's got my back, He is on my side. He forgives me when I mess up. He watches over me. He cares about what I care about. It gives Him pleasure to see me enjoying life, to see me succeeding, to see me trusting in Him despite any hardship this life throws at me. He sustains me; He sent His spirit to comfort and guide me. I am His child. He is my Father. There is not a power in existence that can disconnect me from the love of my Father.

I Am Chosen

God chose you before you were born. He's had a watchful eye on you since before you knew He even existed. God has specially handpicked you; you are God's elect. You are part of His royal priesthood, a brother or sister in His pursuit to bring hope to a world in despair. You have a purpose on this earth, and regardless of the mistakes you've made, where your current situation in life is, what responsibilities you have—no matter how insecure and weak you may feel—God still picks you!

He has big plans for your life, and He is the support you need to accomplish them. God gives you His joy, peace, wisdom, insight, confidence, and strength to accomplish your destiny and to help His people. He's given you all of your gifts, talents, and passions. You are chosen by the Creator of the universe; accept this affirmation and let it empower you to follow the passions and dreams He has placed inside you. The question is, will *you* choose *God*?

It is your choice whether you allow God to play a significant role in your life or not. Don't let insecurity and fear choke the life out of your dreams like it has with so many. Instead, put faith behind your passion and believe that against all odds you will be who God has called you to be. Be the man or woman you have always dreamed you could be! Face the opposition, face the potential embarrassment, and face the fear of the unknown head on with a fiery passion untamed and unhindered by small thinking and small living. God will not let down His chosen.

Scriptures

"But you are the ones chosen by God, chosen for the high calling of priestly work, chosen to be a holy people, God's instruments to do his work and speak out for him, to tell others of the night-and-day difference he made for you—from nothing to something, from rejected to accepted."

–1 Peter 2:9-10 (MSG)

"Even as [in His love] He chose us [actually picked us out for Himself as His own] in Christ before the foundation of the world, that we should be holy (consecrated and set apart for Him) and blameless in His sight, even above reproach, before Him in love."

–Ephesians 1:4 (AMPC)

"Furthermore, because we are united with Christ, we have received an inheritance from God, for he chose us in advance, and he makes everything work out according to his plan."

–Ephesians 1:11 (NLT)

Speak these words over your life

I am chosen by God; I am part of His chosen generation. I was handpicked by God. He has a plan and purpose for my life. I will fulfill the destiny God has for me. God has placed gifts and talents inside me to be used for His kingdom. I will not allow thoughts of my own inadequacies to rob me of the confidence that comes from being chosen of God. I know where I am weak, God is strong. God equips, empowers, and makes me ready for any task which He has set before me. I was chosen to come into this earth for such a time as this; I have a purpose that God has destined for me to fulfill. I will walk in confidence daily knowing just how much I matter in the eyes of the Lord.

I Am Righteous

You are the righteousness of Christ! This statement simply means that you are in right standing with God. When Christ died on the cross, He paid the cost for our sins—past, present, and future—and He replaced them with His own righteousness. Jesus came to this earth to make that trade so that we could have the same relationship and right standing with God that He did. Jesus gave us His ability to approach God any time of day, to talk to God as a friend, to call God Father, and to depend on God without shame—all in exchange for our sin. That's what it means to be the righteousness of Christ—God sees us like He does Jesus, because of Jesus. The Bible says Adam separated us from God by sin, but Jesus connects us to the Father through His righteousness.

When God sees you in pain and being tortured by shame, bound by guilt, and feeling as if you deserve to be punished and not forgiven, it hurts Him. He gave everything so you wouldn't have to feel that way. He loves you, and He sees you spotless, just like Jesus. You are His child, and He wants you to be bold in His presence, not to act like you're a disgrace when you approach Him. Believe that the blood of Jesus Christ is more powerful than any sin you've committed—your past can't haunt you, your present is secure, and your future is bright. Believe you are the righteousness of Christ.

Scriptures

"For our sake He made Christ [virtually] to be sin Who knew no sin, so that in and through Him we might become [endued with, viewed as being in, and examples of] the righteousness of God [what we ought to be, approved and acceptable and in right relationship with Him, by His goodness]."

–2 Corinthians 5:21 (AMPC)

"Namely, the righteousness of God which comes by believing with personal trust and confident reliance on Jesus Christ (the Messiah). [And it is meant] for all who believe. For there is no distinction,"

–Romans 3:22 (AMPC)

"If death ruled because of one person's failure, those who receive the multiplied grace and the gift of righteousness will even more certainly rule in life through the one person Jesus Christ."

–Romans 5:17 (CEB)

Speak these words over your life

The Bible says we have been made the righteousness of God, therefore in obedience to God's Word I boldly confess that I am the righteousness of God in Christ. Not by my goodness, not because I am holy within myself, but through the shed blood of Jesus, my Savior. His righteousness is His gift to me, and I will honor Christ's sacrifice by accepting it wholeheartedly. I have been made righteous and acceptable in the presence of my heavenly Father, and nothing that anyone says to me or about me can ever change that. I can go to God boldly when I need help and obtain grace and mercy. I am righteous not because of what I have done, but because of what Jesus has done for me.

I Am Loved

Whoever you are, whatever you have done, wherever you are from, no matter your station in life, God loves you and will never stop loving you. Neither your accomplishments nor your failures, your victories nor your defeats, qualify you or disqualify you for His love. Nothing you do or don't do will make God love you any more or any less. Let that truth set you free.

When God looks at you, He doesn't think paying with the most precious thing He had in all of eternity, Jesus Christ, was too high of a price for you. He displayed for all creation and eternity His immeasurable and untouchable love for you. That kind of love is difficult to comprehend, because it is so contrary to everything we see in this world. His love cannot be altered, changed, or stopped. It's unconditional. You can't earn it, you can't do enough good deeds to deserve it, and you can't do enough bad deeds for Him to take it away. But it is up to you whether you accept it or not.

When you sin, don't run from God—run *to* Him regardless of how big, bad, and ugly your sins have been, because God is not fazed by it. Nothing you can do is more powerful than what Jesus already did at the cross. Let Him break the bondage in your life, lift the weights off your shoulders, rid you of your guilt, heal your pain, take your worry, and replace your fear with faith born through an intimate relationship with Him. He wants to restore you with His love to a life of peace and joy. Rejoice, for you are loved!

Scriptures

"For I am convinced [and continue to be convinced—beyond any doubt] that neither death, nor life, nor angels, nor principalities, nor things present *and* threatening, nor things to come, nor powers, nor height, nor depth, nor any other created thing, will be able to separate us from the [unlimited] love of God, which is in Christ Jesus our Lord."

—Romans 8:38-39 (AMP)

"For God so loved the world, that he gave his only begotten Son, that whosoever believeth in him should not perish, but have everlasting life."

—John 3:16 (KJV)

"Love never fails [it never fades nor ends]….."

—1 Corinthians 13:8a (AMP)

"But because of his great love for us, God, who is rich in mercy, made us alive with Christ even when we were dead in transgressions—it is by grace you have been saved."

—Ephesians 2:4-5 (NIV)

Speak these words over your life

God's love for me is an unchangeable fact. God's love for me is greater than any sin I have committed, greater than any failure I have had. Nothing I do, nothing other people do, and nothing the devil does can separate me from God's love. Not death, nor life, nor angels or principalities can separate me from His love. God's love for me is eternal. His love knows no boundaries; it never gives up believing in me or reaching out to me. God's love is there for me in the darkest times in my life; when I think I can't go on. His love comforts me, His love sustains me, and His love encourages my soul and restores my hope. God's love endures forever, and He loves me.

I Am an Ambassador

The dictionary defines an ambassador as a diplomatic official of the highest rank who is sent by one sovereign nation to another as its resident representative. The Bible says plainly that we are Christ's ambassadors and God is making His appeal to a lost world through us. We are Christ's personal representatives! This means that you are a divine representative of Christ on this earth; you are an ambassador for Christ and the Kingdom of Heaven.

God touches the broken, brings healing to the hurting, restores relationships, instills peace, promotes joy, and affirms the insecure through you—His spokesperson and ambassador on this earth. As God's representatives, we have a duty and privilege to behave in such a manner that brings honor to God. We are not here on earth to fuse with it, and too often as Christians we try to blend in and exalt our problems in an attempt to relate to those around us. We end up hurt, broken, and confused like the people we are trying to help.

As ambassadors of Christ we are to walk in love like Jesus did, to live *in* the world but not *like* the world so we can help the world. For many people, we are the only God they will ever see, and we are the only Bible they will ever read. With this is mind, the attributes of Jesus should be evident in our lives. It's the joy and peace we have that people crave; it's the patience and gentleness that displays a love that people need; it's self-control and integrity that people respect and trust; and it's our generosity that separates us from a selfish society. That is the heart and soul of what it means to be an ambassador of Christ.

Scriptures

"So we are Christ's ambassadors, God making His appeal as it were through us. We [as Christ's personal representatives] beg you for His sake to lay hold of the divine favor [now offered you] and be reconciled to God."

–2 Corinthians 5:20 (AMPC)

"But our citizenship is in heaven. And we eagerly await a Savior from there, the Lord Jesus Christ,"

–Philippians 3:20 (NIV)

"And He called to Him the Twelve [apostles] and began to send them out [as His ambassadors] two by two and gave them authority and power over the unclean spirits."

–Mark 6:7 (AMPC)

"Therefore become imitators of God [copy Him and follow His example], as well-beloved children [imitate their father];"

–Ephesians 5:1 (AMPC)

Speak these words over your life

I am an ambassador of the Most High God and His Kingdom. I will represent my Father with honor, integrity, and dignity. I will live a life of purity and holiness before God. I am an ambassador of God's love, peace, and mercy to this world. I am quick to forgive the mistakes and shortcomings of others and myself. I am an ambassador of God's healing power, ready and available to be a blessing at all times and speak words of encouragement, hope, and healing to others. I am an ambassador of the power and might of the Holy Spirit and His anointing, and all it represents. I respond to adversity and calamity with a confident and peaceful spirit. I am resolute and undaunted in my faith. God provides His ability and His insight concerning my affairs. I will endeavor to conduct my life at all times in a manner that will be pleasing to Him.

I Am Redeemed

Adam's disobedience opened the door for sin and death to enter the world, separating people from God. Seeing His children suffering due to the effects of sin, God sent Jesus to pay the price of sin and redeem mankind. To redeem something is to gain or regain possession of it in exchange for payment. When you say you are redeemed, you are declaring that **God bought you back!**

This world is in a state of decay from all the effects of sin. Sickness, disease, poverty, pestilence, lack, every kind of hurt, and everything that is diabolical has come upon the earth. Deuteronomy 28 lists every sort of terrible affliction that people face as the result of their disobedience and sin. This list is known as the Curse of the Law. It clearly says that everything that is bad is of the curse. But though the curse may wreak havoc *all around* you, it has no power *over* you because you are redeemed!

You were destined for a life of pain leading to death. But because this misery that was to be our lives was unbearable to God, despite all that you have done to deserve judgment, He bought you back. He ripped you out of the clutches of a doomed existence and accepted you as part of His family. You are redeemed out of the curse and into His blessings. His redemption covers you for the here and now, past, present, and future. You are God's child, bought by the blood of Christ. You are God's once again, for you are redeemed.

Scriptures

"In him we have redemption through his blood, the forgiveness of sins, in accordance with the riches of God's grace that he lavished on us. With all wisdom and understanding,"

–EPHESIANS 1:7-8 (NIV)

"Who gave himself for us to redeem us from all wickedness and to purify for himself a people that are his very own, eager to do what is good."

–TITUS 2:14 (NIV)

"Christ purchased our freedom and redeemed us from the curse of the Law and its condemnation by becoming a curse for us"

–GALATIANS 3:13 A (AMP)

"But it is from Him that you are in Christ Jesus, who became to us wisdom from God [revealing His plan of salvation], and righteousness [making us acceptable to God], and sanctification [making us holy and setting us apart for God], and redemption [providing our ransom from the penalty for sin],"

–1 CORINTHIANS 1:30 (AMP)

I Am Redeemed

Speak these words over your life

I am redeemed. My spirit is full of life and united with God. I am redeemed from any and all failures. I am redeemed from any and all addictions. I am redeemed from the curse of the law. I am redeemed from sin, sickness, and an eternity spent apart from God. Because of the price Jesus paid for my redemption, I can and will declare with boldness:

I am free; I am strong; I am a light in the darkness. I am an overcomer; I am a child of the Almighty. I am chosen; I am righteous; I am loved. I am an ambassador; I am favored; I am protected. I am more than a conqueror; I am healed; I am prosperous. I am the temple of the Holy Spirit; I am rooted in Christ; I am complete.

I Am Complete

It's easy to look in the mirror and notice every flaw about you. If you want to feel bad about yourself, then compare your looks to the top models, your intelligence to the top minds, and your relationship with God to the great leaders of faith.

Yet while you might not be able to compare when you focus on the brilliant minds, the most attractive people, and the most devout believers, if you will shift your focus to Christ, the creator of the universe, you will find they don't even come close to His perfection! Stop comparing the "Goliath" in your life with the "shepherd boy" David you see in the mirror; instead do what David did and compare your greatest obstacle to *God*. Because when you compare anything to God, no matter how big it is, God is bigger still!

You are complete in Christ. Where you are weak, He is strong. Where you have failed a thousand times, with Him you will overcome. When you are sick, He makes you whole. When your heart is broken, His love knits it back together. When you have no more fight left, He's your endurance that picks you up and carries you across the finish line. Forgiver of sins, emotional and physical Healer, constant Companion through every trial, Protector from all danger, He is everything you need. You've been made a child of the Almighty, freed from everything holding you back, and have a promise of a bright future. All this is given to you through the death and resurrection of Christ so that you can be complete! Believe it—no matter what insecurities you battle, what obstacle is in front of you, how inadequate you feel, or how big your mistakes are—with God you are ready and equal to anything. You are complete in Christ.

Scriptures

"And in Him you have been made complete [achieving spiritual stature through Christ], and He is the head over all rule and authority [of every angelic and earthly power]."

–Colossians 2:10 (AMP)

"All Scripture is breathed out by God and profitable for teaching, for reproof, for correction, and for training in righteousness, that the man of God may be complete, equipped for every good work."

–2 Timothy 3:16-17 (ESV)

"But He has said to me, 'My grace is sufficient for you [My lovingkindness and My mercy are more than enough—always available—regardless of the situation]; for [My] power is being perfected [and is completed and shows itself most effectively] in [your] weakness.' Therefore, I will all the more gladly boast in my weaknesses, so that the power of Christ [may completely enfold me and] may dwell in me."

–2 Corinthians 12:9 (AMP)

Speak these words over your life

My salvation is a gift from God. There is nothing I did to earn it. There is nothing I can do to improve on it. I was broken and empty before I met Jesus, but when I accepted Jesus as my personal Savior, He came into me, filling all the gaps of my inadequacies, imperfections, and flaws. He filled my emptiness with His Love; my loneliness with His friendship; my weakness with His strength; my failures with His forgiveness; my worries with His peace; my stress with His joy; my sickness with His healing; my inability with His ability; my insecurity with His confidence; my fears with faith. Any area in which I come up short when it comes to my own ability, God makes up the difference with His ability. I am complete because Christ is in me and He is with me.

I Am Protected

The world is a dangerous place; violent crime is on the rise, terrorism has become a global menace, and sickness continues to plague our society. But we don't need to subscribe to the daily dose of fear the world prescribes, for God refers to Himself as a shield, a refuge, a strong tower, and a very present help in trouble.

The Lord protects us through the power of His Word and by the leading of His Holy Spirit. When you confess His divine protection over your life, you are releasing the power in His words to halt any force that would seek to harm you, and you are increasing your sensitivity to His warnings of danger. God will protect you by warning you to stay away from harmful situations. Listen to these warnings, for they are your answer to prayer and the result of your confession. His protection extends past the physical dangers in the world; He'll also protect you emotionally as well. He'll warn you against harmful relationships, and He'll even guard your heart so that though you hear harsh words, they don't seem to affect you like they used to.

God takes it seriously when you call Him your shield. He cannot and will not allow His child, who is confessing His promises back to Him, to be harmed. He looks throughout the entire world to show Himself strong on behalf of men and women like that. Designate a few moments in the morning to the declaration of His protection over you and your family, and walk the rest of the day free from the fear of this world's ability to harm you.

Scriptures

"My God is my rock, in whom I find protection. He is my shield, the power that saves me, and my place of safety. He is my refuge, my savior, the one who saves me from violence. I called on the Lord, who is worthy of praise, and he saved me from my enemies."

–2 Samuel 22:3-4 (NLT)

"God is our refuge and strength [mighty and impenetrable], a very present *and* well-proved help in trouble."

–Psalm 46:1 (AMP)

"A thousand may fall at your side, ten thousand at your right hand, but it will not come near you."

–Psalm 91:7 (NIV)

"In peace I will lie down and sleep, for you alone, O Lord, will keep me safe."

–Psalm 4:8 (NLT)

Speak these words over your life

Wherever I go and whatever I do, I am walking under the covering of God's divine protection. The angels of the Lord go with me and before me to protect me and keep me from all harm, danger, and calamity. I am attentive to hear God's warnings. The Lord is my refuge and my strength; my fortress and strong tower. I will not fear, for the Lord is with me. I will not fear any evil for I am protected by the Lord! I am protected from financial scams, from violent crimes, from automobile accidents, from adverse weather, and from injuries while at work or at the gym. No evil shall befall me; no plague shall come near my household. My home, my family, and all those who are in my company are protected by God Almighty.

I Am More Than a Conqueror

It is not God's will for you to be defeated, discouraged, or depressed. In fact, it is just the opposite. The Bible clearly tells us that through Christ Jesus we are more than conquerors. That means regardless of what challenges come your way, no matter what life tries to do to bring you down, in spite of the impossible situation you might find yourself in—with God's help you can conquer it. God's will for you is total victory in every area of your life!

Whatever has been holding you back, you can conquer it. Maybe it's bad habits, financial pressure, or a health condition. God is your redeemer, your provider, and your healer. You will conquer it with Him as your ally. Even if you are being held back by internal struggles, such as regret, fear, anxiety, or depression, God sent His Spirit to revitalize, renew, and empower you from the inside out.

You may feel as though you are in a pit of despair that is so deep you could never get out. But God is the God of hope, and He will rescue you. Nothing you are facing is bigger than your God. Whatever the struggle, whether it's external or internal, God is in you and God is for you. You can count on Him to be with you, facing down any obstacle. You can face your problems head on and defeat them. It's time to rise up; it's time to stand strong. You have the Spirit of a conqueror inside you, so awaken the dormant, unstoppable power within your spirit. Begin to speak God's promises over your life. You are more than a conqueror.

Scriptures

"Nay, in all these things we are more than conquerors through him that loved us."

–Romans 8:37 (KJV)

"But if the Spirit of him that raised up Jesus from the dead dwell in you, he that raised up Christ from the dead shall also quicken your mortal bodies by his Spirit that dwelleth in you."

–Romans 8:11 (KJV)

"But thanks be to God, Who gives us the victory [making us conquerors] through our Lord Jesus Christ."

–1 Corinthians 15:57 (AMPC)

"Who is it that is victorious over [that conquers] the world but he who believes that Jesus is the Son of God [who adheres to, trusts in, and relies on that fact]?"

–1 John 5:5 (AMPC)

Speak these words over your life

I am more than a conqueror through Christ; I am ready for anything and equal to anything. The same Spirit that raised Christ from the dead dwells within me. Just as Jesus conquered the grave, I shall conquer any challenge that dares to confront me today. I have the Spirit of victory in me. With God's help, I can and will conquer my problems. I am self-sufficient in Christ's sufficiency. I am well able to endure, battle, and conquer with God as my ally, and my faith in Him as my shield. There is nothing that I face today that can stop me from my relentless trust in my God. I am convinced that God is faithful. He is on my side; He is for me; He is with me; and He is in me. So I stand undaunted, full of vigor, ready for life, knowing that nothing can stand against me when I'm united with God.

I Am Prosperous

God takes pleasure in blessing you, and it's His will for you to be prosperous. God does not want you in lack for any reason, and He wants you to thrive in life, always having more than enough!

One of the names of God in the Bible is *El Shaddai,* which translates into "the God that is more than enough." God is a "too much" God! He doesn't deal in just enough—He deals in abundance. It's His plan for your life to have enough to take care of all your needs and be a blessing to others, too! To be able to take your family out for a nice meal, to live in a good home, to drive a great car, to go on a nice vacation, and to be able to bless others as you have been blessed.

Sometimes it can be daunting to think that you could live this abundant life, but don't be discouraged about your situation, just start where you are. Believe God for a little extra to give, and a little extra to enjoy, and speak His promises of abundance over your life. As time passes, your faith will increase as well as your ability to receive abundance in your finances. Your words have power to shape your life when filled with faith in God. Declare that He supplies all of your needs according to His riches in glory, expect His prosperity in your life, and thank Him before you see any change because you know it's coming! Do this and watch God show Himself strong on your behalf. You are the child of El Shaddai—you are prosperous.

Scriptures

"And God is able to make all grace (every favor and earthly blessing) come to you in abundance, so that you may always *and* under all circumstances *and* whatever the need be self-sufficient [possessing enough to require no aid or support and furnished in abundance for every good work and charitable donation]."

–2 Corinthians 9:8 (AMPC)

"But my God shall supply all your need according to his riches in glory by Christ Jesus."

–Philippians 4:19 (KJV)

"Now to Him Who, by (in consequence of) the [action of His] power that is at work within us, is able to [carry out His purpose and] do superabundantly, far over *and* above all that we [dare] ask or think [infinitely beyond our highest prayers, desires, thoughts, hopes, or dreams]."

–Ephesians 3:20 (AMPC)

"Let the Lord be magnified, which hath pleasure in the prosperity of his servant."

–Psalm 35:27 (b) (KJV)

Speak these words over your life

I am abundantly blessed. God takes care of me. I will not worry or be anxious about my finances, because my God shall supply all of my needs according to His riches in Glory. I always, under all circumstances, have whatever I need. I am sufficient in Christ, for it is He who is able to do far more abundantly than all I can ask or think. God gives me wisdom, insight, and favor concerning all my financial affairs. I am successful; I am prosperous; I declare I have more than enough money to take care of all my needs and plenty left over to be a generous giver towards others and the Kingdom of God. God takes pleasure in my prosperity. I will walk in prosperity all the days of my life, and I will give honor and glory to my God with the abundance He has given me.

I Am the Temple of
the Holy Spirit

The Bible calls you the temple of the
Holy Spirit. The Bible also says that the
same Spirit that raised Jesus Christ from the
dead now lives in you! The Holy Spirit is in
you to comfort you when you are feeling
down. He's in you to remind you who you
are in Christ when your actions dictate something else entirely. He's in you to guide you
through life so that you will be full of joy and
perfect peace as you walk towards the
purpose that God has destined for you. He's
in you to equip you with the knowledge and
wisdom you need as problems arise. He's in
you to give you energy when you run out of
steam. He's in you to unveil the truth and
splendor of God's character as you study His
Word to grow in understanding. He's in you

to infuse life, light, and love into the hurting and dying world—through you!

Being a temple of the Holy Spirit means you house this magnificent blessing within yourself. Living this means you rely on God's direction through the leading of His Spirit. Understanding this tells you that you are not in this fight alone, but rather you have the Spirit of the Lord within you to fight with you and for you.

He is the ultimate help in your time of need. He's your constant companion, your support, and your comforter. He's your friend, and when you need His help He'll show up every time, for it's the very Spirit of your Heavenly Father that lives in you. If you have never let the Holy Spirit play a role in your life, then you are in for a blessed adventure when you accept that you are the temple of the Holy Spirit.

Scriptures

"Do you not know that your bodies are temples of the Holy Spirit, who is in you, whom you have received from God? You are not your own;"

–1 Corinthians 6:19 (NIV)

"Don't you know that you yourselves are God's temple and that God's Spirit dwells in your midst?"

–1 Corinthians 3:16 (NIV)

"If the Spirit of him who raised Jesus from the dead dwells in you, he who raised Christ Jesus from the dead will also give life to your mortal bodies through his Spirit who dwells in you."

–Romans 8:11 (ESV)

"But the Comforter (Counselor, Helper, Intercessor, Advocate, Strengthener, Standby), the Holy Spirit, Whom the Father will send in My name [in My place, to represent Me and act on My behalf], He will teach you all things. And He will cause you to recall (will remind you of, bring to your remembrance) everything I have told you."

–John 14:26 (AMPC)

Speak these words over your life

My body is the temple of the Holy Spirit. God's Spirit lives in me. I am not my own; I belong to Him. I am the temple of the living God. God dwells in me, and works in me and through me. He is my God and I am His child. I choose to treat my body in a way that will honor God. The Holy Spirit in me gives me courage, strength, and power to fulfill God's plan for my life. He gives me wisdom and insight concerning all the affairs of my life. He is my comforter, my encourager, my best friend, my mentor, and my protector. He reveals the truths of His Word and makes them real to me. I am keen to hear and quick to obey the direction and counsel of the Holy Spirit.

I Am Rooted

Victorious strength, unyielding faith, and reckless tenacity come through the Spirit of faith living in every Word of God. Being rooted in Christ is planting your life within the solid ground of His infallible Word and digging your roots deep in Him so you can utilize every gift that has been given to empower and revitalize you.

You are like a tree—the deeper your roots grow, the stronger you are. Not only do a tree's roots draw nutrients from the soil to feed the entire body, but they also act as an anchor when the storm winds blow against it. It's the roots that keep a tree firmly planted! When a crisis roars into your life like a raging storm, it's time to stand on the promises in God's Word. When you are in a drought, the stressful grind of life doesn't seem to end, and your strength is all but faded, you draw the energy from deep within where the streams of living water flow, for when you are weak God is strong. You are rooted in Christ.

His Word is your foundation, but how deep your roots go into that foundation is up to you. The more you read His Word, the more you spend time thinking about it, the more you speak it, the more aware of His things you become, and the more fulfilling your relationship with God becomes, the deeper your roots will go. Identify with the Word of God, draw from it, and let it reshape your mind, repurpose your direction, and rejuvenate your body. The Bible is God speaking to you, so be firmly rooted in God's unshakable Word!

Scripture:

"Then Christ will make his home in your hearts as you trust in him. Your roots will grow down into God's love and keep you strong. And may you have the power to understand, as all God's people should, how wide, how long, how high, and how deep his love is."

—Ephesians 3:17-18 (NLT)

"Blessed [with spiritual security] is the man who believes *and* trusts in *and* relies on the Lord and whose hope *and* confident expectation is the Lord. For he will be [nourished] like a tree planted by the waters, that spreads out its roots by the river; and will not fear the heat when it comes; but its leaves will be green *and* moist. And it will not be anxious *and* concerned in a year of drought nor stop bearing fruit."

—Jeremiah 17:7-8 (AMP)

Speak these words over your life

I am rooted deeply in the Word of God. The Word of God is my foundation. It is my source of strength, confidence, hope, and faith. My life is secure because its foundation is the unchangeable and unshakable truth that is the Word of God. The Word of God will keep me anchored when the storms of life come. Because I am rooted in Christ, I will remain strong, stable, and unafraid in the middle of even the scariest circumstance. When faced with difficulties and challenges I don't know how to handle, I will not fret or be dismayed. I will remain resolute, with my eyes fixed on Christ, and my faith rooted deep in His Word. I shall not be moved. His Word gives me courage and fortitude to endure, preserve, and overcome whatever comes my way.

Jake Provance is an avid reader and an aspiring young writer, who has written four books and has plans to write several more. Jake's first book, *Keep Calm & Trust God,* has sold more than 400,000 copies. Jake is a graduate of Domata Bible School in Tulsa, OK, and has a call on his life to work in pastoral care ministry, with a particular passion to minister to young adults. Jake and his wife, Leah, live in Tulsa, OK.

Check out Jake's blog at
Life-Speak.com

Keith Provance, involved in Christian publishing for more than 30 years, is the founder of Word and Spirit Publishing, a company dedicated to the publishing and worldwide distribution of scriptural, life-changing books. Keith served as president of Harrison House Publishers for more than 20 years and currently works as a publishing consultant to national and international ministries. Keith and his wife, Megan, have authored a number of bestselling books. They reside in Tulsa, Oklahoma and are the parents of three sons, Ryan, Garrett, and Jake.

NOW AVAILABLE

VOLUME 2

KEEP
CALM
AND
TRUST
GOD

JAKE PROVANCE & KEITH PROVANCE

TOPICS INCLUDE . . . HOPE, LOVE, STRENGTH, PEACE,
COURAGE, CASTING YOUR CARES, FACING A CRISIS,
PRESS ON, FORGIVENESS, AND JOY